ALSO BY EDWARD BALL

Slaves in the Family
The Sweet Hell Inside

PENINSULA of LIES

A True Story of
MYSTERIOUS BIRTH AND TABOO LOVE

EDWARD BALL

SIMON & SCHUSTER
New York London Toronto Sydney

SIMON & SCHUSTER
Rockefeller Center
1230 Avenue of the Americas
New York, NY 10020

For information regarding special discounts for bulk purchases,
please contact Simon & Schuster Special Sales:
1-800-456-6798 or business@simonandschuster.com

Designed by Jan Pisciotta

Manufactured in the United States of America

1   3   5   7   9   10   8   6   4   2

Library of Congress Cataloging-in-Publication Data

Ball, Edward.
Peninsula of lies : a true story of mysterious birth and taboo love / Edward Ball.
p.   cm.
1. Simmons, Dawn Langley. 2. Authors, American—20th century—Biography. 3. Transsexuals—South Carolina—Charleston—Biography. 4. Interracial marriage—South Carolina—Charleston. I. Title.
PS3537.I56Z55 2004
813'.54—dc22
[B]
2003066617
ISBN 0-7432-3560-6

To Janet Rowley Ball—
my mother, who loved to laugh

Contents

THE THIRD SEX

Chapter 1

DEATH OF A SO-CALLED TRANSSEXUAL

THE COMMUNIQUÉ

The year before she died, Dawn Langley Simmons, a person I'd never met but knew from her infamous reputation, sent me a letter. I learned later she'd asked someone to draft the letter for her, despite being a published writer, because she suffered from Parkinson's disease and could no longer type. Dawn Simmons said she'd gotten my address from a friend, and she had a question.

I was living in Charleston, South Carolina, Dawn's adopted hometown, an old city where she'd settled after sampling its atmosphere of forgotten manners and antique buildings. Dawn explained that she was a lover of antiques, and some years earlier she'd bought a piece of eighteenth-century furniture previously in the hands of my family. "I once owned the Ball commode chair, which was Chippendale in style," she said.

> It was stolen with everything else after my marriage, which *Newsweek* said "shook the cradle of the Confederacy." It disappeared in a fake auction, turned up in an estate, and was featured in *Antiques* magazine. I would still like to know where the commode chair is. I would be quite happy to find it in a museum, as I did my harp, Palmetto mirror, and grandfather clock.

A Chippendale commode once used by family members was a bond I didn't share with many people, but what, exactly, is a commode chair? There are two types of commodes in furniture. One is a paneled chest that was popular in Victorian drawing rooms. The other is a chair with a big hole in the seat and a bowl underneath, used at night to empty the bladder. Dawn was asking about the Ball family toilet.

Although I had no idea where the thing might be, the chair created a link between this stranger and me, through the warmth of the seat, you might say. I answered the letter with a friendly note but didn't promise to locate the commode. When I had more time, I'd get back in touch.

Too many months passed, however, and Dawn Simmons died. When I heard the news, I reproached myself for letting the chance pass to meet one of the most unusual people ever to put down roots in the South, a region with a flair for the bizarre. Even among the South's strong crop of weird personalities, Dawn's life had been exceptional, the kind of thing with which people marked the passage of time, like a hurricane or a war—as in, "Charleston was such a dignified place until Dawn came to town."

Dawn Simmons, the sexual enigma, had led a lopsided life. She was celebrated in her first incarnation, that of an author of biographies, who happened to be male. Later, she made it known she/he was a transgender person whose identity fell somewhere between the sexual poles, a revelation that led to her ostracism. She faced her punishment with a smile, like an actress catching trash thrown by the audience. In the end, however, she found a kind of vindication and surprised even her detractors.

With all this, I wondered whether there was another reason she'd written. Had she really just wanted to talk toilets or did she mean her letter to convey some message in code? I recognized too late that perhaps what she'd wanted was a listener, someone who might pay careful and not mocking attention to her fascinating and unlikely story.

*   *   *

SHE'D BEEN BORN in England sometime before World War II as a boy named Gordon Hall, and raised in modest circumstances. During the 1960s, Gordon Hall, who'd grown up to become a slight, handsome man and who'd acquired a small fortune, moved to the moldy, provincial American city of Charleston, South Carolina. A picturesque enclave very in love with its Southern heritage, and slow to change, Charleston was still getting used to air-conditioning and airplane travel. In those years, the city was so out of date it felt like an island adrift in time. Some people still kept chickens in the yard, while a few rich whites lived in decaying mansions surrounded by antique silver and old black servants. Gordon Hall arrived into this motionless setting with a lot of money, and he began spending it like a river in an effort to soak open the city's closed, stuffy society, to which newcomers were, on the basis of their newness, refused admission.

It helped that Gordon Hall was a modestly successful writer who'd published a couple of chatty biographies (including a royal one on Princess Margaret, sister of Queen Elizabeth), plus a memoir. In Charleston, where few people actually read books, this entitled the Englishman to the kind of respect that goes to a magician who can pull things from his ear. It helped also that at every opportunity, Gordon Hall dropped the name of Margaret Rutherford, a dotty English movie star who he said was his adoptive mother, and whose reputation suited the local society, where dowagers had special influence. (Rutherford became known to Americans as Miss Jane Marple, the lady detective in big-screen adaptations of Agatha Christie novels, like *Murder, She Said* and *Murder Most Foul.*)

All that was a long time ago. But it was still impossible in Charleston, after forty-odd years, to speak coolly of these things, because of what the British writer did next.

In 1968, Gordon Hall surprised everyone when he began living as a woman, and took the name *Dawn* Hall. To change to the other sex was not a very Southern thing to do, and it was particularly out of line in Charleston, the queen city of the old Confederacy, where men and women were considered two species who met only in church. Doubling the shock, Dawn Hall claimed she *already was a woman*. She said she had actually been born a girl but, due to a genital anomaly, had been misidentified as a boy. Therefore, the surgery she'd decided to obtain had merely *corrected* her sex, not changed it.

This was a lot for people to digest, and the local reaction fell somewhere between bewilderment and fear. Many Charleston people could not even pronounce the T-words like *transsexual*, and *transvestite:* yet here was a trans-person many knew and had shaken hands with. The figure of the trannie had not yet emerged from the secret barrooms of downtown New York, and certainly she'd never showed up at the fake Civil War battles that pass for weekend entertainment in South Carolina. Among people who knew a little about medicine, the term *sex reassignment* had been spoken only in whispers, referring to the strange new practice of one or two sleek hospitals—and fortunately, those were in the North.

Soon after the news of the sex change (or sex correction, as she insisted), Dawn Hall introduced a further nuance into her character, for she was beginning to live like an actress whose audience was a small city. As a fresh, rich white woman, Dawn decided to marry a young black man named John-Paul Simmons. By different accounts, John-Paul was a mechanic, fisherman, or gardener. (A popular rumor, which Dawn vehemently denied, was that John-Paul was her butler.)

Around town, the lady's marriage to "a Negro" aroused even stronger feelings than her evolution from Gordon to Dawn, if that was possible. This time, magazines ran stories, and television crews appeared at Dawn's door. Those few white people who'd remained her friends during her journey from one sex to the next now ceased to have anything to do with her; and Dawn Hall, the new Mrs. Dawn Simmons, passed from one side of the invisible wall that separated the two races to the other. She entered black society, joining an African

American church, becoming a regular at civil rights meetings, and in other ways making herself into an honorary person of color.

But the third act and the climax were yet to come. Two years after her marriage, Dawn Simmons began to appear around Charleston in maternity dresses. And in October 1971, her baby, Natasha, was born. Pictures showed that Natasha was a striking mixed-race child, the perfect creation of a white mother and a black father—that is, if the couple had been capable of conceiving. Dawn Simmons claimed that yes, she had conceived—that Natasha was her biological child, proof of her natural state as a woman—and it was her prior incarnation, Gordon Hall, that was the invention, the costume, and the sexual prop.

Now she was gone, and no one knew the truth.

A LIVING MYSTERY

When Dawn Simmons died, in September 2000, a friend invited me to the funeral; but because I'd never met her, I was reluctant to go. The friend persisted, however, and I justified my appearance with Dawn's letter to me.

We drove to the J. Henry Stuhr Memorial Chapel, where the better sort in Charleston had been embalmed for generations, and threaded our way between the limousines to the canopied door. I'd asked my friend to lend me a tie, and he'd brought a stained blue one with repeating fleurs-de-lis.

A few mourners mingled and murmured in a room with mahogany furniture and Regency curtains. I talked to the two or three people I knew until suddenly, Joe Trott appeared in the room.

Joe Trott had an amiable, lined face and walked with a cane. He was dressed in a linen jacket and string tie, and his long gray hair was pinched back in a ponytail.

"Dawn, Dawn," Trott said. "She was sweet to the bone. Such a dear heart, with no idea about handling money, or handling her life. I knew Dawn before all the hoopla. I remember him from when he first came to Charleston, when he was just a cute little cockney boy." Trott looked away wistfully, and then he wandered off.

For many years, Joe Trott had owned a house a block from the one belonging to Dawn Simmons, on Society Street, a row of venerable townhouses and converted slave quarters remade into quaint cottages. A retired florist and antiques dealer, Trott had stood by Dawn through her sexual transformation and rise to motherhood, when many of her friends cut her loose.

People used to say things about Dawn, and as we waited for the service, some of the old gossip popped into my head.

He was just a pansy who liked women's clothes. He never was a woman.

A nervous young minister, wearing a white cassock with colored embroidery, approached the mourners, and we all stepped into the chapel. The room was long, white, and entirely without ornament, with a simple altar at one end. As we took our seats, I noticed an aspect of the scene that seemed to sum up Dawn's story. On one side of the chapel sat the black people, whereas we, the whites, sat across the aisle. This kind of thing was familiar in Charleston, oil separating from water, and we might have all gone along without thinking; but there was something more to the split.

The black mourners were of all ages and both sexes, and were evidently Dawn Simmons's in-laws. On the white side, however, most mourners were men over the age of sixty. A couple of them wore ascots, and one or two wore hairpieces. Their romantic dress and touches of vanity implied these were gay men of a certain age, probably closeted in keeping with their generation. They were Dawn's friends from before her sexual rebirth, when she was still Gordon, an English-born dandy who wore pressed cotton jackets.

That Dawn had a coming-out party for his two Chihuahuas, who were dressed in white gloves and pearls and carried down the stairs on velvet pillows. He was more than eccentric.

With a strained expression, the embroidered cassock cleared his throat. "We are gathered in the presence of God to offer final farewell to Dawn Simmons," he said. "I only met her a few times, but on each occasion she made a strong impression. She was a gentle person who cared for other people, who loved her animals, and especially loved her daughter, Natasha."

There were only about twenty-five people in the room even though, in her best years, Dawn had been on a first-name basis with the entire city. If you'd said, "Dawn's back in town," everyone in Charleston would've known you meant *the* Dawn, and it was a name that provoked a reaction. Some people would smile, and others would roll their eyes, depending (it seemed to me) on how comfortable they were with sex. Given Dawn's notoriety, I'd expected a crowd, not the thin turnout in the chapel. I later learned that Dawn's daughter, Natasha, had placed a misleading announcement in the newspaper, stating the funeral would occur at another location, so that she and her family could escape curiosity seekers. I imagined a restless mob at that false address.

In the front row, and in the position of chief mourner, sat the living mystery of the Dawn story, Natasha Simmons. It's not too much to say that Natasha had been both the culmination of Dawn's life and her greatest ordeal.

She was a tall, thin, beautiful woman whose poise and height, joined with her dark eyes and beige skin, made her the most naturally elegant person in the room. She wore a fitted black dress, and her composure was magnified by grief.

That nigra he, or she, married was a voodoo man, and they used to sacrifice their animals. At night you could hear the damned dogs howling.

The mood in the chapel was somewhat unsettled. There was no casket, because Dawn's body had been cremated, and her ashes divided into three parts. One portion was to go to England, to be buried in the town of her birth; another went to a friend in New Hampshire, who intended to create a shrine with his allowance; and the third part went to Natasha. I saw at the front of the chapel a small metal box, which I assumed held a portion of Dawn's remains.

Someone had set up a pair of card tables in front of the altar and covered them with mementos. Dawn had been an author, and therefore on the first table were several books she'd written, both as Gordon Hall and as Dawn Simmons. Next to these were framed photographs from different stages in Dawn's life. The pictures began with her days as an androgynous young man in a bow tie (the author photo on a book), moved on to her years as a woman (transfigured into a conservative lady in a dress, with beehive hair), and climaxed with Dawn on her wedding day, a bride in a white gown walking with her black (and much younger) groom, the smiling, vigorous John-Paul Simmons. A last picture was a portrait of Dawn as wife and mother, holding her young daughter. In this faded color image, she seemed different, in a way vindicated, her pale white face nestled into the brown cheek of her girl. It also looked a bit like she was holding a trophy.

Common sense said that Dawn Simmons hadn't given birth, but here in the chapel stood her daughter, silent in grief. If she wasn't the child of her mother, then who was she? I'd heard that in recent years, Natasha and Dawn had lived a few blocks apart and seen each other every day. It was what any aging mother would want with her child, an inseparable attachment.

I wondered what Natasha, standing in the front pew, thought of the talk her mother had stirred. Did she know the rumors? How did she feel about the gossip? Obviously, she knew that Dawn had once lived as a man—how did she make sense of that part of her mother's life? I imagined Natasha regarded Dawn as a woman and a mother, because anything else would have been hard to understand.

JOHN-PAUL SIMMONS was not in the chapel; indeed, his family didn't know where he was. A few years after the wedding, he'd been diagnosed with schizophrenia, and he'd drifted in and out of psychiatric care for decades. It was said he was living in New York State.

The minister gave a ten-minute eulogy on the theme of kindness, which ended with a prayer. "Dear God, watch over your servant Dawn Simmons as she completes her eventful time on earth. Keep her safe from those who would torment her, and protect those she leaves behind—her beloved daughter Natasha, and her grandchildren."

That faggot stole that baby and passed it off as his own.

The service ended and we drifted back into the reception room, where my friend introduced me to Natasha. She was the youngest among the mourners, her trim figure fitting just so in her dress. She weakly shook my hand, looking up but not focusing on my face.

"Thank you for coming," she said.

Natasha blinked but didn't really see me. And I knew she was with her mother, whom she'd loved.

I had been thinking that Dawn's claim to motherhood was specious, but Natasha's obviously genuine grief put doubt in my mind.

For SEVERAL DAYS after the funeral, I felt uneasy. People had once watched Dawn from a distance, like drivers rubbernecking an accident, and I felt like one of the voyeurs.

She'd been properly blessed, but she lingered in memory. The chapel scene was a puzzle: the beautiful Natasha, the black and white factions, the incompatible photographs. Dawn's life seemed like a jagged pile of events, with unbelievable pieces—unless, of course, you accepted her version of things, in which case all of it made sense.

When I thought about Dawn's sex reassignment, my instinct said she was a transsexual, a man who'd become a woman only with surgery. And a sex-change patient cannot have children. Thus, her daughter's origin was a mystery.

But why did she insist on having been born a girl? Dawn's explanation of her sexuality had brought her a raft of trouble, yet she stuck to her story till the end.

Maybe she'd wanted the adventure. Even if one rejected her account, Dawn's life had been a fascinating production, like music that keeps changing keys. First, she'd masqueraded as a man for decades, then lived as a woman for equal time, which gave her a panoramic view of things. And besides inhabiting two genders, she'd had the unusual pleasure of experiencing sex on both sides of the bed.

That's just to start. Dawn's claim to sexual ambiguity also placed her in the path of science. The first studies of the topic took place in the mid-nineteenth century, and since then researchers have listed many sexual dispositions other than male and female—from anomalies triggered by hormones to types of genital variation. Her decision to undergo sex reassignment made her a pioneer in twentieth-century medicine, which had been revolutionized by transplant surgery and a willingness to alter the body.

Crossing into social history, in the years before civil rights won the upper hand, Dawn flouted the ban against interracial marriage. She broke a taboo of the Deep South that reached back to slavery times—the one that called for white women to stay away from black men—and she faced down the punishment. In the midst of this, Dawn produced an heir whose life summed up and extended her story. Natasha Simmons was proof of her mother's womanhood—and a guarantee that the enigma of Dawn's identity would outlive her.

All this was like a pageant. From a distance, however, it seemed Natasha would be made to pay the psychological bill run up by her own birth. I wanted to unravel Dawn's story not only because she'd broken all the rules but also because there appeared to have been a human cost. Dawn's daughter was at stake, and perhaps other people I hadn't met. And what about Dawn's husband? Was John-Paul Simmons, a schizophrenic, born into madness? Or had his mental illness been deepened by the events of his marriage?

I STARTED LOOKING into cases of sexual ambiguity and found several examples of women who'd lived in sexual disguise. A jazz pianist called Billy Tipton had grown up in Oklahoma in the 1920s as a girl named Dorothy but started living as a man at age nineteen. When Billy Tipton died, in 1989, her secret was finally uncovered. She had married several women and had adopted children; among those lulled by the deception were Billy's last wife, Kitty, and their sons. (Her biographer said Billy used to bind her breasts with elastic, telling people she had rib damage from an auto accident. In her sex life, Billy Tipton seems to have kept the lights off, and used a strapped-on dildo.)

No, it was ridiculous—Dawn Simmons hadn't been a "passing woman," or female transvestite. She'd lived as Gordon Hall for half her life, so why would she suddenly switch as an adult and invite problems?

Could Dawn have been a person whose anatomy fell between the sexes? The French psychoanalyst Jacques Lacan used to begin certain of his lectures with a question: *Pourquoi n'y a t-il pas un troisième sexe?* (Why isn't there a third sex?) People have long said that there are "masculine women" and "feminine men." Could Dawn have been a blend, an example of a third way?

Sexual variance is a medical fact, unusual but not especially rare. Some babies come from the womb with mixed organs—a vagina and a small penis—and medicine now labels them *intersexuals*. (*Hermaphrodite* was the old word.) These infants can spend weeks in the hospital as distraught parents and excited doctors decide how to categorize them. In earlier generations, some intersexuals ended up in freak shows. (I had a dim memory of seeing a "bearded lady" at a traveling carnival in the South when I was a child.) Did Dawn's parents have a (mostly) girl baby, and mistakenly assign her the male sex? When put this way, it no longer sounded impossible.

If Dawn was a girl *and* a boy, she could not have chosen a more inhospitable setting to realize her nature than Charleston, South Carolina. Dawn's adopted town was a quiet, parochial Southern city whose sense of self was as a still life. Charleston seemed to deny the world had advanced much beyond the Civil War, which had started

in its very harbor in April 1861, when rebel batteries opened fire on
federally occupied Fort Sumter. I tried to imagine Charleston in the
early 1960s, during the days when Dawn was still the handsome Gordon Hall. Many whites had grandparents who'd fought for the Confederacy, as they were fond of reminding you, and a century after that
war, Charleston had still not fully recovered. Gordon had arrived in
town before the boom in tourism, and most everybody, white or
black, was still poor. Only half the people owned cars, and air-
conditioning was for movie theaters. An intersexual in Charleston
would have fit like a snake in a church.

Eyewitness

I asked Joe Trott, whom I'd seen at the funeral, to have lunch and talk
about Dawn, hoping he could shed some light on the mystery of his
late friend.

When I picked him up, Joe was wearing a striped long-sleeve
shirt, buttoned to the neck, and a leather string tie. His ponytail fit
into a silver barrette. He said he was eighty-three, and that he didn't
like it; but he was quick in his movements, and his mind was alive in
his pale, blue eyes.

Joe Trott had been born to an ancient family name, an important
fact in Charleston, where genealogy is an alternative religion, and his
inheritance even appeared on his right hand, where he wore a gold
signet ring.

"It's a Trott family ring, with the family crest," said Joe. "They
used it to seal the wax on documents."

Joe's illustrious forebear had been one Nicholas Trott, an early
white settler who'd written the first body of South Carolina law in
the early 1700s. "I've got one of his deeds on the wall at home," Joe
said, wrapping his status and shutting the car door.

As the lawman's descendant, Joe Trott had grown up in Charleston,
spent several years working in theater in New York City and Califor-

nia, and then moved home, where he went into the antiques business. When Gordon Hall descended in the 1960s, Joe and a partner were running a store called Cobblestone Antiques out of their house, along with a flower business.

Joe wanted to eat where he was a regular, at Kitty's Fine Foods, a homey place much liked for its lunch counter, dirty tile floor, and 1970s paneling. The restaurant stands on an industrial strip across the street from the longshoremen's union building, on East Bay Street, which runs along the Cooper River through the wharf district. At Kitty's, construction workers and salesmen yell at each other from across the room, the walls are decorated with dozens of pictures of cats, and a hand-lettered sign reads, "BFIC."

"Best Food In Charleston," said Joe.

As we slid into a vinyl booth, the greasy table stuck to our hands. Joe said, "Yeah, the clean problem. Some customers started bringing in toilet paper, because the restaurant never bought it, and we still bring it. But they keep coming to Kitty's. If this place could talk, a lot of people would have to leave town."

The salty feeling of the place got stronger when a middle-aged waitress stepped up and recognized Joe. "Come on, you shit ass! What you want?"

Joe nodded, used to the attention. "The honey ham, okra, and sweet potatoes," he said.

The waitress turned to me—"I've been waiting on him for thirty-five years!"—and disappeared.

"She likes me," Joe said, smiling.

Retired from the antiques business, and having buried a lot of friends before Dawn, Joe didn't mind turning over memories. He had the soft accent of coastal Carolina, with slightly nasal vowels and a low-decibel delivery. His face looked well kept, and although it was lined, his skin didn't sag. There was a strong jaw and heavy eyelids, but the most distinctive part of Joe's appearance was the gray ponytail.

This aging furniture expert was one of the few witnesses to the whole of Dawn Simmons's journey—from British immigrant, to social gadfly and proprietor of an antebellum mansion, to woman, wife, and mother.

"I was devoted to Dawn," Joe said, "and I miss her. But she had her problems. The main problem was that she let her heart run away with her good sense. When Dawn came to Charleston, I mean Gordon Hall, he was a little English boy. He was very, very slight, and a very happy-go-lucky type of man. He made people feel good when they were around him.

"I assume you know she inherited all this money from Isabel Whitney, in New York," Joe went on, switching back to the female pronoun. "The Whitneys were the cotton gin people, Eli Whitney and all that. Isabel Whitney, who was an artist—she painted murals—she befriended Gordon in New York, and left him extremely wealthy."

Gordon Hall's money had come suddenly, in an inheritance, and his benefactor was the unlikely figure of Isabel Whitney, an elderly and unmarried member of a venerable American family whose fortune had come from silk mills. (Another from the clan, at least by marriage, was Gertrude Vanderbilt Whitney, a sculptor who used family money to create the Whitney Museum of American Art in New York.)

"Along with Gordon, Isabel Whitney also befriended another person who worked for her, and that was her butler," Joe said. "He's now dead, but he was a New Yorker, an Italian fellow. He'd worked in one of the bigger auction houses, in addition to being Whitney's servant. That's why he and Gordon thought, with all the money Isabel had left, they would go into the antiques business. And they thought the best place to do it was Charleston, South Carolina." Joe chuckled, as though this was a strange scheme.

I studied Joe's appearance as he talked. He had two rings on his left hand, in addition to the one on his right, and his fingernails shone as though they'd been painted with clear polish. I noticed his hairline had been powdered, and it looked like it had been stitched.

"It was 1961 or '62," he said. "Gordon came down as a guest of the Historic Charleston Foundation, which was trying to promote the cleaning up of Ansonborough, and which had sold him his house." As he spoke, Joe sometimes gestured with his hands, marking out spaces on the table for emphasis.

The Historic Charleston Foundation is an architecture preservation group; Ansonborough is Joe Trott's (and Gordon's) neighborhood. A little "borough" six blocks long and three blocks wide, it takes its name from Captain George Anson, an eighteenth-century English sea captain who acquired the land in colonial times. It is now one of the moneyed sections of town, full of beautifully restored nineteenth-century townhouses.

Gordon gave lovely parties in his renovated mansion, Joe said, and well-heeled Charleston couples wanted to be known as his friend, "this fabulous little English man, who was an author."

Joe's voice suddenly became thick with emotion, and tears formed in his eyes. "Later on, people criticized Gordon so unmercifully for his manners, and the way he acted! They were so cruel to him! And some of those people didn't amount to a fucking row of beans!"

Kitty's Fine Foods had filled up, and the lunch rush rose to a din. The waitress delivered corn bread and refilled our glasses of iced tea. Joe composed himself and continued, "Oh, he was so naive. Very naive."

I asked whether Joe had an opinion of Dawn's claims about her sex.

"He swore that he was a *he-mor-pho-dite* when he came here. Gordon said to me, 'You know, I have the two sexes already.'" Joe mimicked an effeminate voice with a cockney accent, like an actor playing a drag queen from East London. "He said, 'I have the two sexes. We just have to make one more ready than the other.'"

Delivering Gordon's lines, Joe managed to look both amused and disturbed.

"I told Gordon, 'Good luck!' And he said, 'I know you don't believe me, but it happened to me. I have two sexes! I can take my choice.' So I told Gordon, 'Be my guest!' "

The subject made Joe raise his voice, and he grew louder and more emphatic.

"The truth is, I didn't give a shit who he slept with, or what he did when he got there! He would say, 'Well, now I can have babies.' I said, 'Go on and have 'em. But you're either gonna have to spit it up or shit it out, because you ain't gonna have a baby through that thing you've got on you now!' "

Our food arrived. "Here you go, shit ass!" said the waitress.

DAWN HAD WRITTEN ABOUT what she called her "condition," but she didn't give anatomical details. In 1970, she'd had this to say:

> There was only a midwife present when I was born. Although she had a physically healthy little baby on her hands, because of the shape of the genital organs the midwife had been hard pressed to determine the child's sex. Finally she had decided to call it a boy.

How strange that Dawn, talking about herself, used the pronoun *it*. She added:

> In America, this [being labeled a boy] would never have happened, for babies born with genital defects can be treated almost immediately. In my own case, I should have been registered as a girl. Up until the age of five, when I started school, I truly believed that I was a little girl.

*   *   *

MY LUNCH WITH JOE TROTT had failed to help me make sense of Dawn; the library of the local medical school offered another resource.

The medical literature on intersex births was limited, but the books held my attention. Most had pictures of naked patients whose eyes were covered with a black box and whose genitals looked abnormal.

In a standard text on the subject, *Hermaphroditism, Genital Anomalies and Related Endocrine Disorders*, Howard W. Jones and William Wallace Scott explained a syndrome that sounded like what Dawn said she had. Congenital adrenal hyperplasia (CAH), the most common intersexual condition, occurs when the endocrine system in the fetus secretes excessive androgens, or male growth hormones. With female babies in utero, the hormone spurt triggers masculine traits and enlarges the sex organs (the extra growth being the hyperplasia). A girl with CAH will have ovaries and a uterus—but also an enlarged clitoris that might stick an inch out from the body, and possibly fused labia that could look like a scrotum over the vaginal opening.

A biologist had compiled studies and determined that as many as fifteen births in one thousand are of infants with varying degrees of congenital adrenal hyperplasia. Was Dawn Simmons a CAH baby?

Reading around some more, I found that history offered some remarkable cases of apparent intersexuals who'd lived before the routine diagnosis of sexual variations, including that of an Italian soldier who'd become a mother. In 1601, Daniel Burghammer, a blacksmith and infantryman from the town of Piedra, Italy, gave birth to a baby girl (much to the surprise of his wife). Daniel had been baptized male and had served in the army for seven years. His wife requested an investigation, and under questioning by church authorities, the blacksmith said that he was, as he put it, *half female and half male*, and that the father of his baby was a Spanish soldier. The child was christened Elizabeth, and she was weaned at Daniel's breast. Eventually, the Vatican declared the birth a miracle, though the church granted a divorce to Daniel Burghammer's mystified spouse.

*   *   *

STILL DIGGING FOR BACKGROUND, I went as far as Duke University Library, in North Carolina, where I found one thing that really undermined my doubts of Dawn's version of her life. In the reading room of the Duke archives, I opened a file of papers, and the birth certificate for Dawn's daughter, Natasha, fell out onto the table. As I picked up the green document, I felt new trust and belief coming on slowly, like a ship approaching a dock. The birth certificate had been issued by the state of Pennsylvania, and dated October 17, 1971; it was a true copy, embossed with the seal of the Pennsylvania Department of Health. It named Dawn Simmons as Natasha's mother, and John-Paul Simmons as her father. It made no mention of adoption.

Vital records, like birth and death certificates, are used to settle disputes over such issues as when a marriage took place, or how a person died. People trust the records because they exercise two hands of authority. Not only does a birth certificate carry the clout of medical science, with many professional controls, but the government backs it as well, with presumed neutrality. Birth certificates are supposed to give answers, but that of Natasha Simmons raised questions. Was Dawn really Natasha's mother? What was Dawn, anatomically speaking? How could this have happened?

Natasha's birth certificate teased me with its implications. *While they laughed, the trannie became a mother.* Dawn wasn't just a novelist; she was the man who became a woman and gave birth.

Dawn Simmons was like the riddle of the sphinx—only in this case, the riddle was not the question posed by the creature to the traveler, but the sphinx herself. Dawn was the enigma, half-human and half-divine.

The gossip came back to mind.

What do you get when you cross a castrated male with a Negro? I don't know, but it's probably against the law.

Dawn's identity was still a secret. People who knew her story were too upset by her to have a reasonable opinion. I should have stayed away from the funeral, but now it was too late, and I'd been drafted into the case. Dawn had sent me her message in a letter, and then she'd died, leaving behind her unsolved mystery. I had the idea that for some personal reason, which I might never know, she'd wanted me to unlock her riddle. I would have to investigate Dawn Simmons and follow her story all the way to the naked truth.

Chapter 2

HER DEMISE AN INCONVENIENT FACT THAT MIGHT BE OVERCOME BY TESTIMONY

I'd lived in Charleston, South Carolina, when I was a boy, but my family moved away before I grew up, and I only came back to live as an adult, alone. A returning Southerner, I needed to refresh myself in the folklore; and for this, there was no more reliable informant than my friend Ted Phillips.

He was the one who'd taken me to Dawn's funeral (he'd known the right location, despite the false ad in the paper) and lent me a tie. A lover of the offbeat, Ted had gathered a mental encyclopedia of curious facts about his South Carolina home. I imagined Ted could provide further clues to Dawn Simmons, so one day I walked across the old part of town, along blocks of aged buildings with their tiered porches, and down a cobblestone street to his front door.

Ted Phillips made his home on a street with townhouses that looked about the same as they had during the American Revolution. The block also smelled like historic times because carriage rides for tourists clip-clopped down the street every few minutes, leaving blasts of horse urine.

He answered the bell dressed in the uniform of a Southern gentleman—blue blazer, khaki pants, blue oxford shirt. But Ted's blazer had some polyester in it, the pants didn't fit, and he wore old eyeglasses that slipped down his nose. To his friends, his disheveled style was endearing, a sign he didn't care for gentility, whatever that was.

"Come on in out of Disneyland," he said, a buggy easing past.

Ted had been raised in South Carolina but had abandoned his native state to attend Harvard, where he worked on the cool school magazine, the *Lampoon*. Straightening up to go to law school, he'd come home to a job in the Charleston public defender's office, which he later quit. He now lived somewhat at loose ends, with his wife and young daughters, and was writing a book about a cemetery.

Sitting in his book-lined living room, whose front door opened onto the sidewalk, Ted projected the aura of a bard, with the belly of Falstaff and the experienced face of Walt Whitman, even though he was just forty.

"I was a boy when Dawn was the town freak," he said. "I used to see her around in her lacy dresses, and people would cross the street to avoid her. My parents didn't have anything to do with her. Nobody had anything to do with her."

Harvard had failed to dilute Ted's accent, which was loud and country, owing to his early years in a two-stoplight town fifty miles from Charleston. But despite the diction, Ted was one of Charleston's rare cosmopolitans, and a serious collector of Southern art and furniture. He got up to pour a drink and then walked over to a small desk with an old leather surface. The desk had belonged to Josephine Pinckney, he said, a once-famous but now long-dead and nearly forgotten Charleston novelist.

"Auctioneer didn't know what he had!" Ted said. "After I bought it, another bidder called and said he'd pay double. I said forget it! He was just going to fix it and sell it to some New Yorker!"

From the old desk I could see, through a window, the walled garden behind Ted's house. Beyond the wall was the graveyard of St. Phillip's Episcopal Church, the city's first congregation, formed in the 1600s. Charleston is the kind of place where reminders of the past are everywhere, giving the city an amber atmosphere. But Dawn's story was like a mind-altering substance that changed one's frame. Thinking of the graves, I wondered whether there had been intersexuals in the colonial days. The city was young then, when the

men wore breeches. Couldn't there have been, among the first families of Charleston, a person or two with ambiguous genitalia?

Ted sat down on his brown leather sofa and became uncharacteristically quiet.

"She was born Gordon Hall, in a village in England. She fudged
dates, so I don't know if it was the 1930s, or what. Dawn said she
spent a lot of her childhood, as Gordon Hall, at Sissinghurst, the
estate of Vita Sackville-West. Vita was the novelist and poet, and her
friends were all in the Bloomsbury group—though they didn't know
it at the time. Vita was part of the pack of all those artists and writers
who were sleeping together, and then writing it up in their diaries.
Unfortunately, Vita was just as well known for her affairs as she was
for her novels, at least later on, and Virginia Woolf had a thing with
her. Then Virginia threw herself in a river and drowned. All this is
what Dawn saw when she was growing up—a bunch of messed up
artists."

A horse-drawn carriage clattered outside the door, and the muted
words of the tour guide—something about pirates who used to live in
Ted's house—echoed in the living room.

Ted resumed, "Dawn, or Gordon, moved to America, and eventually ended up in New York. The 1950s? In Greenwich Village, heart
of New York City, Gordon got involved with a rich old woman. She
was from the New York Whitneys—the Whitney Museum and all
that—and Gordon moved in with her. And when she died, she left
him a house here in Charleston, on Society Street, and two million
dollars—or so Dawn said. Beaucoup money back then."

Society Street is a few blocks north of Ted's house, an east-west
road that runs through Ansonborough. The street starts at the
Cooper River, one of two tidal rivers that empty into the Atlantic at
Charleston harbor, the other river being the Ashley. (A much-
repeated geography of Charleston: "where the Ashley and the
Cooper come together to form the Atlantic Ocean.") Society Street,
in other words, cuts across the heart of the city peninsula.

Charleston occupies a peninsula between its two rivers, and the land is longer than it is wide, about six miles from north to south and two miles across at the thickest point. As it appears on a map, the peninsula seems to hang down, pointing south, and it looks as though the Ashley and Cooper Rivers hold a shaft of land between cupped hands.

Ted leaned forward, his volume went up slightly, and his accent thickened. "Gordon filled his house with antiques, including bed steps he said were owned by Robert E. Lee, and a pair of mirrors belonging to George Washington! He wangled invitations to dinner parties." Ted caught himself. "I meant she. She wangled invitations."

He got up, poured another drink, and sat back down. "I think the operation was in 1968. I know it took place at Johns Hopkins Hospital. She left Charleston as Gordon Langley Hall and came home six weeks later with a new name, Dawn Pepita Langley Hall. Pepita was the name of the grandmother of Vita Sackville-West, Dawn's idol."

The names Vita Sackville-West and Sissinghurst, her estate, were two clues about Dawn's childhood in England. The gardens at Sissinghurst were now open to the public. And although Sackville-West was dead, maybe someone else from Dawn's past could be found in her wake.

Ted continued, "Then, right after the operation—I mean a few months—Dawn married John-Paul! He was much younger than Dawn, and he was deep black. The newspaper reported the marriage on the obituary page." He sat back and laughed, pleased at the ways of Charleston.

In an interview, Dawn had said more about her wedding. She claimed that threats made her move the ceremony from a church to her house, and that her wedding gifts were burned up by a firebomb thrown into her garden. But Ted couldn't verify those things.

"She started appearing around town pregnant, her tummy out to here," Ted said, his hand over his belly. "Time passed, and people were unkind. They said the pregnancy lasted twelve months. But eventually she walked around with a baby carriage, and her little girl, Natasha. That was it for people in Charleston! Dawn said a burglar attacked her after that. She ended up in the hospital—fell behind on her mortgage—bank foreclosed on her house. Most people lose track of her there." Ted looked drained. "Too much, too much."

If he was so affected by Dawn's life, what was it like to have actually lived these things?

In a minute Ted disappeared, and when he returned, he had something clenched in his hand. "Who knows? She might have had something wrong with her, physically," Ted said. "You ought to look at Duke. They might have a hint."

He meant Duke University, in Durham, North Carolina.

"She always said her papers were going to Duke. Nobody knows what's there, because her things were sealed until her death."

Ted opened his fist and released a crumpled piece of paper. "Also, try this person." The scrap had an address and phone number.

SCENTS OF PAPER

The city of Durham, North Carolina, an early capital of the cigarette, has notable remnants of the smoking industry. Vacant tobacco warehouses and sagging bungalows for the workers who cured the leaf are necklaced through town, strung between frequent truck dealers and barbecue joints. In this old piedmont setting, Duke University looks like a medieval monastery that fell from the sky. The campus appears from nowhere, all Gothic spires and stone quadrangles, like a monks' cloister.

The papers of Dawn Simmons were in the Duke library, in a building that looked like Westminster Cathedral. I approached the counter, where a solid, fifty-something woman in glasses and coiffed hair stood watch.

"I'm so glad someone's seriously interested in Dawn's life," she said. From the look in the woman's eye, I imagined the letters of a possible hermaphrodite made one of the more unusual collections in her care. The woman added, "You're not going to make it stupid, are you?"

A more intriguing question seemed to be this: Why did the school have forty-three boxes of letters, photographs, diaries, and manuscripts from the desk of Dawn Simmons?

"Dawn would send us her papers in dribbles and drabs," said the librarian. "Sometimes it cost us money, because she would send a few letters and a picture, along with an invoice. We always tried to pay her less than she asked." I later learned Dawn had used Duke as a piggy bank when she was broke, and the amounts she asked for were small: a hundred dollars for one packet of letters, fifty dollars six months later for some pictures.

I guessed from the woman's accent that she'd been born in Georgia. She walked away, then turned around and came back. "What do you think?" she asked. "Was it her baby?"

The Dawn Simmons Papers are part of Duke's Special Collections Division, which shelters rare things. I sat down at a brown table in the glass-enclosed reading room, where surveillance cameras peered from the corner. At other tables, thin graduate students rattled their fingers on laptops and perused yellowed papers. Every so often, a researcher would walk to the copier, carrying a piece of old paper as though it were the Shroud of Turin.

The librarian lifted a box onto the counter, leaned forward, and whispered, "We were collecting the papers of Southern writers, and Gordon Hall was writing novels and biographies." She was trying to answer the question about the library's ownership of Dawn's things. "Gordon Hall was considered a Southern writer, even though he was English, because he lived in Charleston. That's why we have his papers here—or maybe I should say, her papers."

The first box contained stacks of photographs, and halfway down the pile was a picture of the young Gordon Hall. His face had an arresting feminine aura: a white dew-kissed brow, pastel pink cheeks, red lips. In a moment I realized the photo was originally in black and white and had been hand-tinted with paint.

In other boxes were scrapbooks Dawn had kept, along with typed manuscripts for her books, including that of a memoir, *Man Into Woman: A Transsexual Autobiography*, published in England in 1970. She'd held on to hundreds of letters, typed notes, receipts, and clippings. She seemed to think someone, someday, would want to read her every grocery list. My amusement at her vanity faded somewhat when I realized that person had turned out to be me.

I noticed that many of the older papers, at least ones with her signature, had one alteration. Dozens of times, Dawn had struck a line through the name Gordon Langley Hall and written Dawn Langley Simmons in its place.

The librarian with the Georgia vowels came over to the table. "These papers used to be under restriction, which was part of the agreement we had with Dawn," she whispered. "Until now, you couldn't even look at them without her permission! But she's dead, so I guess it's okay."

To TALK ABOUT DAWN SIMMONS, and about other trans-people, you have to make a rule for the use of personal pronouns. There is no alternative to gender in pronouns, and the language hasn't made room for a compound term like *s/he*. The simple approach is to refer to Gordon Hall as he, and Dawn Simmons as she, whatever this person's physical sex might have been.

After days of reading, I began to see glimpses of Dawn's early life. Gordon Hall was born in Sussex, England, to a sixteen-year-old girl named Marjorie Hall Ticehurst. (No credible date, as yet, although Dawn would later say it was during the 1930s.) With no husband, the teenage mom gave her child away, and Gordon didn't see much of her while growing up.

Dawn Simmons would write, "My mother's nine-pound baby 'boy' was turned over to its maternal grandmother, an energetic, good-natured, unpredictable, naturally explosive widow of forty-one. She is said to have tied me, at three days, into a basket on the back of her bicycle and taken me for a ride."

Gordon's grandmother, Nellie Hall Ticehurst, was the widow of a butcher who'd died young. She lived alone in the little village of Heathfield, a hundred miles south of London, in a brick bungalow she called Havana ("after a box of cigars," said Dawn). Havana was just four rooms, plus a bathroom. Gordon's bedroom was in the back. It was painted pink, and there were beech trees outside the window.

For Dawn's mother, an unmarried village girl, the shame of the birth was so great that she chose no name for her child, leaving it to Nellie to call the baby Gordon, after an English war hero. General C. G. Gordon was a nineteenth-century imperial governor of the Sudan who had lost a siege to insurgents in Khartoum, after which the Sudanese rebels speared and decapitated him. "I never liked my name—or poor beheaded General Gordon either," Dawn said.

Although Grandmother Nellie called him Gordon Kenneth Ticehurst, years later Gordon would discard most of this. He tossed out Ticehurst and replaced it with Hall, Nellie's maiden name. Then he dropped his middle name and replaced it with Langley, to become Gordon Langley Hall. I tried, but I couldn't find the name Langley in any family context. Eventually, a cousin of Dawn's told me there was a street called Langley in a neighboring town. Was Gordon piecing himself together?

Dawn said Grandmother Nellie accepted the child's congenital abnormality: "Knowing that because of my affliction I would never be able to contract a proper marriage, she decided early to fortify me with so much knowledge that I would be able to hold my own with anybody."

LITTLE HANDS, LITTLE FEET

A friend in Durham had invited me to dinner, and one day I left the Duke library for his house, where the guests were to include people I'd never met. Knowing of my research into sexual ambiguity, the host took me aside and said, "You might find one of the men interesting, because he started life as a woman."

The dinner took place in a one-story house decorated with handsome modern furniture, with a sitting room of Japanese design. Hors d'oeuvres got started, and the transgender guest—I'll call him Robert (not his real name)—sat with his wife, a scholar who'd known her husband both before and after his surgery.

It was hard not to watch Robert, the more so because of his jolly personality. He was about five feet, nine inches tall, firm at the waist, with a square face and dark eyebrows. His clothes consisted of a brocade vest, white shirt, brown tweed jacket, and wool pants, the combination projecting the image of a country squire.

Robert was amusing, telling jokes and keeping the talk under his control in masculine fashion. He had the body language of a man (ninety-degree leg-cross instead of calf-to-calf) and even the laugh, which was loud. He had a full head of hair and sideburns. Everything about his maleness was perfect, except his voice (a little high) and his hands (small and soft). When we shook, there was the gentle grip of a woman. His feet also seemed less than full-sized.

In the kitchen, my friend said, "No one talks about it, least of all him. She was born in Durham and went to high school here before moving away. When she came back, she was a man. Everyone knows, but no one mentions it."

Female-to-male transsexuals are less common than male-to-female. No accurate count exists, but there seem to be about four male-to-female surgeries for each female-to-male. The reasons are debatable, but the sex change subculture has a vulgar saying: "It's easier to make a hole than build a pole."

The table was set for seven, and we took our seats around the polished surface as pizzas emerged from the kitchen, one at a time. Robert, at the head, told funny stories, each with a big laugh at the end. One concerned his former job in New York City as a bookseller. The job went on for years, and when it ended, Robert had to decide whether to come home to North Carolina.

"I made a list of reasons for and against living in the South," Robert said. "And the pros and cons were the same! Pro number one: it's far from the big city. Con number one: it's far from the big city! Pro number two: everyone knows you. Con number two: everyone knows you!"

A big laugh. Women rarely commanded a dinner table like this.

Robert's marriage looked conventional: the couple added to each other's remarks, laughed at each other's jokes. But the way he held forth implied the husband held the balance of power.

At the end of the meal, Robert and I found ourselves alone. When he asked what work I was doing, I mentioned Dawn Simmons, the trans-person who was possibly intersexed. "Yes," he said, expressionless. "So tell me about your other work." We weren't going near the subject of Dawn.

The night went on, and I searched in vain for the woman underneath Robert's surface, but I couldn't see her because she'd been exiled. Or perhaps she was never there.

To JUDGE FROM DAWN SIMMONS's diaries, notes, and photographs, spread out on the table in the Duke library, Gordon Hall's childhood had been full of vigorous women. Dawn said that her grandmother Nellie, a messy, feisty extrovert, made a sideline as a freelance journalist, writing obituaries and wedding reports for a little weekly paper. A photograph of her showed a sinewy figure with flyaway hair, seated on a bicycle, the family being too poor for a car.

There were more strong women. Nellie had an identical twin, the superbly named Mrs. Claradoom Hall Ticehurst, whom Gordon called Auntie Doom. (The two women had married brothers, and so had the same last name.) Where the widowed Nellie was often broke, Auntie Doom had married a successful businessman and lived in an impressive house, called Beecholme. In other words, a close relative lived up the road in splendor, while Nellie and Gordon had hardscrabble lives.

A third looming sister, Gordon's great-aunt Elizabeth, lived in an ancient cottage known as Spicers. (Beecholme, Spicers: in rural England, it was customary to name even modest houses. Eventually,

Dawn would carry the habit with her to America, naming almost every place she lived.) Gordon remembered Aunt Elizabeth as "a tiny person with large hazel-colored eyes" who wore her hair in a bun, and who had an invalid husband, George Ditch, or Uncle Ditcher. Ditcher was wheelchair-bound and entirely dependent on his wife. Some years before, while on a rabbit hunt, Ditcher's gun had exploded, crippling an arm and paralyzing him from the waist down.

The most independent woman around, however, was Gordon's beefy cousin Rosamanda Stanton (Cousin Rosy), who must have been the manliest woman in Sussex. Cousin Rosy worked as a fire-fighter—the only woman on a fire company that anyone knew about—and later, for a pay increase, joined a carnival, making a dare-devil living by riding the "wall of death," driving a motorcycle around the inside of an empty oil tank, while smoking a cigarette for effect. Cousin Rosy's photograph showed a stout, ruddy figure wearing a cap with fake bullhorns—a smiling village Brunhild.

With all these swaggering women, a picture of Gordon came into view, straight out of dime-store psychoanalysis. Strong women plus weak or absent men equals sexual trouble for sons. Of course, if he were intersexual, and anatomically different, trouble would have come in any event.

Feminine women in Gordon's world seemed as rare as visiting fairies, and this is just how he saw them. When Gordon was going on five years old, his natural mother, Marjorie, was just twenty-one, and she looked to him like a shimmering angel: "All I wanted to do was to grow up and be a beautiful lady—"

> —like that exotic mother who once a year flitted like a bird of rare plumage across my less colorful horizon. What she wore was always of great interest to me; in my dreams I copied her. I can recall her long jade earrings, the red dress embroidered with large white daisies, the perfect black—including the veil—what she always wore for relatives' funerals.

Gordon was a small, fine child with ringlet curls and pretty features. While other village boys played outdoors, he collected dolls and played house. Gordon cherished his teddy bear, named Happy, and cut coupons from cocoa cans to buy Happy a friend, "a most elaborate lady doll named 'Lupe.' "

And there was another feminine theme, which was Gordon's love for animals. A photo showed him surrounded by his pets, including a guinea pig, a turtle, and birds. The pets offered companionship, according to Dawn; weirdly, they also echoed Gordon's life. Of the four cats in Grandmother Nellie's cottage (Charmaine, Josephine, Marina, and Nero), Nero was the one "who we thought was a boy but who wasn't," Dawn wrote, locating her own syndrome in the pet family.

Many years later, Dawn said her "affliction" had colored her whole childhood:

> I could never do physical training at school because, owing the malformation of the genital organs, I could not undress in front of others. I could never go to the lavatory during break; I always had to excuse myself during lessons when it would be empty. It was all so frustrating. I adored my teachers but was always thankful for weekends and holidays when I no longer had to be on my guard against being "found out." My voice never did break in the church choir, it just remained treble. Back in those dark days the secret of what I was not was always with me. I cried when I could not go to camp like other children. From an early age I hated war pictures, only because I thought that when I grew up I might have to go into the army. I wasn't afraid of fighting, but of the medical examination that would reveal to unfamiliar eyes the fact that Gordon Langley Hall was, in fact, nothing but a vegetable.

A week of digging through Dawn's papers had yielded a few grains of biography, but only firsthand testimony could turn up the stones of evidence. The scrap of paper wadded up by Ted Phillips contained the scribbled whereabouts of Natasha Simmons, Dawn's daughter. By now, two years had passed since Dawn's funeral. I'd hardly spoken to Natasha then, but if she would agree to talk, she might say something about the mystery of her mother.

When I reached her on the phone, I knew it was an intrusion. Even if I showed interest in the riddle of her origin, there was no promise she'd share her thoughts. Fortunately, Natasha was patient and a little resigned—she was accustomed to strangers' prying questions. We arranged to meet for lunch. And what Natasha said about her mother, the transgender Southern belle, deepened the enigma.

Chapter 3

MOTHERLESS CHILD

Thin and graceful, Natasha Simmons stepped into the restaurant foyer, having finished a cigarette outside. She was dressed in a beige crewneck sweater and dark pants, clothes too conservative for her tall beauty, and her manner was restrained. This was her day off from work, and she'd left her children with her boyfriend so we could meet.

The lunch place had yellow walls, brass chandeliers, and, scooping down from the ceiling, green-and-white-striped bunting. We sat and ordered salads. Natasha said her mother had spoken about me, which made it more agreeable to talk. Her mother's life had attracted a lot of attention, she said, much of it unwanted; after she died, reporters had called until Natasha stopped answering the phone.

Natasha's short hair was pulled back in a way that stressed her slender neck and oval face. Her eyebrows arched high, and her eyes protruded a little, sensuously. Whether she was Dawn's daughter or someone else's, her skin color was the plausible outcome of a black father and white mother.

She said, "For a long time, I carried my birth certificate with me, just to prove to people, 'Yeah, this is my mom. You sit there and talk about me being adopted, but here she is!' "

Although she had the poise I remembered from her appearance at the funeral two years before, Natasha was tense. She still missed her mother, and disliked opening her life to inspection.

The idea that a child would flash her birth certificate to other kids, like a teenager fishing for ID at a liquor store, struck me as sad. But living in the shadow of her mother's infamy meant getting used to odd requirements.

"I don't have early memories of Charleston. My first memory is of the Skyline Motel, in Catskill, New York," she continued. "It was a flea-ridden place, with a lot of low-down people there, and stuff going on."

The story I knew was that Dawn had lived in a mansion in Charleston, not a dingy motel in New York; but in fact, Natasha's speech sounded more like the Yankee uplands than coastal South Carolina. It turned out that a few years after she was born, Natasha and her mother had moved out of the South and settled in upstate New York.

At the Skyline Motel, the two shared a bedroom with a kitchenette. "There was no playground, so I played in the parking lot. But I had Vita—she was a water spaniel, beautiful, that had been abandoned by somebody." At this memory, Natasha's restraint lifted slightly, and she flashed a smile.

The daughter had inherited her mother's love of animals. "We had dogs, cats, mice, rabbits, guinea pigs, and birds, and snakes. And Mommy gave them people names, like Jimmy, Fay, Camilla, Priscilla, and Vita Sackville-West."

More smiles, but her body language remained taut. She rested her hands in her lap, bringing the left one up to gesture with long fingers before returning it below.

When she and Dawn moved to New York, they left John-Paul Simmons in Charleston, but he soon followed. Natasha said her parents' marriage was a mess, and they didn't have much money. Mother and daughter moved around ("a lot of different apartments"), sometimes with John-Paul, often not. Dawn would buy a sagging piece of real estate and then rent a cheaper place when money was short; the pattern repeated itself for years.

When she was about seven, Natasha went to England with her mother because Dawn wanted her daughter to see where she'd grown up. "I have a picture of my mother and me at Sissinghurst, but I don't remember much, except it being cold and damp—and the fish and chips."

On this same trip, Dawn had brought Natasha to see her English family, but I couldn't imagine what their feelings might have been when the former Gordon Hall showed up in a dress, with an African American daughter.

Natasha said she knew some of her mother's friends from her years in Charleston. "Like Joe Trott—he was at Mommy's funeral. And there was John Zeigler—I remember his name, anyway." The two men had known Dawn when she was Gordon.

The mood was better, the speakers in the ceiling played Beatles songs, and our salads arrived. Natasha ate first with her left hand, then with her right, and she changed back and forth throughout the meal.

When I asked what Dawn was like as a mother, Natasha said, "My mother was my Brownie troop leader!" This was strange, she said, because Dawn hated to go camping. Nevertheless, Sunday afternoons were spent in the woods. "We picked berries and flowers, and Mommy would always point out the names of different wildflowers and trees."

In the Duke library, I'd seen little essays Gordon Hall had written as a young man, and some of them had described the English countryside. It seemed he'd shown an interest in flowers and gardens from an early age.

Dawn was "a proper woman," said her daughter. "She didn't like games, or television. And she always wore dresses or skirts. It wasn't until the last couple years of her life—when she got sick—that she put on a pair of pants!"

The ladylike mom that Natasha described brought to mind the pastel photograph of Gordon Hall, delicately painted and feminine. Had the hair been longer, it could have been a picture of a woman.

"Mommy was also socially conservative," said her daughter.

This surprised me, because I'd assumed people pushed to the edge of society by their sexuality would be liberal.

No, said Natasha. She'd encouraged her mother to leave her father, but the answer had been a dogmatic no. "She would say, 'That's my husband. I married him, and I'm going to stand by him.' "

Natasha shook her head, smiled, and described more of Dawn's prim habits. "Mommy was active in the church, and she liked to go to the functions, like the church carnivals—and she'd get on the planning committee for the tag sale. She got me involved in church camps, and she taught arts and crafts at the church school."

A picture was taking shape. After leaving Charleston, Dawn Simmons had made herself into an upright single mother, a church lady who worked on bake sales and helped with Christmas toy drives. Arranging this person next to the others—the young Gordon Hall and the scandal figure Dawn Hall—I felt a kind of information nausea, the result of ingesting contrary facts. How many lives had she lived? Could they be compressed into one identity?

"Mommy was traditional," Natasha insisted, laughing. "We didn't talk about sex, but we would joke about it. When things got graphic, she would say, 'I don't want to hear that!' I used to laugh, because she was a trip. She wouldn't ever curse, but she would say, 'Damn!' And if you really got her mad, she might call you a bitch. When that happened, I said, 'Mom, are you okay?' "

The salads were gone, and Natasha put down her fork. From being polite and friendly, she suddenly seemed to become vulnerable, and the detail started to flow into her memories. I asked about her mother's beauty regimen, and Natasha described something that befit a lady of modest means.

"She used to go get her hair fixed, maybe once a month, in a French roll, especially if something was going on—and I'd be the one to touch it up, put the pins back in. When her gray started, I'd touch that up, too, and trim her ends. I'd also do her nails. She didn't like bright colors. She wore costume jewelry, and she liked big earrings and big necklaces. She used basic cover-up makeup, but other than that, nothing. Except her lipstick—which was always red, and she felt naked without it."

Near the end of Dawn's life, mother and daughter had moved from upstate New York back to Charleston, where they lived in separate apartments but within walking distance. It was as though Dawn had returned to her adopted home, the city where she'd experienced a kind of ragged glory, in order to tend to something unfinished.

Natasha smiled. In those last years, she and her mother had seen each other every day. And as she spoke, her fingers twirled a ring hanging from a necklace.

"This is her wedding band," Natasha said thickly. "The doctors wanted her to take it off for an X-ray or something, and she would refuse. At the end of her life, it was falling off, because she'd lost so much weight, and she taped it to make it stay."

Natasha's eyes welled up, and she looked down at the table to avoid crying.

I offered to give her a ride to her boyfriend's house, where her children were waiting.

LANGUAGE LESSON

Dawn Simmons's life seemed to call for a map; but in my address book, I could positively identify no one who might outline the ways of sexually ambiguous people. Looking for a diagram of Dawn's world, I decided to talk with some of her latter-day peers.

The International Foundation for Gender Education, a transgender group, was holding its annual meeting at an airport hotel in Philadelphia. I made reservations.

The Hilton was one of those comfortable and antiseptic hotels built within convenient earshot of the runway. Why an adventurous group of transvestites, transsexuals, and a sprinkling of intersexuals had chosen to congress there was anyone's guess. But the trans-world appeared to be something of an island kingdom, with its own laws. The meeting would show me who, aside from my woman of special interest, inhabited its shores.

At the reception desk, two male-to-female transsexuals outfitted in wigs and conservative dresses sat behind stacks of literature. As we talked, the feeling of being a voyeur struck me again. (The more I deepened the dragnet through the trans-world, though, the sensation faded; eventually, it went away.)

A printed program offered a word of advice for conventioneers: "Public restroom use is always a touchy subject where transgender people are concerned. Always use the restroom appropriate to the gender role you are presenting, and use it as a person of that birth gender would. (Hint: women never urinate standing up.)"

At midday on a Friday, the conference gathered for lunch in a ballroom, where, seated at round tables, three hundred people dined on tepid chicken. Surveying the scene from a corner, a chatty red-haired transsexual named Nancy Cain, former executive director of the group, who told me she'd crossed over from male to female in 1994, talked about the basics.

"Transgender people make a distinction between gender and sex," said Nancy with a wry tone. "I talk at high schools, trying to widen the kids' world, and I boil it down for them this way. I say, 'Gender is between your ears; sex is between your legs.' "

Nancy looked to be about forty, and stood around five foot nine. She had an aquiline nose, milky skin, and a sassy demeanor. Her dress was feminine-professional.

She was a believer in the laws of her island, which could be laid out as follows: Most people are born anatomically male or female (sex), and only after puberty do they end up with a psychological apparatus (gender) that echoes their sex organs. But the vicissitudes of biology and childhood mean misfires happen all the time. While the majority of people, as adults, hit the gender target predicted by their sex, a lot hit a point between the poles of masculinity and femininity (the "manly woman"), and a few have sex organs and a gender identity way out of sync. A physiological male with the gender or mental life of a woman is not a rare person, and in Nancy Cain's world she is the norm.

"Not all people transition the whole way," Nancy said. "Most stop somewhere on the path, like me." Nancy touched her breasts, and said, "These are homegrown," meaning she'd developed with estrogen supplements. Brushing her cheek, she groaned. "The electrolysis was the worst. How would you like a hot needle in the face a thousand times?"

When asked, Nancy said she'd had her testicles removed, but had kept her penis. "And the same with my partner," she added. Her live-in companion had also transitioned from male to female, but stopped "at that point."

Transsexuals with completed surgery seemed to represent only a fraction of people who start to change sex. The anecdotal report of one scholar who spoke at the convention was that fewer than one in four "finish the job" with genital operations. Most find other ways of living in between the sexes.

The transgender world has a phrase that applies to all of its many tribes: *gender variant*. To whom is this phrase suited? About half of those present in the ballroom appeared to be middle-aged men in drag; they showed little sign of feminization with hormones and seemed content with wigs and heels. Perhaps 10 percent at the lunch were female-to-male transsexuals: women who had become men. Most had facial hair, but with feminine cheeks and chin lines, and most were of small stature. All but one or two had had their breasts removed.

The most conspicuous in the room were the thin, younger women. They had breasts, but some also had Adam's apples and flat lines for hips. They were young men on the road to femininity.

"It's hard to get good numbers," said Nancy Cain, "because we get treated like a freak show by everybody." She waved off the idea, more amused than irritated. "I was invited on a network talk show, and they asked, 'Is there anyone you can bring to fight with?' I didn't go. People who make the change melt back into their lives and don't become a statistic. Why should they come to these meetings?"

*   *   *

JOE TROTT WAS WEARING his familiar string tie, striped shirt, and ponytail. He opened the front gate to his house in Charleston, which stood near the eastern border of Ansonborough, Dawn's old neighborhood, within shouting distance of the Cooper River. This placed him at the edge of the city, a good point from which to keep a skeptical eye on the movements of the peninsula.

Easing along with a cane, Joe was happy to answer a question about his health: "Terrible, terrible."

He looked up at the wooden house, a square, dignified building that sat on a high basement foundation. It had two floors of porches in the Charleston style, and a row of Doric columns on each. When he opened the big front door, an ancient scent drifted out.

"House was built in 1803, burned in 1835, rebuilt in 1838, then doubled in size in 1840," said Joe, giving the one-sentence summary of a Charleston homeowner. "When I bought it, fifty years ago, it was a flophouse for prostitutes and barkeeps."

He walked through tall mahogany doors into the front parlor, which was the size of a trailer, although one trimmed with flocked wallpaper and wainscoting. In the formal rooms, a grandfather clock faced a Victorian sofa ("from Scotland, with thistle carved into the wood"), and there were miniatures under glass in a table case. The assortment of things said the house belonged to a professional furniture picker.

"That's by Sebastian Erard, the French keyboard maker who operated in England," Joe said, touching a magnificent grand piano. "It was done for the Duke of York, but the man who restored it used plastic instead of ivory for the inlay, and did a shit-ass job."

In the corner of the parlor was a typical Charleston item, the family portrait, whose existence conferred bragging rights. The man in the frame, an eighteenth-century gentleman in a red waistcoat and lace collar, was Joe's distant ancestor, the lawmaker Nicholas Trott.

Joe said that he and his wife lived on the first floor of the house, and his business partner lived on the third. His upstairs friend had been a companion for forty years, almost as long as Joe's wife. "At one time he had twenty-one cats. We had a house full of pussy!" said Joe.

The old man's obscenity struck a dissonant note inside the grand rooms of his house, ornamented as it was with formal things. Except, as he said, the building had been a flophouse at one time; and (as Joe didn't reveal, but I'd heard) up the street was the handsome old house that certain Charleston residents had fondly named the Homo Hilton, a meeting point for drag queens.

For many years, Joe and his upstairs partner had run Cobblestone Antiques out of this house, using the old mansion as a furniture showroom. "Our parlor floor was furnished as though someone lived there, but everything had a price tag on it," he said. The business ended when the men retired, but the leftover furniture made the house look like fine things could still be bought.

We finished the house tour and ended up in the kitchen, sitting at a breakfast table covered with a lace cloth.

"When Gordon came to Charleston, Ansonborough was still a slum," said Joe. "It was poor, and seventy-five percent black, twenty-five white." Joe said the Historic Charleston Foundation, the preservation group, had bought a lot of beat-up houses in the neighborhood. The foundation was glad to find someone who wanted to restore one, "so they catered to Gordon hand and foot."

Gordon Hall bought the house at 56 Society Street, a short walk from Joe's place, on the same street. He'd arrived in town in 1962 with another man, the butler from the Whitney mansion in New York. "Scaltro was his name," Joe said. "It was Joe Scaltro. But after a while, Scaltro returned to New York, and Gordon stayed." Their plan was to run an antiques business between the two cities. From New York, Scaltro used Isabel Whitney's money, which Gordon had inherited, to buy eighteenth-century furniture. He then shipped the furniture down south to sell out of Gordon's house on Society Street. About the merchandise, Joe said, "It was the real thing, no jokes about it—they weren't getting department-store furniture and scarring it up."

But the nature of Gordon's relationship with Scaltro was vague. Scaltro didn't want people to know his intimacy with Gordon, outside the business. "He'd come down here from New York, and you'd think he was some tourist staying with Gordon," Joe said, laughing.

To the three personas of Dawn—the boy in England, the sexual convert, and the church lady—I now had to add a fourth: the cosmopolitan from New York.

While Joe Trott ran his showroom in the house where we sat, Gordon did the same a block or so distant. "But in Gordon's house, nothing was priced, so it was even more convincing it was a residence," said Joe.

I mentioned how Dawn had once said she owned bed steps that had belonged to Robert E. Lee, and mirrors that had belonged to George and Martha Washington, and Joe laughed again. "He had more stories about the furniture, good stories, but you could not prove or disprove them. It was amazing how Gordon could create these fantasies! He told me that he was the illegitimate son of an aristocrat, or something. He said his mother, or his stepmother, was the upstairs maid to this Earl Somebody or that Lord Someone—and he was the illegitimate son!"

And Joe's amusement was a clue: Gordon was a fabricator who wove stories about his merchandise. Did he also make up his life?

In addition to selling antiques, both Joe and Gordon had sidelines. Joe Trott ran a floral business; Gordon wrote books and also opened his place as a house museum, charging admission to tourists.

At the time, the city's preservationists handed out brochures on private houses that tourists might visit, and Gordon's antebellum mansion was one of them, with a plaque on the outside that identified it as the Dr. Joseph Johnson House, after its builder. A steady flow of gawkers paid a dollar or two to traipse through Gordon's living rooms, which meant a good income stream, whether anyone bought a tea table or not.

"I met Gordon because he called me and said someone had recommended me to keep his house full of flowers when he had the tours," said Joe.

And there were the pets. "Some people thought Gordon had too many animals," Joe said. "Well, he loved them! But some talk started going around when he began with the birthday parties for the dogs. The dogs got all dolled up, and I provided the flowers for the parties. He had a big German shepherd named Jackie, and he had Chihuahuas. The dogs would have clothes on, and there would be servants with hors d'oeuvres."

This meant one thing I'd heard but never believed—that Gordon had a coming-out party for his dogs—was actually true.

In a memoir, Dawn had said that she (or rather, Gordon) was a sought-after guest for dinner in the great houses in downtown Charleston.

Not so, said Joe. "The high Charleston society were much more insular than we were, and they didn't want peons like us hanging around, so Gordon didn't penetrate that society. He thought he was going to come down here with all this money and be quite the item, but the Charleston society wouldn't let him in. They wouldn't even crack the door!" Joe made a gesture like peering through a peephole.

Part of Dawn's story, which she helped foster, depicted Gordon sweeping through the gentry's chandeliered rooms, leaving a wake of admiring gossip. Was this, too, an invention?

Whether Gordon dressed the truth, or provided nonexistent facts, Joe said, he was a sweet and giving person. "I never felt—never, never, never—that he would be talking behind my back. He was very tolerant about everybody."

I took out a photograph of Gordon with rosy cheeks, and Joe looked at it. "Well, he obviously wanted to be a girl from way back. He used to tell me, 'I'm in disguise. I'm not what I want to be. I have two sex organs.' "

Next I pulled out a picture of Isabel Whitney. "She wanted him as a protégé, someone she could play with," Joe added. I asked about their relationship, and he said, "He was a servant—that's my understanding."

Joe picked up a photo of Dawn, after the sex reassignment, standing with her fiancé, John-Paul Simmons. He slowed down his talk, and his face grew sad. "And when he met—Gordon met—he naturally met him, because he was in his yard doing the garden. He met this black fellow, John-Paul Simmons. He was a gardener. Gordon picked up with this black fellow, and brought him in the house, and fell in love with him. Or so he said—and all this shit."

Joe wrinkled his brow and looked out the window.

Finally he studied a picture of Dawn with a big tummy beneath her white dress, and rolled his eyes.

"I told him, 'Dawn—.' Or, I said, 'Gordon'—because I never could get accustomed to *Dawn*. I said, 'Gordon, what are you trying to prove? Who are you trying to convince?' "

Joe Trott was a doubter, but he missed his beloved old friend.

DAWN SIMMONS SOMETIMES said she was a transsexual, sometimes a hermaphrodite. In fact, she seemed to have belonged to almost every tribe that inhabited the transgender world. I composed a glossary in my mind.

Transsexuals take hormones (mainly estrogen or testosterone) to modify their biochemistry. Occasionally, they seek surgery to change their sexual anatomy so it comes into line with their "gender of conviction." There are no good figures for the number of transsexuals in the United States; but according to European data, about one in thirty thousand adult males and one in a hundred thousand adult females seek sex reassignment surgery. If the ratios were similar in America, this would put the number of male-to-female transsexuals in the United States (in the year 2005) at about ninety-nine hundred, and the number of female-to-male around three thousand. The smaller number of women who opt to transition to male bodies lets them carry their own banner, and many call themselves *transmen*.

Cross-dressers are men or women who inhabit the gender of the other sex, part-time or full-time, but who usually want nothing to do with hormones or surgery. (Dawn Simmons said she was never a cross-dresser until she actually came out as a woman, in the late 1960s.) The majority of cross-dressers—transvestites, trannies, TVs—maybe 90 percent, according to one study—are men in women's clothes, and most of them are heterosexual, as well as married. The rest are women dressing as men. Drag queens, or men who spoof feminine style, have an opposite number: drag kings (women in macho dress, like cowboy gear). Drag queens and kings are the most visible cross-dressers, but not the most common. The classic transvestite remains the husband who puts on frilly things at home.

Most cross-dressers are only part-timers and thus live double lives. But the smaller phenomenon of the *passing woman* or *passing man* seemed relevant to Dawn's life. This is the full-time cross-dresser who inhabits the other sex year-round, sometimes passing so successfully that no straight eyes can tell.

For reasons of concealment and shame, no reliable figures on cross-dressers exist, but groups with an interest in elevating the total put it at about 2 percent of adult men, which would mean millions of American guys. Considering the popularity of humor about men in drag, which never goes out of fashion, there may be a kernel of truth in this high number.

Dawn Simmons claimed she'd been intersexual, born with anomalous genitals. *Intersexuals* have an anatomical condition or hormone disorder that causes sexual variation later in life; they don't necessarily live as transgender people. Their biological differences place intersexuals between men and women, but not by choice.

Until the mid-1900s, intersexuals lived under the name of hermaphrodites, but medicine has largely replaced that term. Medical literature estimates that genital anomalies occur with roughly one in fifteen hundred live births, which would place the number of intersexuals in America at nearly two hundred thousand, far higher than the incidence of transsexuals.

When Dawn Simmons transitioned from male to female in the late 1960s, she was very much in isolation, as one of the first Americans to do so. The thousands who followed hadn't yet joined to hold hands at conventions; and no language told Dawn how to imagine herself, because the vocabulary hadn't been coined.

In the end, she preferred cute metaphors to describe what she was experiencing. "I felt rather like the double-daffodil that we dissected so many times during nature classes at school in England," she once said about having physical exams.

NATASHA SIMMONS SAT in the passenger seat, looking straight ahead, as we drove toward her boyfriend's house and her three waiting children.

"I had my first, my son, when I was fifteen," she said, "and it really upset my mom. But before it happened, I'd told her, 'Mommy, we need to talk about birth control.' She didn't want to hear about it."

Natasha, now thirty-one, had grown up in the towns of Catskill and Hudson, New York, two old settlements on the Hudson River, ten minutes apart, whose factories had closed, leaving many people with hard lives. She had attended public schools and had become pregnant when she was still in eighth grade. "I wish my mom had used more supervision on me," said Natasha, "because I was coming and going, and she didn't know what I was doing."

Her first child took her out of high school, which Natasha later finished with an equivalency test. When she was still in her teens, she had a daughter by a different father. Her third child, with a third man, came in her late twenties.

Dawn had loved Natasha's children and had spent much time with them, babysitting so that Natasha could work as a waitress in Hudson and, later, attend college at night.

When Dawn and Natasha moved back to Charleston, in the late 1990s, Natasha went back to waiting tables. When we met, she was working at a motel restaurant and attending a school of cosmetology, hoping to start a beauty career. "It's been almost two years since Mommy died, and it's been the hardest years of my life," said Natasha, still looking out the windshield.

We arrived at a low white building with a beat-up car in the drive. "That's my piece of junk," she said.

Walking to the door, Natasha added, "I don't know what you'll find out at Sissinghurst." I had told her about my plan to go to England. Now I said that I hoped to visit her mother's grave.

IN HER PAPERS AT DUKE, Dawn often mentioned Sissinghurst Castle, in England, where her parents had been servants. When she was the child named Gordon, Sissinghurst was a crumbling brick manor, already five hundred years old, an atmospheric place and home to the eccentric writers who owned it, Vita Sackville-West and her husband, Harold Nicolson. At that time, Sackville-West, the poet and novelist, and Nicolson, a historian and biographer, were possibly the most famous literary couple in England. They were celebrated for their books and for their unconventional lives, which involved curious sexual arrangements, a fact not lost on the young Gordon Hall. Sissinghurst Castle had been Dawn's childhood playground. I had a hunch the place might hold some clues to her identity—if there was anyone there who still remembered.

Part 2

THE MAN

Chapter 4

THE THIN LORD OF SISSINGHURST

DINKY AT THE MANOR

You leave London and drive south, and soon you come to the rolling farmland of Kent, skimming past hedgerows and clumps of indifferent sheep. First a small, whitewashed village and then, lying in a clearing like a red train, Sissinghurst Castle.

Clack!

"Or what remains of it!"

Nigel Nicolson smacked the stone path with his wooden cane. The heir and occupant of Sissinghurst had agreed to talk about Dawn Simmons, whom he'd known when he and she were both children.

"Yesh, what remains," Nicolson said with his upper-class diction.

Handsome and deferential, and eighty-five years old, Nicolson stood several inches over six feet. He was dressed in a gray turtleneck and wool herringbone jacket, its two leather buttons fastened over a little paunch. His face was rectangular and long, and on his crown a tuft of white hair grew this way and that.

Inside the brick manor, he pointed the way down skinny corridors, past a half-dozen rooms with exposed ceiling beams, giant fireplaces, and Gothic windows. The walls were lined with books and tapestries.

"Tudor," he said. "This part of the building was put up in 1490. The tower and the other part were built about sixty years later. The house was rather grand in the 1500s, when Queen Elizabeth I visited here. But there was a long decline, and most of the place was demolished after your War of Independence. What remains are these pieces."

He meant the locomotive of a house in which he lived, which was a hundred yards long, plus a tall brick tower that stood behind it and a pair of substantial cottages a little bit away.

Nigel Nicolson had lived at Sissinghurst, with interruptions, since 1932, when his parents moved to the estate, bringing their two young sons. At that time, a pair of married servants named Jack and Marjorie Copper also moved in. And this made Nigel Nicolson, in his early teens, an eyewitness to Dawn Simmons's youth, because Gordon Hall was Marjorie's oldest child.

But Gordon was not always around. He'd been born to Marjorie when she was just sixteen, before she married the Nicolsons' handyman, Jack Copper. Because Marjorie had given Gordon to her own mother to raise, her son lived fifty miles away, with his grandmother, and visited Sissinghurst only on holidays.

Nigel Nicolson's office was no bigger than a large bed. It was bright outside but dark in the room. A tiny medieval window threw a shaft of light on bookshelves and a small desk. As he sat down, I noticed Nicolson's khaki pants were stained: the master of the manor felt at ease and had no one he needed to impress.

Nicolson leaned forward in his chair, chin on palm, gripping a wadded white handkerchief. He put on a pair of square tortoiseshell glasses and looked over the top of them.

"Now to this 'Dinky' business," he said. "What possessed you to take an interest in such a *minor* subject?"

"You mean Dawn Simmons?" I said.

"Yes, he was the boy we called *Dinky*."

I said that Dawn Simmons had grown into an unusual person since leaving England, and in America—at least in the little city of Charleston, three thousand miles away—she was a memorable figure.

"He's admired in Charleston? Famous?" A look of disbelief.

"Dawn was infamous," I answered.

"You mean he had a sort of resilience, and survived," said Nicolson. "In my opinion, although he had undoubted charm, he had no great gifts. In any case, yours is an amazing undertaking!"

Nicolson threw his head back and stroked his neck.

Sitting in his little office, surrounded by signs of family accomplishment, I had the feeling of having brought a trivial matter to the attention of an impressive man. The name Dinky made it undeniable.

Before our meeting, I'd browsed Nicolson's memoir, *Long Life*, and seen that in his four-score years, he'd been a publisher, politician, and writer. (Whereas Dinky had been—?) In the book, Nicolson described his education at Eton and Oxford, and then his marching off, at age twenty-five, to serve as an officer during World War II. After the war, in which he commanded troops in Africa and Italy, he was elected to the House of Commons as a Conservative. He also formed the publishing partnership Weidenfeld & Nicolson, which produced the first edition of Nabokov's *Lolita* in England. The furor around that event—the book was thought pornographic—encouraged voters to remove Nicolson from Parliament. Which was just as well, because afterward he wrote a number of books of biography and history, several of which were best sellers.

Resuming his forward lean, Nicolson said, "Dinky was small and perhaps a bit childish. Maybe effeminate, too, I'm not sure about that. I have no idea where the name Dinky came from. It was very convenient, however, because it would do for a boy or a girl. Let's look it up in the Oxford English Dictionary, see what they have to say about *dinky*."

He reached for the big book, flipped the pages, ran his finger down.

" 'DINKY: a small contrivance, like a small boat.' I never heard that, have you? Or, 'as an adjective: trifling, insignificant, unimpressive.' "

Snapping the book shut, he chortled. "The general feeling is childish," he said. Then, moderating, "But rather lovable, I think."

The book went back on the shelf, and Nicolson looked over his glasses. He was familiar with Dawn's public story—the move to Charleston, the sex switch, the birth of Natasha. In fact, he said, a few years earlier he'd written a review of one of Dawn's books. In the piece he'd acknowledged his connection to Dawn and reflected on what had become of the boy he once knew.

Ending the mouseplay, Nicolson mused on the subject.

"Here's what I know of Dinky. He was one of the village boys. His father, Jack Copper, I knew perfectly well, because he was still here when my mother died, in 1962. Copper was my parents' driver. He was a bit of a rogue. My mother adored him. I never did. I thought he was a cheat, lazy, and an untruthful man. He had a certain style, a braggart style that my mother liked. When I inherited him, so to speak, after my mother died, he didn't do a stroke of work. He'd been unkind to his wife, and Dinky hated him. He was a good mechanic and looked after our cars. My father couldn't drive, and Copper met him at the train station. He did odd jobs around the house. A handyman. But his private life was a matter for suspicion. He drank a lot. It was said that he had an affair with a girl in the village, things like that. He had a poor reputation. His temper was violent, and he was a bully. There was one terrible incident where he had a fight with the head gardener here. They really came to blows. My mother said she thought he would have killed him. My mother ordered the gardener to leave at once, even though he was the victim! Because she preferred Copper."

Although Jack Copper, Dawn's rakish father, was a driver and handyman, Dawn had written that her family had also once included Spanish aristocrats. I pulled out one of Dawn's accounts of her lineage, and read aloud: "My ancient great-grandmother on my mother's side was Condesa Elisabeta de Mendoza."

"Good God!" said Nicolson. "I mean, how are you going to check that? You're going to have to go to Spain!" He stroked his neck and laughed.

"I remember Jack Copper's wife, Dinky's mother, was a dim, pathetic, very plain, thin, wasted-away woman. Not particularly noticeable. She never emerged very much from their rooms, and when she did she sort of scurried around." He shook his shoulders to suggest a scampering animal. "We had very little to do with her, and I never had any prolonged conversation with her. That she had this noble ancestry, I never heard of that. She didn't give that appearance."

The person he described did not sound like the beautiful "bird of rare plumage" that Dawn remembered swooping down into her childhood.

I asked whether Nicolson had an early memory of Gordon/Dawn.

"He would be around. My brother and I befriended him in a sort of way. There was no class problem about it, as there would have been had we been older. I remember him vaguely as a sort of sprite. I think I would compare him to Puck. He was naughty, but rather engaging. Made no bones about it that he hated his father, who ill-treated him very much. I don't know about his feeling for his mother. Fishing and swimming are what I mostly associate him with. I don't think he ever had a meal with us; I don't think I saw him in any context other than the fields and farm and lake. There were other working-class boys we knew on the same terms. But we used to go fishing and swimming in the lake, with Dinky. And, as there was nobody around, we swam in the nude, you see. Of course it didn't occur to little boys to look for anything strange. It was prepuberty. The possibility that Dinky might have female organs never occurred to us—that is, to my brother and me. I don't think Dinky, who must have known about it, would have told anybody."

Had Dinky been a hermaphrodite?

"I'm not quite sure what a hermaphrodite is," said Nicolson. "Is that someone who has sexual organs of both sexes?"

A crackle of discomfort in the room. We shifted our weight in our chairs, and he went on. "We didn't even know that such a thing existed! It never occurred to us that such a thing happened to Dinky, or such a thing happened at all in the human race! The problem never arose. Anyhow, I have no light to throw upon that at all. Of course, when Dinky was an adult, I never knew him."

That Dinky, or Gordon Hall, had made little impression on young Nigel Nicolson was not altogether surprising. Gordon didn't live at Sissinghurst, and only visited rarely, never mind the class barrier.

"Retrospectively, he was a rather unusual, active, pugnacious character. Sprightly, rather likable—like any other village boy, with a little bit added. The extra added was his undoubted intelligence. That's what my mother saw in him. I think this is true: he read poetry. He was interested in the history of this place. For my mother, her feeling toward Jack Copper was transmitted to his boy. 'Oh, Copper's child! What a nice little one!' That sort of thing."

The eyeglasses went onto the desk.

To MOST ENGLISH PEOPLE, Sissinghurst Castle is not Nigel Nicolson's home but that of his parents, the writers Vita Sackville-West and Harold Nicolson.

Vita Sackville-West was nearly as unorthodox a person as Dawn Simmons. She was born Victoria Mary Sackville-West, in 1892, into an aristocratic family at Knole House, the largest private house in England. A great brick pile ten times larger than Sissinghurst, Knole had 365 rooms, fifty-two staircases, and seven courtyards. A regiment of servants took care of its art and antiques. Vita was the only child of Lionel Edward, third Baron of Sackville, and Victoria Josepha Dolores Catalina Sackville-West, his first cousin. As a girl, Vita was androgynous and tomboyish, and her mother considered her ugly. Her upbringing was pampered. She was privately educated by tutors and nannies, and produced plays she had written—either on a stage set up on the lawn or in one of Knole's drawing rooms.

In 1913, at age twenty-one, Vita married a young diplomat, Harold Nicolson, and by 1920 she had produced two sons, Benedict and Nigel. It was after motherhood that Vita became a well-known writer. Her books, such as *All Passion Spent* and *Family History*, charted the customs of the upper class, while her poetry, including her famous twenty-five-hundred-line "The Land," tracked her heart.

When Vita's father died, in 1928, the title of fourth Baron Sackville fell to a male relative, who therefore inherited Knole. Throughout her life, Vita declared she wished to have been a man—not from some transgender drive (although she appears to have been a masculine woman), but for reasons of property. As a woman, she could not inherit her childhood home, and she was bitterly disappointed. It was at this point that she and her husband bought Sissinghurst Castle, a then-derelict estate.

The couple moved in, restored the living spaces, and created their own world. Harold Nicolson left diplomacy and began writing, but books were only half of their life. Much of the day during the warm months was spent on the garden. Over thirty years, Vita and Harold created a garden of enormous personality, which covered many acres, with various courtyards, each in a distinct style, and hundreds of varieties of flowers and plants.

Professional gardeners were hired full-time, and the servants were conscripted to help. In one place Dawn Simmons wrote, "I was, according to V. Sackville-West, 'a good weeder,' and many were the hours I spent as a child weeding her flower beds."

After his parents died, Nigel Nicolson persuaded the British government to take over Sissinghurst, and the result was the creation, in 1967, of Sissinghurst Gardens, part of the National Trust, the government-run collection of worthy buildings and lands. The gardens became the most famous in England, visited by two hundred thousand ticket buyers a year. In the summer, the crowds walked beneath Nigel Nicolson's tiny office window on their way to the lavish flower beds, Vita's enduring monument.

ORLANDO

Nigel Nicolson put on a checked overcoat and green cap with earflaps. "I'll show you where Dinky would have stayed," he said. He grabbed his cane and made his way outside, where it was winter, damp, and nearly freezing. The separate gardens marked by walls and hedges stretched out in every direction. In their center was a tall brick tower that Nicolson's mother once used as her writing studio.

The public grounds were closed for the season, and empty; a single gardener walked between clumps of brown plants. "I'm sorry everything is dead," said Nicolson.

I was imagining the young Gordon running along the hedgerows, when Nicolson wheeled around and pointed with his cane.

"When we first came here, Copper, and therefore Dinky, had half the flat on the upper floor of that wing of the house. Those two windows were the Copper establishment."

What were his family's relations with their servants?

"My mother couldn't boil an egg," Nicolson said. "She was totally dependent. We had four servants and five gardeners. It was small staff, although today it would be regarded as large.

"You see, we were an unusual family, because my mother was an aristocrat. We would have been called then 'upper class.' The term has been dropped now. There is no such thing as an upper class. We were what people today call posh. We talked the way I talk"—he meant his Oxford cadence—"and the relationship with the village people was minimal. But my brother and I were a little less class-conscious. Therefore, our relationship with Dinky was much easier."

I asked whether Nicolson possessed a title, and he smiled for the first time. "I could become a peer if my cousin, who is two years younger than me, dies. I would become Lord Carnock. But hereditary peers have no right to speak or vote in the House of Lords, so what's the point of them? They say the only advantage of being a lord is that you get a good table in a crowded restaurant. It's not worth having, you know, the title. You're just an anachronism, like a dodo bird."

Dawn's writings expressed her awe at Sissinghurst, and she'd never stopped talking about it. This was partly because she could use the glamour of the place to persuade people to listen to her; but it was also that in her youth, her parents' employers and their famous friends strode around her like giants.

"Oh, I never showed you the place where Dinky and I used to swim and gambol around," said Nicolson. "We have to go back a bit." We passed through an opening in a brick wall and into a courtyard of shriveled plants. Statuary and urns stood sentry by the flower beds, covered with green cloth against the frost. We turned onto a path lined by trees whose branches had been trained to grow at perfect right angles, parallel to the ground.

"My father liked symmetry, and he designed this, which is called the Lime Walk. He was the designer, and Vita planted." I thought it was curious how Nicolson referred to his mother by her first name.

Again the cane pointed. "There is the lake, two halves separated by a bank of earth. We used to swim from the isthmus between the two lakes. As I said, we never suspected he wasn't a boy."

Nicolson ended his narration, and we walked back to the house. "After that, Dinky vanishes from my life. I never knew him, or her, as an adult."

We passed the tower where Nicolson's mother had worked and entered the house.

THERE WAS ONE FACET of Dawn's childhood I was reluctant to bring up, and that was the sexual life at Sissinghurst, before World War II.

Harold Nicolson and Vita Sackville-West had an unusual marriage, which made them the subject of much gossip. Unhappy as a diplomat's wife (her husband was sent to Istanbul, then Tehran), Vita had affairs with women. Her first lover, Violet Trefusis, was the daughter of Alice Keppel, mistress of King Edward VII. The affair lasted three years, and Vita kept a secret diary of it. Meanwhile, after her children were born, Vita's husband carried on affairs with men, and continued to do so for many years. The family worked like that for decades.

Vita met her mature love, Virginia Woolf, in the mid-1920s.

Woolf soon paid Vita the compliment of writing a book about her, the novel *Orlando*. Suggestively for my transgender protagonist, the book tells the story of a young male aristocrat, Orlando, who changes into a woman.

After Vita's death, her son Nigel discovered the diary of his mother's first lesbian adultery. Fifty years after the affair (and after his father had died) Nicolson published the account in his book *Portrait of a Marriage*, causing a media furor. The book was a best seller, and the BBC made it into a four-hour film.

THE YOUNG GORDON HALL was aware of the sexual turmoil at Sissinghurst—or, at least, Dawn later wrote about it as though she'd witnessed everything. "Vita's lesbian activities were known to all of us," she said. "We would peep out of the window to see Lady Nicolson's 'new lady,' as my mother diplomatically called them. Jack Copper was a little more earthy. To him they were simply, 'the Missus' old women.'"

Elsewhere, Dawn remembered:

> At Sissinghurst, Vita Sackville-West and her husband, Harold Nicolson, took a friendly interest in my writing. I often posted Sir Harold's *Observer* book reviews for him, cycling with them to the village post box. I believe that Vita Sackville-West would have been fascinated had she lived to hear the end of my story, for it is coincidental that her close friend Virginia Woolf wrote *Orlando*, the story of a man who over the years changes into a woman. The boy she knew as "Dinky" became a real-life Orlando.

The novel *Orlando* became a beacon in Dawn Simmons's fantasy life that helped guide her sexual journey. Virginia Woolf published the book, *Orlando: A Biography*, in 1928, and it became her greatest commercial success. The author took Vita Sackville-West's ancestral estate, Knole, as a model for the novel's setting and included pictures of Vita and her family as illustrations in the text.

Orlando's story spans three hundred years and follows the super-human life of its protagonist. The character Orlando begins as a young sixteenth-century aristocrat in the court of Queen Elizabeth. In the eighteenth century, having hardly aged, Orlando matures in a romance with a Russian princess. During the 1800s, he becomes an ambassador to Turkey—at which point Orlando transitions to femininity. As Lady Orlando, the protagonist meets the English writers Pope and Addison. Finally, she gives birth.

Many suggestive passages of cross-dressing and same-sex encounters punctuate the novel, and it's easy to imagine Dawn Simmons under the influence of Woolf's hypnotic and ambiguous prose. From chapter 4:

> The difference between the sexes is, happily, one of great profundity. Clothes are but a symbol of something hid deep beneath. It was a change in Orlando herself that dictated her choice of a woman's dress and of a woman's sex. And perhaps in this she was only expressing rather more openly than usual—openness indeed was the soul of her nature—something that happens to most people without being thus plainly expressed. For here again, we come to a dilemma. Different though the sexes are, they intermix. In every human being a vacillation from one sex to the other takes place, and often it is only the clothes that keep the male or female likeness, while underneath the sex is the very opposite of what it is above. . . . For it was this mixture in her of man and woman, one being uppermost and then the other, that often gave her conduct an unexpected turn. . . . Whether, then, Orlando was most man or woman, it is difficult to say and cannot now be decided.

What do we make of the resemblance of the novel to Dawn's biography? I suspect Dawn identified both with Virginia Woolf and her fictional heroine. Like Orlando, Dawn imagined herself on a journey from maleness to femaleness. Like Woolf, she focused her desire on Vita Sackville-West, especially the grand lady's sexual ambiguity and noble inheritance. (Unlike Woolf, however, Dawn was a spectator, outside Vita's life.) As an adult, Dawn often let it drop that she'd known Virginia Woolf from visits to Sissinghurst, although she failed to mention she'd been a five-year-old boy named Gordon when she made the writer's acquaintance.

RETURNING TO HIS DESK, Nigel Nicolson pulled some yellowed papers out of a file. "I don't know whether you want to take these letters from Dinky. They are of no use to me anymore."

The letters, which Dawn had written a few years earlier, were typewritten and signed "Dawn Langley Simmons." One contained news of Dawn's life in Charleston; another asked Nicolson's permission for Dawn to publish a book about Vita. (He discouraged her.)

There was one last thing. "Oh yes, I'd forgotten," said Nicolson. Suddenly the retired publisher thought of a visit he'd once made to Charleston, where he'd been invited to give a talk. "This must have been in the 1970s, at the very height of the Dinky scandal. I think it was just after he married. Maybe after the alleged baby was born. The city was humming about Dinky, and people were fascinated by me—not because of my lecture, but because I'd known Dinky as a boy! I was quite a figure in Charleston, for a day."

On the visit, Nicolson's American hosts offered to show him where Dawn was living, and he went along for the ride, looking at the house from a car window. "I didn't want to ring the bell. I didn't want to make contact with him—or by then I suppose it was her. Because, what would I have said?"

For his own reasons, this estimable man, who had little to gain by

talking about Dinky, had agreed to reminisce about the former servants' boy. His motive seemed to be a sense of duty and regret.
Nicolson was like the others in that he'd shunned Dawn, whose
behavior was embarrassing. But unlike the rest, he wanted to make
amends.

Nicolson leaned forward, handkerchief in hand, and his eyes
widened. "Whether he had this condition, this sexual anomaly—his
sister would know! She was ashamed of Dinky. She is a more or less
uneducated woman—a simple person, but not crazy in any way. She's
merely withdrawn and suspicious, like village women always are. But
she might be willing to talk."

The old gentleman put on his glasses and pulled out a phone book
for southern England. He riffled to the right page, read out a line. It
was the name of Dinky's sister, which I'd seen on letters that Dawn
had saved in her files.

Chapter 5

MORE SPEAK, EVEN THE DEAD, WHO KNEW THE POSSIBLY DUAL-SEXED YOUTH

Dawn Simmons's sister lived in a village in southern England, a place where the grocer was also the postmaster and knew everyone around. I learned that she was in her seventies, had a house nearby, and that her husband of many years had recently died. The couple had run a hauling business, carrying wood and vegetables in a truck the family had struggled to buy and then repaired, and repaired again, for decades.

I wrote her a letter, saying I was interested in her brother's life and that I'd attended Dawn's memorial service (which she hadn't). No reply. When I called, no one picked up, and there was no answering machine. I thought turning up at her door might backfire, so I set aside the pursuit to look for other clues.

SNOWDRIFT

Gordon Hall had grown up fifty miles from Sissinghurst, in a town called Heathfield, halfway between London and the English Channel, in Sussex. The handsome settlement, population fifteen thousand, had a Victorian section, built after the railroad came through, and an ancient quarter, with tilting old cottages and a medieval church.

At the center of the old part stood All Saints Church, a Gothic stone beauty at the top of a hill. It was here that one-third of Dawn's ashes had been buried, in a graveyard behind the sanctuary.

Near the cemetery gate, a burly man approached with a small Yorkshire terrier. I bent to pet the dog, and the jumpy, bread-loaf-sized animal strained at the leash.

"He's named Chi, as in the Chinese word," said the owner. "It means cosmic breath, the thing the Chinese believe blows around the earth. In China, chi is the prime mover of life."

The furthest thing from this mossy village setting was Chinese cosmology, but the dog walker seemed local enough: stout, with a cheerful manner, dressed in a gray sweatshirt with a red tartan cap on his head, which was mostly bald save a few spindles of gray.

I asked about the church, and he said, "There's an unusual person buried here. He was called Gordon Hall, or Dawn Hall, or something. A man who became a woman in America. My wife is fascinated by the story." It seemed Dawn's notoriety had come home with her ashes.

The chi-sensitive walker went on in a tumble of words. "He apparently wrote about himself somewhere in his books, and the places he mentions are all still in the village. I think he used to live in a house on the main road, past the Jack Cade pub. The house is on the left, near Hugletts Lane. He said in his writings it was a lot grander than it actually is. Strange."

The cosmic terrier yapped for attention and pulled his owner away.

The church was gray stone, with a spire, and dated from the thirteenth century. A door was open. Inside, a list of vicars posted on the wall began with the first priest, who'd come to town in the year 1236.

An inch of snow covered the graveyard, which ran down a slope from the rear of the building. I started to hunt for Dawn's grave, and then remembered I was wearing good shoes and was about to ruin them in wet snow. I found a pair of plastic grocery bags, tied them around my feet, and walked into the cemetery, the bags flapping in the wind.

Here and there, brown leaves surfaced from under the white carpet, and there was a snapping sound in the air from ice melting in the trees. A hundred tombstones later, no Dawn Simmons. I trudged up and down for an hour, until I'd read every inscription.

Cold and frustrated, with my bagged feet soaked, I felt ridiculous. Standing with my back to a clump of tall evergreens, I ducked under the branches to get out of the snow. The limbs made a quiet, dark enclave the size of a room, with an area of clear ground. Here, hidden from the churchyard, were the last few graves. One had a new stone the size of a briefcase, and an inscription: "In loving memory of Dawn Langley Hall Simmons, 1922–2000."

One-third of my subject.

Beside Dawn's grave was the headstone of her grandmother, Nellie Ticehurst, who'd raised the young Gordon Hall. And then something that didn't fit—a large stone with a detailed inscription:

> Isabel Lydia Whitney—the beloved of Gordon Langley
> Hall—Died February 2, 1962—First American woman
> fresco painter—collateral descendant of William Penn—
> She is more precious than rubies—Proverbs 3:15.

Isabel Whitney was the woman Joe Trott and Ted Phillips had talked about, the rich old heiress in New York who'd left Gordon a millionaire. Why was she here? And why "the beloved of Gordon Hall"? This subplot would have to wait.

Abandoning the churchyard, I drove around Heathfield to see the places Gordon had lived. The dog walker at the church had mentioned Hugletts Lane, and near the corner of that little street and the main road was an imposing brick house with a little sign, "Beech Holme." Although Dawn had spelled it *Beecholme*, this was the former home of Gordon's rich aunt, the one with the blue-ribbon name, Claradoom Ticehurst. She was the aunt who'd lived in splendor while Gordon and his grandmother scratched out a life.

I later learned that after he got rich in America, Gordon had come back to Heathfield to buy Beecholme. He'd used the house as an English getaway and to lord it somewhat over the old neighbors.

A quarter-mile away, across from the Jack Cade pub, stood the cottage Gordon called Spicers, home of the wheelchair-bound hunter, Uncle Ditcher. Spicers was a quaint brick townhouse, modest and low, with a slate roof; but Gordon's family was long gone, and a sign outside said "Spicers B & B," giving a Web address and a phone number.

Pieces of the past had survived, just as Dawn described them, even though others were altered. Havana, the house named after a box of cigars, where Gordon's grandmother raised him, stood in the newer part of Heathfield. Enlarged and modernized, it was no longer a quaint cottage with a garden.

Gordon's grandmother, Nellie Ticehurst, possessed an old Sussex name. According to maps, Ticehurst was actually the name of a town twenty-five miles away. Asking around Heathfield for remaining Ticehurst families, I was led to a cottage where a friendly woman answered the kitchen door. Inside, the woman's children ran around the room and called for their mommy. She wanted to help, she said, but she and her husband had only recently moved to Heathfield; and as far as she knew, they were the only ones called Ticehurst living in the area.

ABSENT FATHERS

I had only a few days to look for people who might know things about the mysterious boy named Gordon Hall, who'd left England some fifty years earlier. Word of mouth led me to a couple in Sissinghurst village, just a few miles from Nigel Nicolson's estate.

Geoffrey Hattersley-Smith, a retired geologist, and his wife, Maria, a former geneticist, invited me over for tea. The idea that they were scientists came as a relief, because in theory this meant they'd be credible witnesses.

The couple lived on a leafy corner in an ancient farmhouse that had half-timbered walls and a slate roof. Sagging a little, pleasantly squatted in green hedging, the house could have been a backdrop for *The Merry Wives of Windsor*, and it would not have seemed strange if a minstrel in brocade jacket had appeared at the iron gate.

Instead, Geoffrey Hattersley-Smith came to the door, a vigorous older man, thin as a pole, with excited speech. His long, trim nose and darting blue eyes accented a rapid, youthful stream of words.

"There you are! Don't mind the dog!" (A big black one.) "Come in, come in! Tea or coffee? We have both. And call me Geoffrey."

He wore a crewneck sweater and green corduroys, and his hair, which looked as though it had once been red, was salt and pepper.

Geoffrey said he was in his late seventies, and he and his wife had moved back to Sissinghurst Village after many years abroad. He walked energetically into a large, low-ceilinged living room. Heavy beams jutted from the walls, and there was a fireplace large enough to roast a pig. "The house was my father's," Geoffrey said, adding that it dated from the 1500s, like Nigel Nicolson's place, only this one had belonged to farmers and not peers.

After just a few days in England, this sort of atmosphere had already given me a feeling for Gordon's childhood: he'd come from a placid, olden society, sealed away from everything modern.

Geoffrey sat in a straight-backed chair, just as Maria appeared in the room. She was a petite woman in wire-rimmed glasses, with gray hair parted on the left and combed over. Wearing a sensible brown sweater and a brown beaded necklace, she carried coffee and a plate of homemade baklava. The big black dog followed her, and then put his nose in the dessert.

"Rollo!" said Maria.

Geoffrey and Maria were retired scholars who'd spent much of their married life in Canada, where Geoffrey had made survey trips to the Arctic and Maria had worked in a genetics lab in Ottawa. They seemed cosmopolitan and not thoroughly of rural England. In fact,

Maria had been born in Greece and educated at Oxford, which made her spoken English sound Mediterranean.

I mentioned the difficulty of finding witnesses to Gordon's youth, and Geoffrey gave his theory. "The families in the villages are a little clannish, and wary of talking, especially about people who are out there, or way out there, as this person was—Gordon Hall, or Dawn, or whatever you want to call him, or her. And outsiders who ask questions are thought dangerous. If they're American, that makes it worse. Sorry."

I asked Geoffrey to describe Gordon Hall, and he said, "I never was aware of meeting the boy or girl. I only saw him from a distance. But our housekeeper is from an old local family, and they knew him."

Maria interjected, "I've just learned from her, our housekeeper, that his or her mother was the daughter of the butcher! I'll go ask more!" She jumped up and left the room.

"Not that there's anything wrong with being a butcher!" said Geoffrey after his wife. Then he continued, "I also heard that Gordon Hall's grandfather, the butcher, was run over by a car while he was delivering a joint of meat." He made an effort not to be amused.

These pieces fit with what I knew. Gordon's grandmother, Nellie, had been married to a butcher, but this was the first I'd heard about the way he died.

Maria reappeared with the housekeeper, a solid woman in her fifties, wearing a pink sweater. She had a straight line for a mouth, brightened with red lipstick, and a strong working-class accent. She clung to the room's edges, looking for an escape; it was plain she didn't want to talk.

"My husband said Gordon Hall's mother was the daughter of the butcher," the woman said, averting her eyes, "and that his sister is his half-sister, not his full." The housekeeper moved toward the door.

Dawn Simmons had always maintained that her father was Jack Copper, the driver at Sissinghurst, but the reluctant housekeeper had just implied otherwise. I mentioned that Dawn Simmons said Jack Copper was her father.

"He would, wouldn't he?" answered the woman. Glint of a smile.

I asked the housekeeper if her husband would be willing to talk, but she looked down. "He's a bit worried about that. Doesn't want to upset anybody."

The woman slipped out the door. Dawn Simmons had disturbed people here, just like in Charleston.

Geoffrey resumed. "Our housekeeper's husband was brought up in the village, lived in it all his life, and is head of the neighborhood watch association. Responsible fellow. He knew the creature Gordon Hall. He said quite definitely that Jack Copper was not the father, and moreover that Jack Copper was paid by the family to take on this illegitimate child! No one knows who the father really was. He waxed quite eloquent about it, sitting here yesterday, with a glass of sherry."

Dawn's story was shaping up to be an extended piece of hearsay. He *saith* she was a woman. She *sayeth* not. If the hearsay about Gordon's paternity proved true, it would be a revelation that would throw a new light on things. Eventually, I assumed, the lies and the truth would make themselves known.

Or would they? Would Dawn's life turn out to be a species of her gender variance, in which each version of events called into question the others? Would the whole be more than its parts?

In the seventh edition of *Black's Law Dictionary*, there is this definition of *hearsay*: "Traditionally, testimony that is given by a witness who relates not what he or she knows personally, but what others have said, and that is therefore dependent on the credibility of someone other than the witness."

The business about someone paying to give Gordon a credible father was double or triple hearsay. The housekeeper said that her husband said that he'd heard what Gordon Hall had said about his father was untrue.

Who was Gordon's father, if not Jack Copper, driver for Vita Sackville-West? Had the family kept alive a fiction for decades?

Geoffrey went on. "This man, who knew Gordon or Dawn but doesn't want to talk, said you could tell. He said he knew Gordon was a *poofter.* You could tell just by talking to him, just by his manner. A poofter, you know, not pointed toward women."

More hearsay—Gordon Hall was queer because "you could tell."

In their youth, Geoffrey and Maria had known the famous couple at Sissinghurst, Vita Sackville-West and Harold Nicolson. "After Maria and I married, in 1955, Vita took us up into her private study, in the tower at Sissinghurst," Geoffrey said. "She gave Maria a blue Persian bead, and said, 'Keep this, because it will bring you luck.' Maria still carries it when she travels."

I asked idly who had cared for the Sissinghurst gardens in those days, and Geoffrey released a rush of words in the style he preferred for conversation.

"There were two Dutch women who were the head gardeners. They were a couple of lesbians, I think, but never mind. They were there for thirty years. And there was an undergardener at Sissinghurst named William Taylor, who grew vegetables. He hated flowers! He said, 'The only good flower is the cauliflower!' Anyway, there is a coincidence in that he had a niece that turned into a nephew. Normally it's the man-to-woman thing, but this was the opposite way, a girl to a boy. It's a strange business, isn't it, that these two transvestites—or transsexuals, whatever—would be associated with the same place?"

Maria, sitting on a striped chair, said she had never seen Gordon Hall. Having grown up in Greece and gone to Oxford, she was elsewhere in those years. "I've heard that Gordon Hall came back to visit several times from America, but he was not well received," she said. "The trouble was that he had gone away, and he was in the newspapers, and it was said he had gotten a lot of money. But he didn't help people where he came from, you know, people who needed it. So he didn't have the best reception. He didn't die in poverty, did he? Or rather, she didn't die in poverty?"

It now seemed that in Gordon's hometown there'd been several spurts of gossip, each lasting a few years. The first concerned Gordon's father, whose absence, and possible abandonment of a teenage mother, threw a shadow on the boy in the small village setting. A second wave erupted when Gordon Hall came back from America to buy the biggest house in town, Beecholme, in vindication of his difficult childhood. The last and biggest geyser of gossip erupted after the sex reassignment and birth of Natasha, when Dawn Simmons became a regular subject in the British tabloids. Taking the long view, I could see that Dawn's life, where she came from, had played about as well as a series of explosions.

Maria Hattersley-Smith was a retired geneticist, and as the conversation shifted to her own past, she grew nostalgic. She'd once held a job in gene research, during the early 1950s, in the pioneer days of the science. "We, our lab, had the first photograph of human chromosomes!" Maria's small hands gripped the air triumphantly.

I mentioned a gene condition I'd read about, one of the intersexual disorders, known as Klinefelter Syndrome. Named for an American physician, Harry F. Klinefelter, who first observed it, the condition seemed to be another possible diagnosis for Dawn (in addition to the more common intersex condition, congenital adrenal hyperplasia). Klinefelter has to do with an extra chromosome. Normally, women have two X chromosomes at the end of the DNA chain, and men an X and a Y chromosome. Klinefelter Syndrome occurs when the individual's DNA possesses forty-seven pairs of chromosomes instead of the usual forty-six. The spare is an additional X chromosome, which produces a so-called X-X-Y birth, a boy who acquires feminine characteristics, including enlarged breasts and sparse facial and body hair.

We talked a few minutes about genetic testing and the difference between contemporary science and the field Maria had pioneered.

"The labs are everywhere now," Maria said, offering a piece of baklava.

In theory, one could test Dawn Simmons's DNA for signs of Klinefelter. But I balked at the thought of asking Natasha, grieving for her mother, to search for stray hairs on brushes or some other trace of Dawn's leftover cells.

Around the living room, deep niches had been cut into the old walls, and in them Geoffrey and Maria had placed little sculpture and figures. In one dark corner of the room, I thought I could make out the small figure of a naked male, with prominently modeled genitals.

MUTE WITNESSES

The vital records office for this part of the country stood in the town of Crowborough, not far from Sissinghurst, and the scrupulous English way with documents gave me hope that birth and death records might hold some answers.

In a memoir, Dawn had said she'd been born on October 16, 1937, which sounded wrong, especially because her gravestone put her birth year at 1922. The age discrepancy of fifteen years was either a misprint in stone or a fat fiction Dawn had perpetrated for decades.

In a small, modern building, two helpful clerks disgorged Gordon Hall's birth certificate from the files. Then, in short order, they uncovered a second, nearly identical document. It seemed Gordon's data had been filed twice.

The first certificate put the birth of a "male infant" named Gordon Kenneth Ticehurst on October 16, 1922. This not only confirmed the earlier birth year but also corresponded with the name I had found among the Dawn Simmons papers at Duke University. He was tagged a boy, the label Dawn said she'd been stuck with. However, while Gordon's mother's name appeared on the certificate, the space for the father was blank.

A second birth certificate had been issued in 1939, seventeen years after the first. It was identical to the original, except for one detail: the name Jack Copper now appeared as Gordon's father.

A clerk explained that this was an instance of birth re-registration, a rare but legal action permitted under a regulation designed to assist so-called illegitimate children with no father of record. If the mother or child desired, and a father had come forward, his name could later be added to the official papers. In other words, when Gordon was seventeen, he refiled his own birth record, giving himself a father.

Here was circumstantial evidence that someone, perhaps Marjorie's richer relations, had paid Copper to claim Gordon as his own child long after the fact. This was speculation, but had Jack Copper been Gordon's biological father, he would likely have attached his name to the birth record after he married Marjorie rather than waiting until Gordon was seventeen. What's more, if Jack was not Gordon's father, that would also explain why Marjorie and Jack did not have Gordon live with them after they got married, when the child was just four years old. The identity of Gordon's real father remained a mystery.

The birth records contained at least one and possibly two inventions. Dawn had lied about her age, and she had perhaps also helped her "father" to falsify government records. How trustworthy were Dawn's other stories?

BITTER SISTER

Before leaving England, I gave Gordon's sister another try. This time she picked up her phone, recognized my name, and started talking.

I'll call her Frances, although that isn't her real name. "It's done and I wish it were behind me," Frances said. "He's dead and resting in peace."

The sharp working-class voice on the line sounded aggrieved. I asked whether Frances would sit down for half an hour to talk, and she said, "I'd rather not." I'd heard from several people there was antagonism between Dawn and her sister, and the tone in the voice implied this was right.

"I'll tell you what I know, and it's the truth." With this opening, Frances then let go a monologue that lasted fifteen minutes.

"Dink was born on the sixteenth of October 1922. The reason he went to my grandmum's is that my mum was going on seventeen when he was born, and from a middle-class family, and the embarrassment in those days was strong."

Frances called her sibling *Dink* (for Dinky) and *he*, but never Dawn or she.

Describing the circumstances of Gordon's adoption by Nellie, Frances sounded defensive that a twist of fate meant her mother had raised her, whereas her older brother had been handed off to relative poverty.

"Dink stayed with Grandmum, and when he was in his teens, my parents wanted to take him back, but my gran begged for him to stay. Mum said all right, and it was the worst decision my mum ever made."

In other words, Frances was the real daughter with a real home and Dinky was a cast-off child, and everyone including the child knew it.

Dawn claimed throughout life that she'd gotten her writing skill from her grandmother, who was a country journalist, but Frances dismissed this. "Well, my grandmum, Nellie Ticehurst, never did newspaper writing, despite what Dink said. She read the paper, that's it, and she would roll in her grave if she knew what Dink said about her."

Frances's voice sometimes rose in anger, of the kind that wants to settle old scores; but her annoyance seemed to fade when I showed sympathy with her situation.

Dawn's papers included no pictures of Frances, and I couldn't meet her. The only impression she gave came over the phone.

"When Gran died, we packed up the house, and Dink moved with us to the castle," she said, meaning Sissinghurst. "But he wasn't happy, and he got a flat with a friend in an attic. He went away to America in the 1940s, and came back in 1956, with money, and bought the house, Beecholme. He sold that in 1964."

Frances punctuated her talk with dates and family events that normally no outsider would know, but she assumed I would. She was in a hurry to tell her brother's story, which she seemed to have arranged in bullet form, for brevity. It was as though she'd thought about it for years, and had made sense of the mystery by shrinking it to capsule size.

Bringing up Dawn's sex operation, she said, "We didn't hear about the sex op until it happened, and it was shocking. Or rather, it was all right—until he sold the story to the *News and World*. Then the photographers came and camped outside our house."

The scene Frances described sounded pretty bad. Men with cameras lurked around her garden and followed her down the street to get pictures of her family for the tabloids ("the transsexual's relatives"). In her village, the photographers caused a breakout of gossip even before the stories appeared. What was worse, said Frances, her sons, then in their teens, took abuse from their schoolmates for being the nephews of a "sex freak."

After that, the family was tormented for years, Frances said, "which is what happens when you live in a small place, where everybody knows everybody."

This was the kernel of her dispute with Gordon—that her brother had humiliated her.

The sex reassignment and media flurry that followed—with reporters calling at strange hours, and Frances's boys taunted at school—wrecked her relationship with Dink. Things deteriorated further when, six months after the surgery, their mother died. "Which I think had to do with the op," said Frances, sighing. She thought Dawn's sex reassignment had rushed her mother to the grave, a belief that provided plenty of fuel to feed a smoldering family dispute.

When Majorie Copper died—the birth mother of both Frances and Gordon—Dawn couldn't get to the funeral, because the call from England came on the day of the burial.

"I took the blame for that," said Frances, "but me dad didn't want him, because Dink would have brought that what's-his-name. Can't remember his name—the black."

"John-Paul Simmons?"

"Yes, John-Paul. Dad didn't want that."

Jack Copper had barred his alleged son from the funeral because he didn't want Dawn's black husband to come along. Frances and Dawn didn't speak for ten years, during the 1970s, and afterward they'd only repaired things slowly. I'd seen many friendly letters in Dawn's papers from Frances, but most of them dated from the 1990s.

In the background, on the phone, I heard the sounds of a door opening and then a voice. Frances said it was her neighbor, and she took this as a chance to wrap up. "Can't make my friend wait," she said.

To talk with Frances was to speak to someone who knew Dawn well, but about Dawn's anatomy Frances had little to say. She'd never seen her brother with his clothes off, and in any case the embarrassment Dawn had brought down on Frances's family was more important to her than an accident of birth.

"Dink had a vivid imagination, you see, but I don't think he was unstable," she said. "I went to see his grave last October, and he's resting in peace, Dink is."

The neighbor in the kitchen said something, and Frances sped to the end.

"That's it, I've said it. I've talked to you. And I've told you the truth."

The next day, I flew back to America.

Chapter 6

PSYCHOPATHIA TRANSEXUALIS

THE FIRST WITNESS

Dawn Simmons was sitting at a mahogany table in her living room, in front of nineteenth-century pictures and a fireplace with a Federal period mantel. She was a poised middle-aged woman with high cheekbones and a thin nose, and her body was fencepost straight, as in an advertisement for posture lessons. She looked at you with intense dark eyes, and her voice was scratchy but not unfeminine.

"Somebody said to me the other day, whatever happens to you, you always seem to have the last laugh," she said.

I'd found a videotape of a TV interview among her papers. She'd done many interviews with reporters—she liked the attention—and in this one she looked established, matronly, and composed.

"Anybody can have a sex change operation if they have the money to pay for it, but that was not true with me," she said. "I was wrongly sexed as a baby when I was born. The fact was that my natural mother's brother had kicked her in the stomach when I was coming. My clitoris was so swollen that the midwife who was present, she couldn't tell if it was a boy or a girl."

The show was taped in the 1980s, and to signal her Englishness, Dawn wore a large beehive hairdo, apparently in deference to the then–prime minister, Margaret Thatcher, whose hair was similar, like a frozen tsunami. Dawn had on a white half-sleeve dress with a black flower pattern. Around the scooped neck, a long string of fake pearls accented her thin collarbones, and she wore red lipstick and a gold bracelet.

"I was taken to a Harley Street gynecologist, a very eminent man," she went on. Harley Street was a road in west London where, by tradition, the city's most capable doctors were thought to practice. "And he stated it was as I thought, I was wrongly sexed as a baby. And you couldn't blame the midwife or the young mother, because they probably had never seen such a thing before in their lives. As a child, I was different, and I was also the tiniest thing in school. I liked to play with dolls, and I loved to keep house. Later, I knew in my heart I was really a woman. I *felt* as a woman."

Dawn laced her fingers in front of her. On a near table was a two-foot-tall wooden statue of a robed woman. I recognized it as a figure she'd described in her letters. It was Saint Teresa of Avila, an icon from Spain she'd acquired when she was still Gordon and carried with her through life.

The interviewer, having none of the quaint setting, maintained a sarcastic air. He made a cross remark about the smell of Dawn's animals, which he told viewers infested the house, and hustled her story along. But Dawn stayed detached.

"Menstruation started late, actually with random bleedings," she said quietly. "I had a very bad one when I was living in New York City, and I was in hospital for three weeks. Nobody would venture an opinion there. When I moved to Charleston, things started sort of regularly. One morning the housekeeper came to work and found me in bed lying in a pool of blood. I was rushed to the hospital, and they pumped this blood out. And I always remember the doctor at the time saying, 'I can't understand why this is not fresh blood.'

"I went to a lady doctor, and she sent me to a gynecologist, and I had to sit there in the waiting room, dressed as a man, with all these matrons. He X-rayed me, and he told me that there was this six-and-a-half-inch vaginal tract! And he told me that if something wasn't done about it, psychologically, I was going to commit suicide within a certain period. Or something would just corrode inside, and I would die anyhow."

The camera cut away to Natasha, Dawn's daughter, sitting alone on the stoop in front of the house where the interview was taking place. She was a young girl at the time of the TV show, in little braids and a cute madras dress, and she looked bored.

Dawn had been adept with the media. When she traveled, she often wrote a press release and sent it ahead to the local paper. Sometimes she got an interview, and when the piece appeared, she would cut it out and send copies to friends.

The business about the hidden vagina was a flashy detail, and I was inclined to believe she'd used it before as a lure to fish for reporters. But was there a chance it could be true?

"I was working on a biography of Mrs. Lyndon B. Johnson, and physical changes started with a vengeance. Suddenly there were great changes in my breasts, for instance. The doctors have described it, that I was like a fourteen-year-old girl. There was a burning sensation in my breasts, and the only relief I could get was by massaging them with old-fashioned cocoa butter, which somebody told me about. I would be walking downstairs, and you know when you miss a step, you get an awful jolt? I realized something very much wrong was going on."

Dawn smiled lightly, an acknowledgment what she was saying strained belief. But her manners never broke, and her hand movements were so faint as to be measured in centimeters. She was a lady, consenting to the public's attention.

"I went to the women's clinic in Baltimore, to get my mind prepared for possible marriage," she went along. "They said the thing most necessary for me was to fall in love with somebody who would give me a quiet and balanced life. But it turned out in my marriage, sex was about the only successful thing!"

A polite laugh. She'd married a much younger man, John-Paul Simmons, and in good lady form she spoke indirectly about her marital problems, and also about her husband's sexual craft. "Then the baby came," the story continued. "The Catholic nurse who was present, Nurse Hardy, she was sent up to be the private nurse for 'Gordon Langley Hall,' which was a mistake, of course. And when she went into the room and pulled back the sheet, there was the body of a beautiful woman!"

With pinched fingers and elevated pinkies, Dawn mimed the movement of a prim woman pulling back a sheet.

"It didn't faze her. She was a Catholic, and she thought she had seen a miracle!"

The camera cut away and cut back. Now it was time to bring her proof home, and to do so, Dawn made a final appeal to science.

"There were always one or two doubters," she said. "I am very pleased that recently we had DNA tests to prove that Natasha is my child. One of the large magazines had these tests done, and they all came out positive. They used various techniques. I had a sampling of my natural mother Marjorie's hair, and I had my grandmother Nellie Hall Ticehurst's skin. I actually had the caul, the extra skin that was covering her face when she was born, many years ago, in Withyham, Sussex."

Dawn didn't reveal the location where for all these decades she might have stored her mother's hair. And the caul—the membrane stretched over her grandmother's face when she emerged from *her* mother—that also must have had a special hiding place. But the revelation went out on the airways, and either the tests took place or this was a new fable with the smell of the laboratory.

She gave a slight red-lipstick smile. "It's all come right in the end, hasn't it?"

DAWN SAID SHE was wrongly raised as a boy and became a woman in midlife, when she was about thirty. To my surprise, I uncovered one case history that gave her the benefit of the doubt.

The intersexual condition called congenital adrenal hyperplasia had produced some extraordinary patients. The monograph on hermaphroditism I had found in the medical school library included the case history of "R.S.," an individual with the adrenal syndrome. R.S. was an eleven-year-old whose parents had consulted Johns Hopkins Hospital in 1915. The patient, who'd been raised as a boy, had no scrotum or testes but did have a small penis bent down between labial folds, as well as excessive body hair and a deep voice, the result of early-onset puberty. The urethra did not run along the underside of the penis, the doctors said, but was between the labia, at the base of the shaft. R.S.'s parents consented to exploratory surgery, and the examining physician, a Dr. Quinby, opened the abdomen to find a uterus, two fallopian tubes, and two ovaries. Dr. Quinby removed one of the ovaries and found it to contain egg-forming follicles, which led Quinby to conclude that R.S. was not a son, but a daughter. The stunned parents insisted their child not be told she was female, and they took their "son" home.

Twenty years later, R.S., now thirty-one, returned to Johns Hopkins as a rich businessman engaged to marry his mistress, with whom he'd been accustomed to frequent intercourse. R.S. told physicians that even before meeting his fiancée, he was having coitus with women two or three times a week. He said he found the sex satisfying; it always produced an orgasm and the ejaculation of fluid at the base of the penis.

The bride-to-be, who doctors said was present at the medical interviews, seemed to be in love with R.S. and was keen to marry him. But the couple were upset about a dispute they'd had with their priest. It seemed the father of R.S. had told the cleric his son was actually female, and the priest had subsequently refused to perform the marriage service. R.S. said, "A mistake must have been made," and, citing his ejaculations, "I am really male."

Another examination was done. This time a catheter was inserted through R.S.'s urethra, opaque fluid injected, and an X-ray taken, which revealed a heretofore hidden vagina inside R.S.'s pelvis. The patient was told that the tests confirmed the determination of twenty years earlier, namely, that she was female.

Three days later R.S. committed suicide. She took a large dose of mercury, which triggered acute nephritis, and died of kidney failure. An autopsy revealed another surprise: a prostate gland, which had produced the seminal fluid.

The big lie she told about her age made Dawn untrustworthy. There was also the caul story. But some of her claims—mistaken for a boy, a vagina tucked away—were remarkably similar to the facts of R.S.'s case. Could it have happened twice?

"I KNEW IN MY HEART I was really a woman," Dawn had said to the interviewer. "I *felt* as a woman." Dawn was trying to get the story past her questioner's skepticism. "The only release came in my writings. I liked to write as a woman, in the first person—and I've written about women in my biographies."

I'd looked at Dawn's manuscripts at Duke. Indeed, from his earliest attempts at writing, Gordon Hall had chosen a female narrative voice. An unpublished novel called *The Green Orchid*, from 1947, had a narrator named Melanie Maw. In 1949, a character named Orleanna narrated Gordon's long poem "Song of the Wilderness."

"I was scared of sex in my twenties," Dawn told the camera. "I shudder when I think today how I felt. I hated anybody even to kiss me. My real mother was a very loving person, and I would even draw away from her. I suspected sex, and I suspected all kinds of love. I realized I had to grow up without it, and I was steeling myself against it."

Dawn smiled lightly, remembering her youth. If her sexuality had been so confused, as she said it was, it was at least credible she would have recoiled from touch. "After my transformation, I got sexual feelings. And for the first time, I began to notice one certain young man. He seemed to light a fire from within that has never gone out."

A GOOD HISTORY OF SEX, if one could be written, would have a plentiful chapter on transsexualism. One section might describe the priests called *gallae*, followers of the ancient goddess Cybele, whose cult appeared in Anatolia and spread to Greece about 500 B.C. Cybele was a child of Zeus and a hermaphrodite whose male organs were cut off; and on the goddess's annual feast day, in March, crowds gathered at her temple, where men who wished to become her acolytes would publicly cut off their own testicles and put on women's clothes (one assumes after they recovered). The chapter on transsexualism might also touch on the mythic Amazon women and their queen, Penthesilea, whose warriors severed one breast, entered the phallic world of combat, and lived like sexual predators. There could be some pages on the men of the Skopzty sect of Christians, in Russia, who practiced amputation of the genitals and whose cult flourished for two centuries. (In the mid-1900s, one eunuch follower, named Malenkov, worked as a clerk for Stalin.)

These and other weird chronicles would seem to support the view that transsexuals—some of whom used to mutilate themselves—suffer from a rare pathology. Not surprisingly, trans-people have a different opinion, turning the thing around. If illness lies anywhere, they say, it resides in the cruel laws of masculinity and femininity, which drive people to extreme acts.

Until lately, those who physically crossed from one sex to the other have had only one role in the culture, that of the pariah. Transgender behavior stood outside society until the 1900s, when medicine first got involved with its hormone pills and surgery, and the trans-world, after centuries, started to be tamed.

Medicine and psychiatry have come to regard transsexualism as a mental illness that can be treated. In 1998, the World Health Organization published its tenth revision of the *International Classification of Diseases (ICD)*, a standard medical reference worldwide. In chapter 5, within a list of the "mental disorders," there appears this definition: *"Transsexualism:* A desire to live and be accepted as a member of the opposite sex, usually accompanied by a sense of discomfort with, or inappropriateness of, one's anatomic sex, and a wish to have hormonal treatment and surgery to make one's body as congruent as possible with the preferred sex."

In the United States, the *Diagnostic and Statistical Manual of Mental Disorders (DSM)*, issued every few years by the American Psychiatric Association, contains a similar description. Although the term transsexualism doesn't appear in the fourth edition of the *DSM*, published in 1994, an alternate phrase, *gender identity disorder*, takes its place. This disorder is indicated when a psychiatric patient shows "evidence of a strong and persistent cross-gender identification, which is the desire to be, or the insistence that one is, of the other sex," as well as "evidence of persistent discomfort about one's assigned sex."

To be a transsexual means you suffer from a syndrome, and the threshold of belonging .is high. You can't just want to be like the other sex, as men envy women the power of motherhood, or women want to be listened to as men are. You have to feel unbearably bad that you're not the other sex. For you to get treatment, specified as hormones and surgery, a psychiatrist must examine you and agree to write a diagnostic letter naming your disease.

The editors of the *DSM*, obvious lovers of labels, give gender identity disorder a numeric tag, 302.85, to distinguish it within a long numbered list of unrelated syndromes and to give therapists a code to paperclip to the patient's file.

Dawn Simmons underwent several physical and psychiatric exams. I wondered whether her medical records had survived or, better, whether any of her doctors were alive, and willing to talk.

BERLIN 1919

The unlikely pioneer of transsexual medicine, a man who led the first patients from the exile of freak status to the homeland of sex reassignment, was a mild-mannered neurologist named Magnus Hirschfeld. In Berlin after World War I, Hirschfeld, a fifty-two-year-old author and physician, had audacity enough to solicit and treat transsexual patients. Before Hirschfeld, medicine did not distinguish among homosexuality, cross-dressing, and transsexualism. Instead, psychiatrists and the heterosexual public ran them all together. Hirschfeld took it for granted that transsexualism was a behavior (or condition, or diagnosis) that needed to be seen on its own terms.

Magnus Hirschfeld had a walrus mustache and a full head of hair, wore oval wire-rimmed glasses and three-piece suits, and liked florid ties. He was Jewish and gay, two marks of outsider status that may have helped him see the sexual subculture of Weimar Germany as something other than criminal, which was the way many ordinary people, and especially the Nazis, regarded the cabarets of Berlin.

For most of his life, he was an indefatigable student of the libido. In 1897, when still a young physician, Hirschfeld established the first gay rights organization, the Scientific Humanitarian Committee, which unsuccessfully petitioned the Reichstag to repeal laws against same-sex love. By 1910, he was publishing a journal of sexual studies, and nine years later he opened a clinic in Berlin. As an evangelist for sexual freedom, he became the friend and colleague of Havelock Ellis, Sigmund Freud, Wilhelm Reich, and Margaret Sanger; and in the 1920s he published a garrulous five-volume study, *Geschlechtskunde* (Sexual Knowledge). Hirschfeld was an early proponent of the view that two genders could in no way enclose the abundance of natural sexuality. He argued that a large minority of people were what he called intermediates, something in between, a kind of third sex.

Hirschfeld was writing at a time before the physiology of intersexuals had been described, so his categories sound crude. The various diagnoses—from congenital adrenal hyperplasia, to Klinefelter Syndrome, to five or six others—didn't exist. But he was able to recognize and accept that some people wanted to change sex and others swung involuntarily between the sexual poles.

In 1919, Hirschfeld opened the Institut für Sexualwissenschaft (Institute of Sexual Science), a clinic and public health center that combined therapy, physical treatment, a lecture program, and a library. The institute occupied a large, three-story villa in the fashionable Berlin district of Tiergarten, on a tree-shaded corner of

In Sussex, England, sometime before World War II, an unmarried sixteen-year-old girl gave birth to a child named Gordon Langley Hall. Even at age two, Gordon (with his Jack Russell terrier) appeared androgynous, or perhaps girlish. Years later, Gordon said he'd been born intersexual ("a hermaphrodite," he pointed out, using an older word), with unusual genitals that caused a rural midwife to mislabel him a boy.

Gordon Hall's mother, Marjorie Hall Ticehurst, about 1960. The daughter of a butcher, Marjorie had been a schoolgirl when she gave birth to Gordon, and she handed the child over to her widowed mother to bring up. Marjorie soon left Sussex to work as a servant at Sissinghurst Castle, an estate fifty miles from Gordon, whom she rarely saw.

Although Gordon Hall was a sensitive child, the youth's registered father, Jack Copper (who married Marjorie several years after Gordon was born), was a hard-drinking workman at Sissinghurst Castle who hardly resembled the boy.

The 500-year-old house at Sissinghurst, where Gordon Hall's parents worked, belonged to writer and aristocrat Vita Sackville-West and her husband, historian Harold Nicolson. Although Gordon never lived at Sissinghurst, he fell in love with it during visits to see his mother and spoke possessively of the estate for decades.

Vita Sackville-West (1892–1962), the employer of Gordon's parents, was a poet and novelist celebrated for her books, including All Passion Spent and Family History, which charted the customs of the upper class. She became equally famous for her majestic gardens at Sissinghurst, which eventually became public property and the most-visited gardens in England. Gordon Hall idolized Vita, whose unconventional personal life combined a fifty-year marriage and outside affairs with women. The writer met her mature love, Virginia Woolf, in the mid-1920s, after which Virginia paid Vita the compliment of writing a book about her, the novel Orlando: A Biography. The self-described intersexual Gordon regarded Orlando—the story of a beautiful nobleman who transforms into a woman—as a blueprint for his own life.

He said in retrospect he'd been miserable at school due to the "dark secret" of his sexual anomaly. But when Gordon (seated) got the part of a woman in a school play, the role put him in front of an audience for the first time as female, the sex he claimed was the stronger within his alleged dual identity. The play was an adaptation of David Copperfield *and the part that of* Aunt Betsey Trotwood, *a widow who shelters the needy* Copperfield.

Gordon Hall had a lifelong love of animals and threw birthday parties for his pets, including one for his bull terrier, Regina.

By the 1950s, Gordon had left England and moved to New York City to make a career as a writer. For a publicity photo, he struck a pose as a bookworm in Greenwich Village.

In New York, the fortunes of Gordon improved when he found a patron, Isabel Whitney, an elderly heiress. Isabel gave the would-be writer a stipend, moved him into her mansion off Fifth Avenue, and (according to Gordon) accepted his sexual "affliction." In about 1958, Gordon, his pet parrot Philadelphia McCrae, and Isabel chose Delft tiles for a fireplace.

As a young woman, Isabel Whitney (photographed about 1910, when she was twenty-six) had been a successful mural painter. Her clients had included the Brooklyn Museum, as well as family friends who hired her to decorate their townhouses with scenes of frolicking aristocrats.

Gordon Hall with the actress Bette Davis, in Camden, Maine, 1957. His intimacy with Isabel Whitney gave Gordon entrée to privileged circles.

12

Gordon befriended the eccentric English film actress Margaret Rutherford (dressed for a publicity photo in 1962), who became known to Americans as Miss Jane Marple, the lady detective in movie adaptations of such Agatha Christie novels as Murder, She Said *and* Murder, Most Foul. *The actress allowed Gordon to call her "Mother Rutherford" and to treat her as an adoptive parent.*

When Isabel Whitney died, in 1962, Gordon took her remains to England, where she'd never lived, and buried them in his hometown of Heathfield, Sussex. At the grave, Gordon (clutching flowers), accompanied by a pretty cousin (left), wept over the box containing Isabel's ashes. In her will, Isabel had left Gordon cash, stock, antiques, her mansion in New York, and another house in Charleston, South Carolina.

14

Newly rich, Gordon renovated the house in Charleston, a dilapidated beauty with the melodic address of 56 Society Street. The antebellum house (pictured about 1960) stood in the neighborhood of Ansonborough, a largely black section that was also home to the city's white gay elite, especially its decorators and antiques dealers.

15

Charleston Doorway, by Edward Hopper, watercolor, 1929. The American realist painter Edward Hopper had been a neighborhood friend of Isabel Whitney and Gordon Hall in New York. By coincidence, in 1929 Hopper had visited Charleston and had painted the entrance of 56 Society Street, the house Gordon would later occupy.

The dining room of Gordon's renovated house, about 1962. As a newcomer hoping for acceptance in Charleston, Gordon embraced the formal style preferred by local whites.

56 Society Street, Charleston, 2003.

With a bit of his inheritance, Gordon hired a portrait artist to depict him in masculine style.

Gordon Hall at home in Charleston, bethroned with his dogs, about 1965.

Lady Bird &
her daughters
Gordon Langley Hall

*An informal biography of the Johnson women
by the co-author of* JACQUELINE KENNEDY

By the 1960s, Gordon had become an author of society biographies, including several about first ladies, such as one from 1967 on the wife ("Lady Bird") and children of President Lyndon Johnson. The author said that during research he'd taken one of his three Chihuahuas, Richard-Rufus, to an interview at the White House.

Two of Gordon's Chihuahuas, Annabel-Eliza and Nelly, dressed for a party at the mansion in Charleston, about 1967.

With dozens of pets, Gordon faced a burial problem, which he solved by creating a pet cemetery in the garden beside his house, ordering stones for every animal.

Beethovenstrasse. Its pioneering sex surgery made headlines for a decade, until the permissive experiments ran head-on into Nazi repression in the early 1930s.

A history of transsexuality, *How Sex Changed*, by Joanne Meyerowitz, deftly tells the story. According to Meyerowitz, the earliest "complete" transsexual case at Hirschfeld's clinic was that of Dorchen Richter, the son of a poor farming family. Richter, who made his living as a waiter, had his testicles removed at the clinic when he was forty and, nine years later, in 1931, had his penis taken away and a vagina surgically constructed. The same year, 1931, a physician at the institute named Felix Abraham published the first scientific report on transsexual surgery, "Genitalumwandlung an zwei männlichen Transvestiten" (The Genital Transformation of two Homosexual Transvestites), a description of two patients, one of them Dorchen Richter. With illustrations, the report outlined the three-stage treatment: surgical removal of the testicles, amputation of the penis, and the creation of a vagina.

A more adventuresome case was that of transsexual patient Einar Wegener, an artist from Denmark. Wegener underwent castration at Hirschfeld's behest and took the name Lili Elbe. Later, doctors in Dresden removed Elbe's penis and (according to a book about her) allegedly had human ovaries transplanted into her body. The artist's self-transformation was short-lived, however: after a last operation to create a vagina, the patient died of heart failure, in 1931.

The idea that an attempted ovary transplant had allegedly taken place in 1931 gave luster to Dawn Simmons's claim to motherhood. If such things were tried before, why not later? Dawn, however, never mentioned having "borrowed" ovaries.

Hirschfeld treated patients with a rare disregard for taboos. He believed transsexuals had physiological, rather than "merely" psychological, causes for their drives. He accepted female-to-male cases: among his patients were women who requested mastectomy and preparation for beard growth. The Institut für Sexualwissenschaft did not perform phalloplasty, the construction of an artificial penis, a technique that would have to wait another forty years. But physicians did give women male growth hormones, extracted from animal urine (synthetic human hormones would not become available until the 1940s), while giving men the female counterpart.

The Nazis brought all this to a burning finale. In 1929, four years before Adolf Hitler became chancellor of Germany, the National Socialist newspaper *Der Stürmer* called Hirschfeld "the apostle of indecency" and targeted his clinic for action. Nazi brownshirts interrupted his public lectures and made threats to the staff, and the menace escalated after Hitler was elected in 1933. In May of that year, about a hundred Nazi university students in brown uniforms forced their way into the institute—along with a brass band that played marches, to keep up festive morale during the nasty task—and carried off its library in trucks. Under orders from propaganda minister Joseph Goebbels, the collection was burned in a vast pyre in Berlin's Opernplatz. (The most familiar photographs of Nazi book burnings are of this event.) Hirschfeld was in Paris at the time and had the memorable experience of attending a movie theater where he saw a newsreel of the fires consuming his library.

The Institut für Sexualwissenschaft was converted into offices for an anti-Semitic newspaper, and at least three physicians who worked for Hirschfeld committed suicide rather than face Nazi interrogators. Magnus Hirschfeld never returned to Germany, and in 1935 he died in Nice, France.

THE UNITED STATES LAGGED about fifty years behind Europe in sex surgery and transsexual medicine, perhaps because doctors flinched at the fate of Magnus Hirschfeld. There was no American equivalent to the German experiments, no propagandist of sexual ambiguity. In fact, before the late 1950s physicians risked prosecution if they contemplated sex change surgery on patients.

One test case was all that was needed to keep the medical ranks in line. In the late 1940s a would-be male-to-female transsexual named

Lynn Barry sought castration and surgery in Wisconsin. Getting wind of the case, the state's attorney general announced such treatment would constitute the felony of "mayhem." Hunting for a legal weapon to stop what he considered repellent, Wisconsin's top prosecutor had found a remnant statute handed down from English common law. Mayhem laws were edicts used by kings to prevent men from becoming useless to fight in war: whoever maimed a potential soldier could be found guilty of the crime. Transsexual surgery was said to fit under the banner, and the threat worked.

Prior to the Wisconsin case, a handful of American physicians who'd heard of Magnus Hirschfeld had been distributing hormones and contemplating surgery on patients. But after the legal line was drawn, word got around and almost all doctors showed transsexuals the door.

The give and take of gender mixing had not ended, however. In 1949, an editor at a popular pseudoscientific magazine, *Sexology*, used the phrase *psychopathia transexualis* (transsexual psychopathology) to describe the growing clamor for sex change among a few hundred vocal and unhappy patients. The phrase was a play on a famous nineteenth-century study of gay eroticism, *Psychopathia Sexualis*, first published in 1886 by the German psychiatrist Richard von Krafft-Ebing. The word *transsexualism*, therefore, started life in English as a sort of joke. But in a few years it drifted into the mainstream media, and it stuck.

Then came Christine Jorgensen. In 1952, George Jorgensen, a twenty-six-year-old New York–born son of Danish immigrants, had come to despair in his search for an American surgeon who would operate on him so that he could live as a woman. Jorgensen went to his parents' home country of Denmark, where a doctor named Christian Hamburger performed transsexual surgery on the New Yorker. In December 1952, the New York *Daily News* ran the headline "Ex-G.I. Becomes Blonde Beauty: Operations Transform Bronx Youth." Returning to New York from Copenhagen the following year, Jorgensen was met with media frenzy.

Christine Jorgensen (who adopted the feminine form of her doctor's first name in tribute to him) was quite good with reporters and cameras, and played well at being feminine. Capitalizing on her celebrity, she developed a nightclub act and had a minor career in show business. In the 1960s she wrote an autobiography, which was made into a Hollywood movie. She died a rather fulfilled pioneer, in 1989.

The Jorgensen celebrity coincided with years of deep cold-war conservatism, and though it promised much, it didn't open the gates for sex-change operations in America. On the contrary, Jorgensen aroused fears that the government, itching to prosecute anti-Americanism in every form, might make an example of the medical maverick at home (rather than in decadent Denmark) that would tamper with the national manhood.

But by the 1960s, in a climate of wider cultural liberalism, the fear of mayhem began to subside, and surgeons finally experimented with sex reassignment. The first hospital to do so was Johns Hopkins, in Baltimore, which opened its Gender Identity Clinic in 1966. And one of the early patients at the hospital, in 1967, was the British-born writer Gordon Hall.

The Second Witness

Dawn Simmons had said she was a hermaphrodite, or an intersexual (to use the later word), so I went to look for testimony from people in the intersex world.

Cheryl Chase was a former software developer living in California. She'd been born with an ambiguous sex identity, and out of the trauma this event imposed, she'd made herself into an activist. In 1993 Chase had founded the Intersex Society of North America, a nonprofit organization whose goal was to change the way intersex babies were treated by medicine. She agreed to a meeting in California to talk about intersexuality, and I flew out to see her at her home.

A couple of hours from San Francisco, golf courses and mall

sprawl had just begun to cover a long, dry valley that once consisted of grazing land. Cheryl Chase's ranch-style house sat at the end of a two-lane blacktop, with horses in the backyard and pigs across the street. I saw egg hens pecking around a chicken coop behind the house, and brown hills lumping on the horizon. Near the chickens stood a green, one-room building with big windows; inside was Chase's nonprofit, which consisted of two desks, computers, file cabinets, and an assistant.

Cheryl Chase had a scientist's even manner and unflappable confidence. She was in her midforties, stood about five-foot-nine, and acted serious, but her fashion sense was miles from the white-coated specialist. On this day she wore black pants with silver cowboy trim on the leg seams, a brown sweater, and cowboy boots. She had a sharp nose, short graying hair, and thin lips; and on her lean face were oval tortoiseshell eyeglasses. Her voice was husky.

As a teenager Chase had shown an aptitude for science, and in college during the 1970s she'd studied math and physics at the Massachusetts Institute of Technology. She then broke ranks to do graduate work in Japanese at Harvard. The two paths converged in her twenties, when she moved to Japan and helped run a computer business. In the early 1990s she dropped all this and came back to the States, settling in San Francisco. Around the Bay, Chase reinvented herself as the first of a kind: an intersexual activist, not different in righteousness from an antinuke protester, but one with an agenda barely understood outside of obstetrics departments.

We sat at an iron table on a patio in the backyard, which looked out at an unfenced field and the hills a few miles away. Dawn Simmons was not one of the cases that Chase knew from her research. "Did Dawn Simmons have congenital adrenal hyperplasia?" she asked, when briefed.

The absence of a diagnosis wasn't strange, Chase said, because the medical history of intersex people was weirdly treated. "Even when their records should be at an institution, intersex records are frequently missing or incomplete. We're pretty sure, based on the reports of people who have worked in those institutions, that the reason why is that they're fascinating, and doctors just keep 'em."

Chase smiled, leaned back in her chair, and put her thumb and forefinger together in a pinch of emphasis.

"Doctors sometimes pocket the records of patients. I've heard from people at Johns Hopkins that if you treated an intersexual and you didn't keep the notes, you wouldn't get to see them, because the next guy down the line was going to keep them and get to publish research with them."

The records of Dawn Simmons might not have survived if curious eyes had fallen on them.

Chase laced her fingers in her lap and returned to serious mode. "Johns Hopkins created the model of how to manage sexual ambiguity and intersex, but the people who did that are not the same people who worked there on transsexuals," she said. "They used the same basic science, however. They both do surgery and use hormones."

Although I'd read that the most common intersex condition is considered congenital adrenal hyperplasia, Chase maintained that Klinefelter Syndrome is more common. Chase explained that Dr. Harry F. Klinefelter was a physician at Massachusetts General Hospital in Boston. During the 1940s, he and two other doctors published their observations of a group of male patients with enlarged breasts, sparse facial hair, small testes, and a failure to make sperm. These patients became the first Klinefelter cases.

"One in eight hundred men has Klinefelter, but it's not that obvious," Chase explained. "They are always assigned male at birth, and a lot of times not diagnosed. They are born with typical-looking genitalia, but their testes don't function very well. There is an elevated rate of transsexualism among men with Klinefelter."

Dawn Simmons did talk about being an apparent male with enlarging breasts. She also spoke of being indifferent to sexual desire, a possible effect of failed gonads. Was she a Klinefelter case?

The sun had grown stronger, so Chase and I moved to get out of the light. A flock of crows cawed in the afternoon cool.

* * *

CHERYL CHASE HAD PUBLISHED ARTICLES that told her personal story. She'd been born in 1956, the first child of an upper-middle-class couple, but the obstetrician couldn't name the infant's sex. A doctor specializing in intersex conditions examined the child over three days ("and sedated my mother each time she asked what was wrong with her baby") before concluding it was male. The diagnosis was *micropenis* (medicine's felicitous word for a small member) with undescended testes. A male birth certificate was completed, and the infant's parents named him Charlie and began raising the child as a boy.

When Charlie was a year and a half old, however, his parents went to different physicians, who checked the toddler into a hospital for "sex determination." Doctors operated and discovered Charlie had internal gonads, a uterus, and a vagina. The micropenis was renamed a *hypertrophic clitoris* (i.e., a large one). Then, as Chase wrote, "I received a clitorectomy."

Surgeons amputated Charlie's clitoris, saying it was too big, and shaped a vaginal orifice. The baby's parents discarded traces of his boyhood (pictures, clothes), and the name on the birth certificate was changed to Cheryl. Chase's family moved to a different town, and everyone in Cheryl's life started referring to her as female. The crisis was buried.

When she was eight, Cheryl's parents took her for more surgery, and when doctors examined her gonads, they were found to contain both ovarian and testicular tissue. This made Chase one of the rarest of humans. In the language that she dislikes, she was identified as a "true hermaphrodite."

The word *hermaphrodite* arose in Greek mythology. Hermaphroditus was a child of Hermes (the patron of music and messenger of the gods) and Aphrodite (the goddess of beauty and erotic love). One day Hermaphroditus, a remarkably handsome boy, undressed to swim in a lake in which there lived a nymph called Salmacis. Intoxicated by his beauty, Salmacis fell in love with him, but Hermaphroditus rejected her. Salmacis embraced him, and Hermaphroditus struggled while she prayed to the gods they would never be separated. Salmacis's wish was granted, and her body fused with that of her love, creating a sexually ambiguous figure. In grief, Hermaphroditus prayed that anyone who bathed in Salmacis's lake would meet the same fate.

In the 1800s, anatomists familiar with genital irregularity coined the terms *true hermaphrodite* and *pseudohermaphrodite*. The first meant a person with both types of gonadal tissue (ovarian and testicular); and the second, a person with the gonads of one sex but external organs of the other. Chase didn't use these terms, which she considered vague and also offensive, the language of the circus sideshow.

The frequency of "dual-sex" births, people with both ovarian and testicular material, is so low as to be almost impossible to measure. In 1981, a researcher in South Africa, Willem van Niekirk, claimed that only 409 dual-sexed people had been recorded worldwide since 1899, which he said was the year the first true hermaphrodite was reported in medical literature. (Van Niekirk's count is one of the few that exists, and it is flawed: his survey included only rich nations, leaving seven-eighths of the world uncounted, and there were plenty of intersex births before 1899.) The incidence of births like that of Cheryl Chase amounts to statistical zero.

As yet, no individual has been observed who has both a whole ovary and whole testicle. And the fantasy figure that hermaphroditism arouses—namely, a person who can inseminate him/herself and who is therefore self-reproducing—has never been known to exist.

Presented with the eight-year-old Cheryl Chase, a history-making patient, surgeons cut away the testicular areas of her gonads, on the arguments that a "normal life" was paramount and that the testosterone the gonads would secrete could upset the patient's feminization. Meanwhile, Chase was never told the nature of the operation, either as a child or, later, as an adult.

Chase began menstruating in her teens, and her relieved parents stopped the medical interventions. But in adolescence, she became aware she didn't have a clitoris or inner labia, and that she could not have an orgasm. She began to suspect something had happened, but her parents were silent.

At nineteen, Chase started a search for medical records she thought might exist, and after years pursuing a reluctant hospital, and fighting obstructionist physicians, she received a scant three-page summary of her case. The records called her a true hermaphrodite named Charlie, and sketched the treatment given to her in childhood.

"I thought, this can't be anyone's story, much less my own story," she wrote about the discovery, which came in her early twenties. The revelation traumatized her, and Chase tried to erase what she'd learned by repressing it from memory.

In her love life, Chase said that by her twenties she was living as a lesbian, but her relationships tended to sink on the rocks of her maladjustment. She functioned at a high social level, however. Her language skills and hard-science background enabled her to move to Japan, where she became a principal in a firm that did computer and translation work. Ten years passed, and she made money; but she was increasingly frozen, blunted by her nonorgasmic sexuality, in shock and withdrawn. "Thoughts of myself as a Frankenstein patchwork alternated with longings for escape by death," she wrote about this period.

When she reached her early thirties, the trauma of her damaged sexuality and conversion from maleness to femaleness returned, and Chase suffered a breakdown. The crisis ended gradually, and she determined to become an activist, using her outrage to fuel a different kind of life.

In 1992, Chase moved to San Francisco, and the following year she founded the Intersex Society of North America, with the goal of changing the way intersex infants were treated. The group advocates gender assignment for intersex newborns, but not surgery. It also recommends that intersex children be raised as boys or girls, but that decisions about surgery be left to the patient in adulthood.

* * *

WHEN WE MET, Cheryl Chase was living with her partner, a short-haired younger woman with her own work and life; the two shared a house, two horses, a parrot, and a spaniel named Scout.

Sitting in her iron patio chair in the backyard, Chase said she spent her energies on the nonprofit and on writing and giving talks about intersex conditions. I mentioned the story of Daniel Burghammer, the soldier in seventeenth-century Italy who became pregnant and gave birth to a daughter, causing the church to declare a miracle. Chase doubted that Burghammer had been intersexual.

"History is filled with cases of ambiguous sex," she said in her husky voice, "and probably most of them aren't intersex. There are cases of passing women, and these are women everybody thought of as men, and then at some point after death who were revealed to be anatomic women. Intersex is obviously not that. It's a physical status, chiefly."

Chase nodded minimally at markers in the conversation, shaking her short gray hair. She was a focused listener with unwavering eyes behind her brown glasses.

However, she said, there were cases of people who'd apparently and spontaneously changed sex in midlife, which was the experience Dawn Simmons claimed she'd had. "There's a famous case involving a guy called Robert Stoller, who was a psychiatrist who did work on gender and transsexuals, in the 1950s and '60s. He's also well known because he and an anthropologist went to Papua New Guinea and wrote about ritual fellatio. There are a lot of cultures in that region where part of the coming-of-age process involves fellatio. They have women's huts and men's huts, and in the men's huts, the boys fellate slightly older boys.

"Anyway, one of the things Stoller also found in Papua New Guinea was a lot of people with a condition called 5-alpha-reductase deficiency. These are people born looking quite female, and unless you are familiar with 5-AR, you would think of them as girls. The

Papua New Guineans are familiar with it, and can detect slight anomalies in the genitals, and they realize this is one of those kids who looks like a girl, but turns into a boy later. What the babies have is an enzyme deficiency that causes their prenatal virilization not to work very well; but later, their pubertal virilization works just fine. In most cases, these people grow up as girls—and then, at the age of expected puberty, they start to get a beard and a deeper voice."

Chase opened her mouth for a moment and let her tongue dash from the left to the right side.

Under some circumstances, she said, the apparently female genitalia of people with 5-alpha-reductase deficiency can blossom into male genitalia at puberty. "Testosterone acts equally well on girls and on boys," Chase went on, "so if you apply enough testosterone to somebody with female genitals, the clitoris grows quite a bit. I've seen some that are that big." She held thumb and forefinger two inches apart.

Is there a corresponding syndrome that causes male-to-female transitioning? "No, because virilization is a process that goes in one direction, female-to-male," Chase said. "It can't be reversed." In other words, a boy doesn't wake up one day and find he's a girl, and that his penis is shrinking into his body.

And with the image in my head of Papua New Guineans easing gracefully from female to male status, the sun set in the hills beyond Cheryl Chase's horse stable.

IT WAS CLEAR that Gordon Hall didn't have 5-alpha-reductase deficiency, which caused female-to-male realignment. He might have had Klinefelter Syndrome, and still in the running was congenital adrenal hyperplasia. But no condition could be confirmed without more evidence.

After much canvassing, and despite the reports of witnesses in England, I still knew little about Gordon's early life. Had there been physical exams? Photographs?

Parents usually describe their own youth to their children in tossed-off remarks, leaving the children to piece together the father's boyhood or the mother's girlhood from fragments. If anyone possessed the remnants of Dawn Simmons's youth, it would be Natasha Simmons, her daughter. Natasha would have photographs, and perhaps some of Dawn's personal memories. She would have kept alive something of the image her mother had retained of her English childhood—when she was a young boy, or perhaps a young girl.

Chapter 7

THE UNMAKING OF
AN ENGLISH SERVANT BOY

PHOTOGRAPHIC PROOF

Natasha Simmons lived in a rented house in a hardworking section of Charleston that featured chain-link fences around cottages, aluminum siding on buildings, and secondhand cars in the driveways. Her living room had a vinyl sofa, thin flower-print curtains, and a big poster of a leopard on the wall. It was dim, but in the shadows were a handful of antiques, which Natasha said she'd inherited from her mother, and several framed pictures of Dawn Simmons hung on the wall.

Sitting at her dining-room table under a little brass chandelier, Natasha opened a cardboard box full of old photographs. She was dressed in a brown sleeveless blouse, hoop earrings, and a gold necklace, and her gleaming dark hair was held back with a plastic clasp.

"This is Mommy when she's about three years old," she said, waving a picture.

The photo showed a small child with long curly hair, patent-leather shoes, and a pullover that came to bare knees. To my eyes it was a girl, but it just as well could have been a boy in girlish clothes. The child had Dawn's facial features and was standing next to a white Jack Russell terrier.

Flipping to another photo, Natasha said, "but I've always questioned this picture."

This time it was a chubby-faced girl, maybe fourteen years old, whose shoulder-length hair was tied with a bow. The girl wore a gauzy white dress and lipstick, and her plump face and body bore little resemblance to Dawn's spindly form. "My mom told me that it was her when she was a young girl—or guy, boy, whatever—but I don't know."

Natasha had tipped her hand. For the first time, probably by accident, she admitted she had questions about her mother's story: "a young girl—or guy, boy, whatever."

Damari, Natasha's three-year-old, arrived from the next room and climbed into her mother's lap. The girl had little braids and big eyes, and she wore a red-and-green football jersey with the number 28 on the front.

I took out a picture of Dawn as a new mother, holding baby Natasha in her lap, and the photo looked a lot like the mother and daughter in front of me. Damari grabbed the picture and said, "That's your Mommy."

"Yes, that's my Mommy," Natasha nodded.

Natasha fished out a picture of her mother in the 1980s, sitting in a rocking chair on a porch. "That's when we went to Jimmy Carter's farm in Plains, Georgia," she said.

As a writer, Dawn had developed a specialty in biographies of politicians' wives. "My mom did a book on Rosalyn Carter, so we went to see her there," Natasha explained. "I met Mrs. Carter, and I swam with Amy Carter in the family pool. Mommy's got pictures of that, too."

Natasha had never seen her mother's papers in the archive at Duke, and she looked surprised when she heard the extent of what was there. But the sex surgery wasn't fully represented in the papers, with the exception of a list of doctors' appointments and some articles Dawn had written.

"Your mother went to the Gender Identity Clinic, at Johns Hopkins Hospital, in Baltimore," I said.

"I've heard of it."

"It was a place people went to have gender reassignment, and one of the things that comes up in your mother's story is her claim she was born a girl."

"Right," said Natasha, expressionless.

Natasha neither confirmed nor denied that her mother might have been something other than a woman, and it wasn't clear whether she knew the whole truth.

Pointing at a wedding picture of Dawn, who was wearing a white dress and tiara, Natasha said, "She always laughed at this picture, because it was so windy that day, and the wind almost took her tiara off." In the next shot, Dawn and her new husband were cutting a wedding cake. "They got a little plastic bride and groom to put on the cake, but they had to paint Daddy's face black, because they didn't have interracial figurines."

Walking into the living room, Natasha took a framed photo of her mother off the wall. It showed Dawn standing outdoors in Charleston, wearing a bonnet and a billowing antebellum dress made of shiny maroon fabric. She looked like a Confederate widow.

"That's from when Mommy was in *North and South*, the TV series," said Natasha, referring to a network show from the 1980s about the Civil War. "Mommy was an extra, and she was in quite a few scenes." Dawn made a credible Southern belle, a plantation trannie, though her little body almost disappeared in the hoop skirt.

Natasha picked up a photo of herself as a baby, dandling in the arms of a white man. "That man was Princess Margaret's hairdresser," she said.

It took a minute to place the reference. Years before the sex reassignment, Gordon Hall had written a biography of Queen Elizabeth's sister, Princess Margaret. Evidently, Gordon met the princess's stylist while doing research, and Dawn later showed off Natasha to the royal hairdresser.

Next came a picture of Dawn's husband, John-Paul Simmons, who looked to be in his early twenties, and thin as a reed. "One of the few pictures I have of my daddy when he was skinny," said Natasha. "He's tall."

"Which made you tall," I said. A moment passed before I realized that I was saying he was her actual father, which I found implausible at best.

"Yeah," Natasha said with a laugh.

A two-foot-tall figure stood on a table and overlooked the room: the icon of Saint Teresa of Avila that had appeared in the TV interview. Her mother had loved the statue, Natasha said. (St. Teresa was a sixteenth-century Carmelite nun and church reformer; the wood figure wore a long shroud and held an open book, signifying the nun's life as a woman who'd defied the Inquisition and authored spiritual guides.) In a note in her papers, Dawn mentioned that her great-grandmother had come from Seville, Spain, to England in the 1850s and had brought the statue with her.

I asked when Natasha had first been aware of her mother's unusual past, and she said, "Mommy was always open about it." Dawn had answered questions as they arose, her daughter said.

"The first time I remember saying something was after I came across one of her books, when I was about seven years old," Natasha said. "I said, 'How come the name on here is Gordon and your name is Dawn?' She told me, 'That was my pseudonym,' and she said authors don't always write under their real name."

Natasha covered her mouth with her hand, as though contemplating a secret, and then removed it.

Dawn told her more as she grew up. "She was never ashamed of it, and I didn't have to encourage her to talk. Once I could understand all of it, she told me the whole thing, and I asked her questions. The issue of adoption came up, and she was always very adamant. She said, 'No, you were not adopted!' And she showed me the birth certificate, so I went by that."

Natasha's father, John-Paul Simmons, would have something to say about whether his daughter was adopted. Indeed, he was shaping up to be the only person who could give definite answers. But there were big obstacles, beginning with his mental illness. Also, he had been out of touch with his family for nearly five years, and Natasha didn't know his whereabouts. She said she'd last seen him in New York, where, angry over her decision to move to Charleston, he'd said he was cutting himself off from her.

"My grandmother, my daddy's mother, says she knows where my father is," Natasha said. "But I doubt she'll talk."

Natasha added that her grandmother—John-Paul Simmons's mother and Dawn's mother-in-law—was living in a retirement home in Charleston, and she mentioned the street. She said her grand- mother and Dawn had not been close. "But if you want to find my father, you could start with her."

It was a less than appealing prospect, searching for a frail woman to ask about her schizophrenic son and estranged daughter-in-law, but at the moment it was the only thing on offer.

The Soldiers' Cabaret

At the Duke University library, Dawn's papers opened the curtain that still surrounded my subject's youth. What emerged was an eso- teric and creative boyhood. Gordon Hall had made some autobio- graphical notes, and in one place he said his favorite childhood pastime was to put on plays. "Every fine afternoon after school, my special friends dropped in for some kind of rehearsal," he said, "and most of the material I wrote myself."

Gordon said that he first tried his hand on the stage at the Church of England school in Heathfield. For one little sketch, he wrote a script based on a murder legend involving Sissinghurst Castle. The story told of a sixteenth-century nobleman who took a succession of brides to Sissinghurst, where, one after another, he killed them. Gor- don gave himself the part of the murderer—which raised a question: Why was the schoolboy symbolically doing away with femininity by killing brides?

The love for costume and exhibition was telling in another way, since it mirrored the childhood of Dawn's lifelong idol Vita

Sackville-West. Gordon seemed to want to imitate the writer, who'd also grown up staging little plays, only at Knole House, the great manor. If he could do something like she'd done, he thought, he might grow up to be like her, and become an author and personality.

A few years later, in his midteens, Gordon played the role of a woman in a stage adaptation of Charles Dickens's *David Copperfield*. His character was that of Aunt Betsey Trotwood, the widow who looks after the orphaned Copperfield when he runs away from London. A picture in Dawn's papers showed Gordon in stage costume, draped in a heavy Victorian dress and shawl, wearing a wig with corkscrew curls.

The Aunt Betsey role seemed to be Gordon's first appearance in public as a female. And because the show ran several nights, he was able to bask in the experience.

"With the coming of the teenage years I tried hard to live a lie," Dawn said of her adolescence. "I cut my hair short, wore the most masculine tweed jackets I could find and did my best to be like other 'boys.' I tried to shave, with little success. Hair never grew on my chest, and people remarked at the smoothness of my skin."

Aside from this brief remark, Dawn's papers held no other recollections of Gordon's puberty. It seemed strange she'd omitted her adolescence and sexual awakening from her written reminiscences. Or maybe not: somewhere Dawn said she'd never sexually developed, either as a man or as a woman. If this was true, the shame might have been so great that she couldn't have been expected to write about it.

Dawn said that Gordon's appetite for writing came from his uncle Ditcher, who made the boy into a novice travel writer. The disabled hunter was also an amateur historian who loved old buildings and villages. "[He] sent me on excursions to learn about the churches and monuments of Sussex," Dawn wrote. "From these outings I would bring home my notes and snapshots for his vicarious enjoyment. Finally Uncle Ditcher would have me write reports."

According to Dawn, the child Gordon also used to accompany his grandmother Nellie Ticehurst on her job as a wedding and funeral writer for the local newspaper. But Gordon's sister, Frances, had dismissed this claim, saying Nellie never wrote a line. Whether or not Nellie wrote wedding copy, Dawn used to tell a rich tale about one of Nellie's assignments.

In 1940, Dawn said, Nellie and her grandson came face-to-face with their former king, Edward VIII. Edward, the Duke of Windsor, was the man who'd given up the throne to marry a twice-divorced American woman, Wallis Simpson. On this occasion, the Duke and Duchess of Windsor were escaping France, which had fallen to the Nazis, and they'd arrived in Sussex to stay with friends; Nellie Ticehurst was allegedly one of the reporters sent to meet them. According to Dawn, as the royal couple entered their borrowed living room, a florist handed young Gordon a dozen pink carnations to give to Wallis Simpson. The boy dutifully presented the bouquet after first bowing to the lady.

His grandmother had raised Gordon, and he regarded her as a saintly figure, but in 1941 Nellie Ticehurst was diagnosed with cancer. She declined rapidly, and Gordon nursed her in their little cottage, Havana. As his substitute mother was dying, Gordon became hysterical. "She was going to leave me and I would be alone with nobody to share my secret, for nobody else had ever cared," Dawn later wrote. Soon Nellie died in her sleep at age sixty-one, and she was buried with her husband in the Heathfield church cemetery.

Gordon had never been close to his natural mother, Marjorie, and he hated Jack Copper. Grandmother Nellie's death threw Gordon into a depression. But in another respect, the death was liberating: Gordon, who was nineteen, was no longer accountable to anyone.

He stood five feet, six inches tall, weighed 119 pounds, and had the build of a woman. Photographs from these years showed a waiflike figure, with narrow shoulders, stick arms, and a big smile (but alas, no breasts).

My thoughts turned back to the telephone monologue of Gordon's sister, Frances. Brief as it was, this conversation had revealed some basics. According to his sister, Gordon enrolled in a vocational college, Eastbourne Technical School, the tuition paid with his grandmother's money. At this school a half-hour ride from Heathfield in a holiday town on the south coast of England, Gordon learned office skills, but he also took classes in art and theater. Frances said that Gordon had gotten a certificate from Eastbourne and later took an office job.

Then came World War II. At the start, in 1939, Gordon was too young for the draft, but he reached the right age during the Battle of Britain. I found no sign in the Dawn Simmons Papers that Gordon had been drafted, and his sister had said, "I don't recall hearing about Dink's call-up, or a medical exam." Gordon dreaded the physical, for fear of exposure (said Dawn). Could he have been examined and rejected by a stunned physician?

If Gordon *had* been drafted, those papers might have survived, so I tested the availability of service records in England. But the British armed forces kept a viselike grip on privacy. According to the Army Records Centre of the Ministry of Defence, information in service records would be disclosed only to the ex-serviceman/woman or, if that person was deceased, the widow/widower.

I imagined that John-Paul Simmons, were he ever to surface, might be less than eager to read the medical report on his former wife, the soldier. Perhaps Gordon went to the draft office, and for one reason or another—either he was too small, too effeminate, too intersexual—he was given status 4-F, "not fit to serve."

Gordon's sister had said that every adult was required to do something for the war and "Dink worked at a milk depot, doing manual labor." This may have been so, but according to newspaper clippings from the period, Gordon also did something more to his liking: he went on the stage.

In the 1940s, the town of Heathfield, by accident of its location, was transformed from a sleepy backwater into a military center. If

Germany had invaded England, the Nazis would have had to storm through the area on the way to London; therefore, Britain, Canada, and later the United States all stationed regiments in the Sussex farmland. News clippings published in a local paper in 1946 said that Gordon Hall worked around these men in a "soldiers' welcome club" in Heathfield, "entertaining Canadian and American troops."

British welcome clubs, like the USO centers of the American military, were places where soldier boys danced with willing women, drank, and watched vaudevillelike stage shows. Gordon worked at a club run by the Canadian Red Cross; later, he spent time in a similar place in south London, organizing entertainments (the newspaper said) for troops on leave.

So it transpired that a thin, fawnlike twenty-year-old, the former actor in school plays, the alleged boy who dressed the girl, also performed in smoky rooms full of beery, uniformed men. Did he do skits, or was it the showgirl-style song and dance? The clippings didn't say. Neither did they say whether Gordon appeared onstage as a man or a woman.

NATASHA HAD SUGGESTED talking to her grandmother, John-Paul's mother, in order to find her father. I wrote Dawn's mother-in-law a letter to ask for a meeting. To my surprise, she agreed to see me, and I went to her apartment at the appointed time.

When I met her, Elena Simmons (not her real name) lived in a five-story building with a receptionist behind glass and a security guard in the lobby. Most of the six people sitting listlessly on sofas by the elevator were over the age of seventy, and black. I made my way to an upper floor and knocked on Mrs. Simmons's door. Thirty seconds later, a faint voice came from deep in the room.

"Who?"

Another half minute before I heard the clink of an aluminum walker. A crease opened from the top of the door to the bottom, and right about the middle was a round face with vertical lines on the cheeks and horizontal ones on the forehead.

Elena Simmons looked to be about eighty. Her eyes were disturbed and frightened, and she pulled the door shut. I mentioned our appointment through the closed door.

Pause. An answer, "No—I won't go into that."

"May I explain what I'm doing?"

The door latched from the inside.

"No, I won't talk about it. I can't be going into that."

I mentioned her family, her son, her granddaughter, but the clink of the walker moved off into the apartment.

Although I tried again another day, Mrs. Simmons still refused to talk. Dawn had evidently left some scars on her husband's family.

From what I could piece together out of Dawn's notes, John-Paul Simmons had been born in 1948 in Charleston, the son of Elena and Richard Simmons. He was the fourth of thirteen children, and the family lived in a wooden house on Montagu Street. Dawn said John-Paul's father "spent his early years in an orphanage," and then worked for decades at the Charleston Navy Yard, a military installation, operating a crane. But something had gone wrong, and Richard Simmons was arrested in a property-theft ring on the job and landed in prison.

As a boy in the 1950s, John-Paul Simmons had gone to public schools (the "Negro" schools being separate from the white) and had no white friends. His father had run a strict house before he was jailed, and John-Paul had quit school at eighth grade because the elder Mr. Simmons charged rent to his teenage children to live at home. To pay his father, fourteen-year-old John-Paul got a job as a delivery boy at Henry's Cut Rate drugstore, a white-owned pharmacy on King Street, the main commercial strip through the old part of town. Throughout the 1960s, between three in the afternoon and nine in the evening, John-Paul rode his bicycle from one end of the city to the other, carrying prescriptions and sundries to customers for a salary of fourteen dollars a week. When he got older, John-Paul moonlighted at an auto dealership, where he picked up skills in the garage. This was the young man Dawn would later marry, one of the seven sons of Elena Simmons.

In a short typewritten manuscript titled "Portrait of My Mother-in-Law," Dawn called Elena Simmons "Mama" and said she was "a jewel of rare price, a rough diamond to some, a great lady and a real mother to me." But, she added, "Mama can't write." During the first months of their relationship, Dawn had befriended Mrs. Simmons by taking down letters she wanted to send to her husband in prison.

That seemed to be the high point of their acquaintance. After the marriage and the resulting storm of publicity, Elena pulled back from Dawn; things chilled further when John-Paul was diagnosed with mental illness. It seemed Elena Simmons blamed her daughter-in-law for her son's disease.

FROZEN WHITE TEACHER

Gordon's job during the war turned his eyes to America. Dawn's sister, Frances, had said that after the war ended, in spring 1945, "Heathfield was crawling with Canadian soldiers," and many women became war brides as a way to get out of England and make fresh lives. One newspaper story told of an acquaintance of Gordon's from the welcome club, Rita Coakley, who married a Canadian, emigrated, and "has a school of her own out in the wild and rugged country at Batchawana, Canada, [where] the pupils are all Red Indians."

Like many after the war, Gordon looked to start again, and the first step was to escape his village upbringing. Within a year of the German surrender, his family had put the contents of Grandmother Nellie's house on the block. E. Watson & Sons, an auction house in Heathfield, organized the sale, which took place on May 16, 1946. Among the lots up for grabs were Nellie's "2ft. 6in. inlaid mother-o'-pearl tray," a "9 ft. x 10 ft. bordered Axminster carpet," an "old map of London, 1835, framed," and a "statue of Buddha." When it was done, Gordon had no belongings to speak of, but he may have had money to get out of England.

Frances said that her brother left in the fall of 1946 but was gone for just a year before coming back home. This made some sense, because the times were chaotic, with veterans and civilians grabbing what choices came their direction. It seemed the English government had a program with a stuffy name, the British Empire's League Exchange Teachers Scheme, which sent instructors from England to the far reaches of the Commonwealth. Gordon's friend Rita Coakley had found work in the "Red Indian" school in Canada—and when Gordon angled for a similar assignment, he landed one in a distant village in upper Ontario.

Gordon worked as the sole teacher on an Ojibwa reservation, situated on remote Lake Nipigon, nine hundred miles north of Chicago, or two hundred miles north of the top of Lake Superior. Yanked out of his claustrophobic boyhood, Gordon was dropped into a snowbound fishing village, where he ran the one-room school for native children. The weird experience would eventually give Gordon material for his first book, which would be published in America a few years later.

The Ojibwa were trappers and fishermen in the middle of Canada who'd been overrun by the influx of whites, sold their land to the British government, and moved to enclaves that mining companies didn't want. One of their reservations stood on Lake Nipigon, an icy lagoon ringed by black beaches, with a single village at a place called Gull Bay. Gordon went there in 1946, ostensibly to run the school.

As the job required, he moved into a cabin built for "the white teacher," and offered himself as a beacon of enlightenment to some twenty indigenous families. They'd seen plenty of Brits come and go, and they expected this one also to numb them with lessons on the royal genealogy. But the frail and freezing Englishman seemed inexplicably different.

"My doctors have told me that although by braving the rigors of Gull Bay to prove a manhood that wasn't there," Dawn later said, "instead, by working with the children, I fulfilled the dream of many a transsexual child to grow up and become a teacher."

An intersexual incident, if that's what it was, erupted the first week. One night a bunch of boys appeared outside Gordon's window and serenaded him with love songs. The next day, a white-haired man came to the door and reported that a well-built Ojibwa named Buckaroo wanted "to ask a few questions concerning your anatomy." The man said a rumor was going around that the new teacher "was a beautiful blonde English war bride" and "the boys wanted to see her"—which supposedly explained the songs at the window. Gordon presented himself to the Indian teens, and after some discussion, it was settled that he was no feminine catch.

Gordon's comic memoir about his year on Lake Nipigon, *Me Papoose Sitter*, is still in many libraries. Its title sounds like the "Injun talk" of old western movies, in which white actors in feathered headdress said things like "Me Choctaw, trade wampum." In the book, Gordon depicts himself as a bumbling cosmopolitan among the exotic natives, who are dependent on him but who also see him as a naïf they can exploit.

The Englishman called himself "the papoose sitter" because, "When the mothers wanted to go to the warehouse to do the week's marketing or have a look at their fish lines out on the frozen lake,

> they brought their babies to me. I lined them up on the four walls of the sitting room, each snugly settled in his tchnogen (cradle). There they dangled [from] large nails driven into my wall. Each baby was securely strapped in place, resembling a midget-size Egyptian mummy.

In his season with the natives, Gordon claimed to have become a mother figure to his students. Later, Dawn wrote, "Minding the Ojibway babies gave me a satisfaction I had never known before. When I held a child in my arms something warm and wonderful welled up inside. How I needed children of my own!"

The papoose sitter lived alone—teaching spelling and nursing children—with only a wood stove to toast his twiggy body during the merciless winter. And then, after less than twelve months, he was gone.

PROVINCIAL CHAMELEON

"Dink came back to England in 1947," Frances said, "because the job had ended. Mum had to raise money to fly him home."

Back in Sussex, Gordon must have felt stuck. He'd had a taste of travel and wanted more of it, but nothing else like the teaching job surfaced. According to one family member, he lowered his sights and got a job helping in a law firm, where his specialty was to execute the Old English lettering on deeds. After this, he managed again to launch himself away from home, this time moving to London, where he landed a job as a teacher. Between 1947 and 1949, Gordon taught art and theater at the Gregg School, a primary academy in the south London suburb of Croydon, and Clark's College, another school nearby. At both places, Gordon was a master to boys ten to fifteen years old.

Parlaying his years on the wartime stage into classroom lessons, Gordon now wrote more sketches and put his pubescent students up on the boards. In one show at the Gregg School, described in a faded program in Dawn's papers, Gordon and his thirteen-year-old charges adapted a scene from *Uncle Tom's Cabin* into a little playlet called "The New Arrivals." The piece dramatized slave life on an American cotton plantation and depicted the purchase of fresh black workers from the auction block, "with the Negro slaves played by the pupils."

When after two years he left teaching, Gordon's students gave him a going-away party. An item in the paper described the event, a picnic, and observed, "Mr. Gordon Hall was the recipient of several presents from his class. The gifts included a silver inkstand, silver breakfast set, valet razor in presentation leather case, a leather wallet, and a fountain pen."

Gordon was trying anything he could. He went back and forth to his hometown, working in the schools, and also sampling journalism, or something like it. The young man started his writing career modestly, contributing little items to the *Weekly Standard* in Sussex, covering weddings and society. To judge from his output, news reporting didn't come easily. Here is the full text of one of his pieces:

> Town of Waldron—An exhibition of needlework, produce, jam, jelly, flowers, baking and soft fruit was held at the July meeting of Waldron Women's Institute, in the Lucas Memorial Hall. Mrs. L. W. Innes presided, and Miss Una Humblecrofts distributed the prizes. The standard of the exhibits was excellent.

On the strength of such prose, the paper made Gordon a "ladies' reporter," a scribbler on village happenings:

> At St. George's Roman Catholic Church, Polegate, the wedding took place of Mr. Michael Joseph Shannon and Miss Janet Mary Frazer. The bride looked smart in a two-piece suit of a brown shade, and chose as shoulder-spray white Scottish heather.

A year of this sort of thing, and Gordon was able to branch out:

> Twenty-one chickens owned by Mr. F. C. Wadley, and valued at £25, have been stolen from Southover Nurseries, town of Burwash.

In five years: student, cabaret hoofer, office clerk, teacher, and village reporter. It was a fitful life, with only one real adventure and no clear goal. At least possibly, it could have been the life of a woman masquerading as a man. There was also the chance it was the life of a gay man, living in the closet, moving from one thing to the next.

In Gordon's notes from these years, he didn't mention his dual sexual identity. Yet how or why would he write about it? It was remotely possible this was the life of an intersexual. The hidden truth was that something was terribly wrong—and the only thing to do was to try to escape it.

"WHEN SHE FIRST PASSED AWAY," Natasha said, "I had my own monument to my mother, a whole room in the house, with pictures and things." Natasha was standing in her living room, talking about relics of Dawn. "Then I thought it was too weird."

In the months after Dawn died, Natasha had packed away many knickknacks connected to her mother, but Mommy was still very much in evidence. On one wall of the living room was a pastel drawing of Dawn dressed as a bride, wearing a veil and looking demurely at her bouquet. And on a table to the side stood a brushed aluminum container, like an old-fashioned flour tin.

"My mother's ashes," said Natasha.

She wiped the dust off the box with a paper towel. The tin had an adhesive label from the funeral home that said, "CREMAINS OF DAWN LANGLEY HALL SIMMONS #2."

"Even though she didn't say anything about being cremated, I felt she would understand. Because it's a lot of money just for a coffin," Natasha said.

Natasha permitted me to hold it, and the container seemed surprisingly heavy, five or six pounds, perhaps because human remains contain splinters of bone mixed in with the ash. Natasha said she'd never opened the tin, but she felt comforted by her mother's presence in the living room. "She's not out in the open, so nobody freaks out. And it kind of gives a sense of peace to the house to have her here."

I placed the box back in Natasha's hands.

CORN-BELT BRIDGE CLUBS

Gordon made it to America in 1950, sneaking in through a midwestern back door. Trawling for a job in journalism, he received an offer from the *Nevada Daily Mail*, the newspaper of choice in a place that had nothing to do with Las Vegas but instead served the heartland town of Nevada, Missouri.

A farm community, population twenty thousand, Nevada sat smack in the Corn Belt, 150 miles east of Wichita and 300 miles north of Little Rock. Gordon's ticket to Yankeeland was as a society editor, covering the parties, weddings, and bridge clubs of the farmers and their ilk.

Arriving in Missouri, Gordon found an apartment off the two-stoplight main street, and in America Dawn later said her feminization continued. "In my dreams I was always my real self, and the pseudo-man Gordon was supplanted by a real woman," Dawn wrote. "I knew that I was that woman. My diary for the day following that first night spent in Nevada tells of such a dream."

Gordon went shopping for furniture, and in a secondhand store, "One object stood out, and that was a marriage quilt made from a century-old design. It intrigued me for some reason, probably because I thought it would never be possible for me to marry. [After that,] I often found myself looking wistfully at bedroom suites, kitchen sets, and pretty dishes."

He couldn't drive (he would never learn, and neither would Dawn); to cover his farmland beat, the immigrant lumbered across the county by bus. But far from home, he found his English village experiences came in handy. He used his columns to praise the prizewinning squash at the annual fair, comment on the beauty of the rodeo queen, and talk up the bridal chiffon that was frequently on view in church.

Nevada, Missouri, did its service by getting the boy-girl to America. After two years the wheel turned again, and Gordon left Missouri to take his chances elsewhere. This time he'd disappear in a mass of strangers and, as Dawn remembered in cliché, "seek my fortune in New York City."

GORDON ARRIVED IN NEW YORK in the fall of 1952, carrying a few hundred dollars and deep anxiety about who he was. He wanted to keep writing, but standards of journalism were higher in the big city than in Missouri, and he found it hard to get work. He settled on a file clerk's job at Altman's department store, across the street from the Empire State Building, and found a tiny apartment on 103rd Street, on the Upper West Side.

Dawn's papers didn't quite explain the personal trials that had driven Gordon so far from home, but outward signs were that he was restless and fleeing something. He was, in Dawn's words, "a nonentity," and he felt adrift. If Dawn can be believed, Gordon had never had a girlfriend or a boyfriend. "I was a sexual zero," she said.

In New York, Gordon thought, he could overcome his confusion. But it was a risk, because the city answered the desires of only a few newcomers and crushed most of the rest. As things turned out, the young man stepped into the metropolis, and before a year passed, she found much of what she craved.

Part 3

THE WOMAN

Chapter 8

AN HEIRESS AND HER HEIR(ESS)

THE LONELY LADY

On the east coast of Florida, a hundred miles north of Miami, lies the city of Stuart, which is blessed with shimmering bay and a necklace of islands and beaches. Among the retirees and middle-income taxpayers of that place lived two women who'd befriended the transgender adventurer Gordon Hall during his first years in New York.

The melodic name of the first woman was Emeline Paige. She was a retired journalist who'd worked many years in New York City, and she'd agreed to talk on the phone about the gentle newcomer whom she once knew when she worked on a small newspaper in Manhattan. The phone had to be our only means of contact, because Emeline Paige was ninety-seven years old and could no longer withstand a social visit.

Miss Paige, which is how she referred to herself, remembered Gordon Hall as an aspiring writer and man-about-town. In her mind, Gordon had walked gracefully out of the midwestern flatlands and onto the streets of Greenwich Village, the artist colony of New York City, where he soon hustled himself up the social ladder. Until this point, evidence implied that Gordon possessed no great social skills, but he'd made a deep impression on Miss Paige, who called him "a member of our family."

Miss Paige had been a writer and editor at the *Villager*, a weekly newspaper in Greenwich Village. Her caregiver, Janet Hutchinson (the second friend of Gordon's), said that as she approached age one hundred, Miss Paige was sometimes confined to her bed, where she took shots from an oxygen tank. Miss Paige and Mrs. Hutchinson (which is how Dawn's letters to the caregiver were addressed) had been longtime companions and had shared a life in New York City. Mrs. Hutchinson said of her friend, "Miss Paige sleeps most of the day, but she comes alive about 4:00 p.m., and then you can't shut her up."

One afternoon at four-thirty, Miss Paige and Mrs. Hutchinson picked up separate receivers in their Florida home. They said they were sitting across from each other at their dining-room table, sifting old papers.

Miss Paige began, "I started working for the *Villager*, in New York, seventy years ago—"

"And in the 1940s, she became editor," Janet Hutchinson finished.

I pictured the two women in their semitropical Florida house, surrounded by New York memorabilia, most of it out of keeping with blazing sun and sliding glass doors. Miss Paige spoke in rapid streams about her Manhattan years, and her trumpetlike voice sounded anything but hindered by age.

"A hundred years ago, there was a New York family called Whitney," she said, "and you can't understand Gordon without talking about that family. They gave him an entrée."

She sketched the background of Gordon's initial flourishing in New York. Miss Paige said that his life in America made sense only because of the Whitneys. Joseph Whitney was an industrialist and minor captain of industry who'd patented the Whitney Work Stop Motion Silk machine, a device that gave his family a fortune. Not incidentally, Joseph Whitney was also a descendant of inventor Eli Whitney, the creator of the cotton gin, which changed garment making worldwide. By 1900, the latter Whitney, Joseph, owned several lucrative silk mills, and he and his wife Martha displayed their wealth by building houses in New York City and in Massachusetts. The couple had two children, Isabel and Hazel; and when Joseph and Martha died, in the 1930s, their daughters inherited the family money.

"These two sisters," said Miss Paige, "who hadn't married, moved in together in a big old house on West Tenth Street, off of Fifth Avenue, in Greenwich Village—"

"And that's how we met Gordon," Mrs. Hutchinson inserted.

Isabel and Hazel Whitney—now we were in the 1940s—divided their lives between the New York society in which their parents had moved and the cramped apartments of their poorer friends in Greenwich Village. It happened that the older sister, Isabel, had a career as an artist, painting murals and, later, watercolors. These variations in the lives of two feminine ornaments of the robber-baron class gave the rich Whitney ladies an unusual social circle. On the one hand, they moved among other old-money heirs of their own ilk; on the other hand, they befriended relatively poor artists, whom they wouldn't have known had they been more conventional. For example, Isabel and Hazel socialized a good bit with the painter Edward Hopper, who lived around the corner from them with his wife, Josephine.

"The Hoppers lived at 3 Washington Square North," said Miss Paige, "and it was ninety-four steps up to their apartment from the street. Edward would stand at the top and count them off as you ascended."

Isabel and Hazel Whitney grew old together, and when Hazel died, in 1952, she was buried in the family plot in a stately Brooklyn cemetery, leaving sixty-nine-year-old Isabel alone.

The sizable Whitney house, "one of the old-fashioned big brownstones," said Mrs. Hutchinson, was cavernous for one person. "It had four stories, servants' rooms, and a wine cellar that went halfway underneath the street." The unmarried and elderly heiress now roamed alone through dozens of overdecorated rooms, empty except for a uniformed Polish housekeeper.

Enter Gordon Hall. About the time of Hazel Whitney's death, Gordon appeared in Isabel's life. The two had met in an art gallery, and within a week Gordon had moved into the top floor of Whitney's house.

"He became the accommodating male whenever Isabel needed a companion," said Miss Paige. "He went every place she wanted to go that she needed an escort—and in exchange, Isabel gave him a place to live, and paid his expenses."

The December–May partnership between the old lady and the youthful English arriviste seemed to have been a relationship of convenience, at least at first. The chatty, accommodating newcomer was expected to refresh Miss Whitney's dim hours.

"When I first met Gordon Hall," said Miss Paige, "Isabel had sent him over with a note, which she wanted to have published in the *Villager*. He was wearing a beautiful overcoat, and so I said, 'Abercrombie and Fitch?' And he answered, 'Yes, Isabel insisted.' " Miss Paige laughed at this memory, a sign that Gordon had quickly picked up on the benefits of Isabel's money and patronage.

"They had that kind of relationship," Janet Hutchinson inserted.

"But she knew from the beginning that he was homosexual," said Miss Paige.

The laughter stopped. "I don't know that this is true!" Janet spoke up, a little cross. "He had all that horrible experience with being of both sexes—the bleeding, and the pain, and having to hide his real identity!"

The memories of the two women on the phone, which had previously been synchronous, now diverged, and their voices sharpened.

"He was a homosexual," repeated Miss Paige.

"No," said Mrs. Hutchinson, "because Gordon told me about a funny experience he had with his two sexes. He said he was interviewing Mrs. Jackie Kennedy, and writing a book about her. It was about the time when he was changing, and starting to develop breasts. They were swollen and painful, and he didn't know how to manage them, and he said one of them almost popped out of his shirt! But fortunately, Mrs. Kennedy didn't notice."

At this, Miss Paige said, "Yes, I see," but she didn't sound convinced.

SERVANTS' QUARTERS

On a trip to New York, I went looking for the old Isabel Whitney mansion. It still stood, at 12 West Tenth Street, off Fifth Avenue on a block of discreetly magnificent townhouses from the early 1800s. The house had a redbrick facade with a large bay window, and stairs led up from the sidewalk to the parlor-level door. It had been built in 1805 and enlarged later with touches favored by rich Victorians, including a wood-paneled central staircase and a new top floor for the butler and chambermaids. Since the Whitney sisters' time, the house had been cut up into apartments, and the buzzers and mailboxes in the foyer, along with the building's shaggy condition, drained the place somewhat of its grandeur.

Isabel Whitney was enough of a success as an artist to have left a legacy. A collector had acquired her papers and in turn left them to a small museum in the quiet Southern city of Augusta, Georgia. I made my way to Augusta, on the Savannah River, and sifted through her things.

The Isabel Whitney Papers confirmed that Isabel had been a member of an unconventional family. She was born in 1884, the first of the two sisters. The girls' mother, Martha Whitney, became an early feminist, campaigning for the right to vote and marching in suffrage parades in the front row among the women who held the banner. Martha Whitney had also helped to found a women's college in Massachusetts. When Isabel showed a talent for drawing, instead of setting her daughter on the usual path of finishing school, Martha Whitney put her in the Pratt Institute, in Brooklyn, to study art.

After studio training, daughter Isabel decided to paint murals, often landscapes with which she covered whole walls, specializing in fresco. A method of painting on fresh plaster, fresco was thought to be man's art because the artist had to work on a ladder—not to mention yell at men to bring on more heavy buckets of wet mortar, which was continually spread on the wall to receive the paint. Isabel became a regular newspaper subject, attracting reporters when she painted a

mural at the Brooklyn Museum in 1912, and again when she decorated the homes of private clients. The news clippings often showed
Isabel standing on a scaffold, wearing pants.

Isabel Whitney gave up her frescoes after a fall, which left her
dependent on crutches for the rest of her life. (Dawn Simmons said
the accident happened in the kitchen, from a stool.) She started making watercolors of flowers, but they were sentimental and innocuous,
and she dropped from public view. By the 1940s, she'd been reduced
to showing her work at mediocre art associations and ladies' clubs. It
was a cruel descent, and it made the tiny spinster (she stood four feet,
eleven inches tall) lonely and ripe for a friend.

GORDON HALL ARRIVED in New York City in 1952, got his
department-store job, and rented his little apartment. When the job
ended, he worked as a secretary for a news syndicate; after a few
months, he started freelancing as a society columnist for the *Port
Chester Daily Item*, a little newspaper in the northern suburbs. Dupli-
cating the job he'd had in Missouri, Gordon wrote about home-
bound housewives, church bazaars, and garden clubs. One of his
bigger stories, "Port Chester Treasures Wait Only to Be Found," was
about furniture discovered in the attic.

It was a shaky beginning, and life sputtered along until February
1953. "Then, of all things, I took ill," Dawn wrote. "I began to notice
things. My ankles had started to swell out of all proportion; then the
swelling spread upwards, first my legs, then my stomach." Gordon
landed in St. Luke's Hospital, where "tubes were pushed up through
my nose and down into my stomach; countless X-rays were taken."

Years later, Dawn Simmons said the mysterious illness had been
caused by swelling in her uterus. Until this time, she said, she'd never
menstruated—and finally, her body was trying to discharge blood.

Released from the hospital, and weak, according to Dawn, Gordon meandered downtown to Greenwich Village, where he'd heard
that artists lived, along with "people who didn't fit," like him. By

coincidence, Isabel Whitney was having one of her now-infrequent shows at the Pen and Brush Club, an artists' guild on West Ninth Street. She was in the gallery when Gordon walked in.

Dawn remembered, "I fell in love with one of her watercolors, named 'Gollywog's Cakewalk,' after Debussy." The two talked, and after Isabel visited Gordon's little apartment, she invited him to tea at her house downtown.

"Visiting Isabel's home was like entering some Tiffany cathedral," Dawn remembered. "The rooms were lighted for the most part with tall white church candles, while in the drawing room soft shafts of brightness filtered through two enormous silver sanctuary lamps that were embossed with silver cherubs' heads. A fire burned in a white marble baroque fireplace—and Isabel, dressed in an ankle-length gown of delicate white lace, presided over the most enormous silver tea service I had ever seen."

Gordon amused his hostess with stories of the Canadian hinterland and his war years as a "cabaret girl." Within a short time, Gordon had moved in, taking several of the servants' rooms on the top floor.

They became intimates. "Although my frustrating affliction was still with me, Isabel taught me how to live with it," Dawn said. "There was no need to prove I was strong and masculine when I really wasn't. As she had learned to live with her crippled leg, so had she taught me to accept with resignation something that we thought could never be righted."

What started as a commercial transaction (Gordon entertaining the lady) developed into an intense and sexually charged liaison between an old woman and her young attendant. Several photos in Dawn's papers showed Gordon and Isabel gazing dreamily at each other, and sometimes holding hands, pictures that suggest two lovers separated by an age difference of fifty years. In each picture Gordon looks at ease, the diminutive Isabel Whitney at his mercy.

In the end, Gordon maneuvered Isabel into his hands; and when she died, he carried her remains to be buried in his own hometown.

It was her grave I'd found next to Dawn's in the cemetery at All Saints Church, in Heathfield, where the inscription said, "Isabel Lydia Whitney—the beloved of Gordon Langley Hall."

Isabel introduced Gordon to her friends, some of them women like herself, moneyed and alone. One was the actress Dame Margaret Rutherford, who'd won an Oscar as best supporting actress for the movie *The V.I.P.s.* Rutherford was childless, like Isabel, and she would find a similar love for the talkative writer. The friendship with Margaret Rutherford grew until Gordon was calling her Mother Rutherford, and her husband, Stringer Davis, Father Stringer. Gordon the new New Yorker had remade himself from a wedding writer on a farmer's newspaper into a companion to rich women in their twilight years.

"We were involved," said Emeline Paige on the phone, meaning she and her companion Janet Hutchinson, "in the time Gordon met Bette Davis. We bought a house in Camden, Maine, to run as a bed and breakfast, and Davis's daughter was in a private school nearby." Miss Paige said there was a movie shot in Camden at that time, *Peyton Place*, and the premiere was scheduled, so a friend got in touch with Bette Davis, who agreed to do publicity for the release.

Gordon had been fascinated with Bette Davis for years and had even made scrapbooks about her from magazine clippings. (A half-dozen of the scrapbooks, each like a hardbound, hundred-page tabloid newspaper, were gathering dust among Dawn's papers.) In England as a teenager, Gordon would take the train from Sussex to London for the premiere of every new Bette Davis movie.

"Word got back to Gordon that Bette Davis was going to be on hand, so he took the next plane from New York to Maine—without Isabel, for once," said Mrs. Hutchinson. The idea that he might meet his idol would have electrified him. Bouncing with anticipation, Gordon arrived at the Maine retreat and told his hosts he would do whatever he could for the dinner. "He said, 'I can do the dusting,' so when he came in the door, we handed him a dust mop."

Gordon cleaned the dining and living rooms; and when the

actress arrived, he descended on her. Miss Paige said, "They were locked in conversation for hours. No one expected it. She sat on a chaise longue, and he at the foot of it—and when it was time for dinner, we weren't sure we could even break in."

Miss Paige inserted, "Gordon did a lovely story about Bette Davis for the *Villager.*"

WHILE GORDON ENTERTAINED HIMSELF with his new friends, he grew as a writer. "Due to Isabel's loving care and protection, I finished my first book," Dawn wrote.

Me Papoose Sitter, about Gordon's Ojibwa days, was published in 1955 to friendly reviews, and he threw himself into publicity. A clipping from the *Indianapolis Star* showed Gordon bare-chested, wearing a feathered headdress and holding a tomahawk, with a somewhat feminine Indian garment around his hips. The native drag act paid off. The Broadway producer Oscar Lerman optioned the book for the stage, and the *New York Times* reported that *Papoose* was scheduled for the 1956 season. (Something went wrong, however, and the show failed to materialize.) European editions of the book followed. A French translation of *Papoose* brought Gordon to Paris for a week of promotion; the Danish edition was called *Mine Sma Indianere.*

Gordon had made his first acquaintance with fame, thanks to Isabel's support, and he wanted more. In June 1956, flying to London to promote his book, he went on the BBC television show *In Town Tonight.* The interviewer, a woman with the Dickensian name of Pauline Tooth, needled her guest with questions about his sex life (according to the script of the show, filed in Dawn's papers). "Did you have a wife with you on the Indian reservation?" asked Tooth. "Did they regard you as an eligible bachelor?—Describe the three women who were 'after you.' "

Back in England, Gordon flaunted his new money in front of his family. In 1956, he went home to Heathfield and bought his aunt's fancy house, Beecholme, the place he'd once visited as a poor relation. ("Gordon is making great plans for the gardens at Beecholme," his mother, Marjorie Copper, wrote a friend. "He's had a sundial put up and a bird bath, and he's been buying antiques for his top rooms.")

In New York, he became a bit of a personality. The publisher of the *Villager*, Emeline Paige's paper, wrote Gordon, "Do find time to come in to see us once in a while. I think it is good for my paper for a notable like yourself to be seen coming in and out of our basement."

With *Papoose*, Gordon had made a writing career, but instead of finding a new subject as unusual as the Ojibwa, he allowed himself to be drawn further into his fascination with famous women. He developed a sideline writing for American newspapers about the British royal family. In 1957, he published a biography, *Princess Margaret*.

And after that, his writing stayed fixed on the subjects of glamour and women. His output suggests he was drawn by a compulsion to get close to femininity. Gay men sometimes focused their desire on campy femininity, but did people with an ambiguous sexual identity also do so?

One winter night, said Emeline Paige, Isabel and Gordon came home in formal clothes from the opera and found a man crouched under the sidewalk stoop, drunk and freezing. They got him into the house, warmed and cleaned him, then put him to bed. When the drunk revived, "he turned out to be charming," said Miss Paige—and Isabel gave him a job. "He was Italian, and a good cook, and his name was Joseph Scaltro."

According to Joe Trott, Dawn's ponytailed friend in Charleston, Joe Scaltro would wind up years later as Gordon Hall's boyfriend, the man with whom he moved to South Carolina.

Miss Paige said that Scaltro became a kind of butler, living on the top floor (along with Gordon), cooking and doing errands. "He was a charming scamp, and at some point, he started taking things out of Isabel's house and selling them to antique dealers," she said.

It was one of the weirder households in Greenwich Village: the disabled, aging heiress; a sexually ambiguous author; and Joe Scaltro, butler and rogue. Filling out the scene were Gordon's pets. A Christ-

mas card from 1958 included a drawing of Gordon's brood of animals, with a printed caption beneath: "Gordon Langley Hall's pet
parrot, Philadelphia Macrae Hall, sits on top of the Christmas tree
and is assisted in her decorating by Simon the Guinea-pig and the
tortoises Alfred, Scarlett Lee, Arabella, Brigitte and Bruno."

THE BEQUEST

Isabel Whitney was diagnosed with leukemia in 1959, and for three
years, as her condition worsened, Gordon nursed his beloved. About
this time, Gordon told a cousin that he and Isabel were engaged.
This might have been fantasy—I wasn't sure how to judge—but at
any rate, in Dawn's papers I'd found two power-of-attorney documents that the couple had exchanged, each giving control over their
property and well-being to the other. As it became clear Isabel would
not recover (according to Miss Paige), the pair made plans to get out
of New York—and money not being an issue, they looked for a tran-
quil place to flee. Isabel wasn't strong enough to travel, so Gordon
searched for real estate in various other states, with the assignment of
finding a comfortable place for Isabel's last years.

Letters from Isabel Whitney (in the Morris Museum in Augusta)
showed that Whitney had visited family friends in South Carolina
when she was a younger woman, and it was perhaps for this reason
that Gordon went to Charleston in the fall of 1961 to look at houses.
Equally plausible, because Gordon's mind had an obsessive streak,
the city of Charleston attracted him for its name. Charleston was the
name of a country house in Sussex where the Bloomsbury circle and
Virginia Woolf, author of *Orlando*, used to retreat for smart talk and
tête-à-têtes. Whatever the case, a cousin remembered that Gordon
had nearly settled on the sedate Southern city when, in January 1962,
a representative from the Historic Charleston Foundation made a

special trip to New York to discuss the matter. The envoy returned to South Carolina with a signed agreement that conveyed an old house in Charleston to Isabel and Gordon.

The couple wanted to retreat there. They'd chosen a dilapidated brick mansion, built about 1830, with porches and a walled garden. Isabel had signed the papers, buying the dream house sight unseen. Two weeks later, however, on February 2, 1962, she died, never having left her bed.

To judge from the photographs, when Isabel died, Gordon nearly lost his grip on reality. One picture showed a makeshift shrine he made to her in the living room of their New York mansion: on a round table decorated with flowers and candles, he placed Isabel's ashes in a box covered by an American flag.

Isabel Whitney's relatives must have been surprised by Gordon's next move, which was to bury his love's remains in Heathfield rather than the family plot in Greenwood Cemetery, in Brooklyn. But Emeline Paige disagreed that this was an issue. "She wanted to be buried in England; it was *her* idea, and Gordon merely arranged it." The two had traveled together on one or two of Gordon's trips home, and Isabel had apparently felt comfortable in England, home of her partner. Miss Paige added, "And for what it's worth, the ambassador to England at that time, John Hay Whitney, was a relative."

The ashes were flown to Sussex, and Gordon enlisted family members to make a good showing at the funeral. He hired a photographer to document everything, and the result was a glossy "funeral album," a picture record unlike any photo album I'd seen. In the loose-leaf book, with upward of a hundred photographs, Gordon's erstwhile father, Jack Copper, looked anxious to be elsewhere, while other relatives put on appropriately long faces. At the gravesite, Gordon wept uncontrollably.

Not forgetting the publicity moves he'd learned after *Papoose*, Gordon, in Sussex, announced to reporters that he and Isabel had been engaged. (In the clippings that survived, the English papers described Isabel as "the author's fiancée.") One paper dutifully ran a photo of a flower arrangement, on top of which Gordon had placed a card with the words, "From your beloved brokenhearted Gordon— for the one—*the only one*—who truly loved me." Back in America, long obituaries appeared in the *New York Times* and the *New York Herald Tribune.* These, however, made no mention of the engagement.

Was Isabel, who was old enough to be Gordon's grandmother, sleeping with her friend? If so, were they two women, or one woman and an intersexual? Or again (and somehow this was hardest to imagine) were they a woman and a man? I didn't have enough to go on, and the people who'd known them didn't want to speculate.

IN THE OFFICE OF THE SURROGATE'S COURT for New York County, located in a century-old building in lower Manhattan, the will of Isabel Whitney, dated November 16, 1960, was filed in book number 2375 of the Record of Wills. The document superseded an earlier will in which Gordon's name went unmentioned.

Isabel left Gordon the mansion on West Tenth Street, a sum of money, and one-quarter of "all the rest, residue, and remainder of my estate." She gave her lawyer a memorandum that stipulated a large portion of her property be handed over to him—art, jewelry, furniture—and she left him stock in a dozen companies, including Commonwealth Edison, General Electric, Marathon Oil, Sears, and Standard Oil.

Although Gordon Hall was suddenly an heir to the real estate, art, and cash fortune of a distinguished American family, the records of the bequest are too scattered to say how much he was worth. Dawn later claimed it was $1 million; at another point, she said it was $2 million. (One couldn't trust with numbers a person who bumped her age downward fifteen years.)

In any case, soon after the will was filed, Gordon sold the stocks for cash. Next, an announcement of a sale by Coleman Auction Galleries, on East Fifty-ninth Street in New York, advertised the "property of Gordon Langley Hall," including porcelains, rugs and broad-looms, paintings, an Asian art collection, bronzes, and chandeliers. This was some of Isabel's loot, although Gordon kept back a good portion for himself. Finally, just a year after his lover's death, Gordon decided to break up the Whitney mansion into apartments, which would bring a nice rental income.

With the various cash streams, it's likely Gordon carried off something less than a million dollars. Whatever the figure, it was supposed to be enough to live on for a long time.

THE HIRED CAR, driven by a uniformed chauffeur, left New York in September 1962, carrying Gordon Hall, his parrot Marilyn, and his two new pedigreed Chihuahuas, Nellie and Annabel-Eliza. Although temperatures in Charleston, South Carolina, often reached ninety degrees in the fall, the heir had taken the precaution of buying an electrically heated kennel for the almost-naked dogs.

In the years before the widespread restoration of its old buildings, Charleston, in the eyes of newcomers, seemed mysterious and dark. Notably in Ansonborough, Gordon's new neighborhood, paint peeled from the houses and chunks of stucco fell off their sides, leaving holes of naked brick. The house Isabel Whitney had bought for her and Gordon Hall had the melodic address of 56 Society Street, which was perhaps part of its appeal. But a picture taken before repairs showed a dilapidated hulk of a building, gray from dirt and neglect.

The Charleston peninsula droops down like a pendulum into the waters of the harbor, and Society Street runs a horizontal line through the middle of it. Around Society, the peninsula widens, as though swelling up with interest. The street contains the most redolent blocks of Ansonborough, which at that time was one of Charleston's many insalubrious quarters. Four or five houses to the west of Gordon's new place, on the same side of Society, stood the old house known as the Homo Hilton, home to drag queens and street people, including a few hustlers. Several buildings farther, on the corner of Wentworth and Meeting Streets, stood the Coffee Cup, a twenty-four-hour lunch counter where the most loyal clientele tended to stumble in at three in the morning, after the bars had closed.

Repairs to 56 Society Street were just half finished, but the new owner and his animal entourage pulled up to the front.

"When I arrived," Dawn wrote, "there was only one light in the house [and] the first night was spent sleeping upon an air mattress."

Within a few weeks, the immigrant from the foreign nation of New York had followed the custom of the showy rich and hired a black cook (named Irene Ladson) and an elderly black butler (Alex). When the house renovation was done, two truckloads of antiques, the remainder of Isabel Whitney's art and furniture, were moved in. Gordon's new life was ready for display. And his neighbors were preparing to put the handsome stranger through their social and sexual tests.

Chapter 9

THE HERMAPHRODITE OF ANSONBOROUGH

THE INTERLOPER

He had money, an English accent, and he liked to drop three names: Isabel Whitney, Bette Davis, and Margaret Rutherford ("Mother Rutherford," to his new friends). In some places, his list of women wouldn't impress, but Charleston liked its ladies to be grand and past their shelf life. The *Charleston News and Courier*, the city's 150-year-old daily, welcomed the stranger with a posh style who'd fallen into the midst. When Gordon restored his garden, the paper ran a picture of the clover-shaped flower beds and Gordon's blank commentary ("I wanted to create a garden full to overflowing"). When he lent some of Isabel's art collection to the local Gibbes Art Gallery (two drawings of Queen Victoria, signed by her, and a pencil sketch by John Constable), there was a flattering item with a photo of Gordon on his staircase next to Jackie, his new German shepherd.

Local society kissed the newcomer's ring in other ways. Gordon had allowed himself to become a pioneer in an early push for gentrification that would eventually drive poor black people out of Ansonborough. As thanks, preservationists invited him to dinner at grand tables and introduced him to suitable peers.

Meanwhile, said Dawn, her sex organs again began to rumble, as she felt new and mysterious pains. "There were strange sensations in my breasts, as if, deep down, some seed long dormant was stirring. I can best describe the feeling as a burning one, changing for periods to an itching irritation."

I LOOKED AROUND for someone who could bear witness to an older Charleston, and soon found a distinguished man and retired bookseller who'd watched the Gordon-and-Dawn pageant from a storefront seat.

The name John Zeigler had come up in conversation with several people. He lived a couple of blocks from Gordon's old house on Society Street, and, at ninety years old, he'd been in the city for most of the twentieth century.

"My memories aren't flattering to your subject," John Zeigler said on the phone in a gravelly voice. When Gordon first came to the city, he'd often visited the Book Basement, which Zeigler ran with his partner. "At the bookstore, Gordon would talk frankly to us," Zeigler went on, referring to himself and his companion. "So I feel some of what I have to say is true."

John Zeigler was a gentle Southerner from one of the region's rare well-read households. The son of a newspaper editor in nearby Florence, South Carolina, he'd gone to college in the 1930s and later made an attempt to write novels; but Zeigler disliked the result, and chose to be friends with writers instead. In his twenties, Zeigler met a young man by the name of Edwin Peacock, another South Carolinian and the person who would become his life partner. After both men served in World War II, they settled in Charleston, where they ran their bookstore and lived together for forty-nine years, until Peacock's death in the 1990s.

The crape myrtles were in bloom on the street in front of Zeigler's house, and most of them had been trimmed to show off the tiny white flowers at the tips of the branches. Zeigler lived alone in an old Charleston "single house," the type of long rectangular townhouse favored by the Carolina gentry during the slave days. True to the genre, Zeigler's house had its narrow end facing the street, and two tiers of porches on one of its long sides. A black iron fence framed the front yard.

Zeigler stood nearly six feet, had a little paunch, and a good amount of still-resident white hair. As he surveyed the street from the door, his jowls puffed out from his cheekbones and his chin came to a point. He had a handsome nose that ended in a forty-five-degree angle; in profile, it formed a perfect right triangle. He was dressed in a blue oxford shirt, gray pants, and horn-rimmed glasses.

"Gordon was very good at touching old ladies," Zeigler said as we climbed the stairs to his library. "Isabel Whitney was one of the old ladies he touched. There were others." Zeigler's voice was deep and much-used, with a pleasing chafe.

The library had floor-to-ceiling bookshelves filled with actual books rather than pretty things and doodads, as in most Charleston homes. We sat on a sofa that had a pattern of green leaves on a yellow background. I brought out a photo of Isabel Whitney, and he said, "Doesn't she look like the kind of person you could work around?"

He'd warned me that he wasn't going heap praise, and I could sense Zeigler was in a mood to debunk Gordon and Dawn.

"With Gordon, it's hard to cut through the lies and bizarre behavior," he said. "But in the beginning, when Gordon came into our bookstore, we were the people he could talk to that were not old ladies. He told us that his grandmother had started out with a barrow, or peddler's cart, in her village in Sussex, and had finally gotten enough money to open a little store. He never would have said that if it weren't true."

Gordon had often said his grandmother, Nellie Ticehurst, was a freelance journalist, but he'd apparently told John Zeigler otherwise. This new version of Nellie Ticehurst's story, which I'd heard nowhere else, was at least plausible, if you subtracted the caustic telling of it.

He said, "The business of Gordon being the adopted son of Dame Rutherford is probably right, because there are pictures of them together, but one wonders about many other things."

Some remembered that Gordon was celebrated when he moved to town, whereas others I'd spoken to, creating a safe distance from the Dawn phenomenon, had said nothing of the kind happened. Zeigler thought Gordon had been a social success.

"People in Charleston love anything English," he said, "so here is this fairly attractive young Englishman doing over this lovely house, and buying antique furniture. He had a slightly lower-class English accent, but no matter. He had two very good black servants, and he gave very nice dinner parties. People liked going there, to Gordon's house. And old ladies entertained him, people like Mrs. Totsie Middleton, others."

Zeigler named a society figure of the day, a hostess who'd presided at starchy but influential parties. When I asked whether Gordon had been admitted to the Charleston dinner-party circuit, Zeigler said he had. "Yes. I went to some of those parties. These were people I knew."

I remembered another story I'd heard, this one involving a social gatekeeper of the day named Frances Edmunds. As the chair of the foundation that had sold Gordon his house, Frances Edmunds used her formidable charm to work the city's elite in the service of her cause, which was the preservation of the city's architecture. Rumor had it that as Gordon renovated his new home, Edmunds gave him decorating advice. The symbolic moment of his acceptance in Charleston came when Edmunds traveled to New York with Gordon to inspect the Whitney mansion, whose mantelpieces and chandeliers, on her approval, were stripped and shipped to Society Street for reinstallation.

Dawn Simmons said that during Gordon's early days in South Carolina, he was toasted and courted. "Invitations from would-be matchmakers started pouring in," she wrote. "One poor soul who would never see forty again, whose only asset was her family name and her illustrious forebear's sword, delighted in arriving to see me in white tennis shorts. She would tempt me with a pair of legs that should long before have been veiled."

John Zeigler's library showed signs of a life spent around art and artists. There were paintings on the walls of the kind one might have collected in the 1950s if one had known the painters. On a table was a picture of Zeigler with Carson McCullers, the Georgia-born novelist, author of *The Heart Is a Lonely Hunter* and *The Ballad of the Sad Café*. Zeigler and his partner Edwin Peacock's friendship with McCullers had lasted until she died in the 1960s.

Clearing his throat, the retired bookseller offered his low opinion of Gordon's writing. "There was a review of one of Gordon's books, which I'll paraphrase," Zeigler said. "'Mr. Gordon Hall has written a book about Princess Margaret. He has written a book about Jacqueline Kennedy. He has now written a book about Lady Bird Johnson. He must be stopped before he strikes again.'" (I later found this review, by James Reston of the *New York Times*, and Zeigler had cited it almost verbatim.)

The old man laughed at the memory, then looked a little ashamed. "The one thing I really admired about him was that no matter how far Gordon fell, he had a certain push, and he always bounced back." This, at least, was a backhanded compliment.

Zeigler studied a fingernail. "Can I offer you something cold?" he said, and got up to go to the kitchen.

WHEN GORDON MOVED TO CHARLESTON, he had several books in print, which brought in money and also made him a curiosity. After *Me Papoose Sitter*, the book about the Indian village, he published *Princess Margaret*, his biography of the troubled sister of Queen Elizabeth. Then came *Golden Boats from Burma*, a book whose sugary title was matched by the obscurity of its subject, a woman named Ann Hasseltine Judson, a relative of Isabel Whitney and (supposedly) the first American woman to visit Burma.

In his new hometown, sitting like a gentleman at Isabel Whitney's antique desk, Gordon next wrote a book about an artist. *Vinnie Ream: The Story of the Girl Who Sculptured Lincoln* was a juvenile biography on the sculptor who created the statue of Lincoln that now stands in

the U.S. Capitol's rotunda. Then followed a book about Jacqueline
Kennedy, and afterward, *Mr. Jefferson's Ladies*, a portrait of the wife
and daughters of Thomas Jefferson. (The manuscript that I'd seen in
Dawn's papers made no mention of Jefferson's slave, Sally Hemings,
who was almost certainly one of the president's ladies.)

A recognizable thread held these books together: all told inspira-
tional stories about women in the midst of a journey of self-discovery.
It took no special insight to see that Gordon identified with his subjects, women struggling to flourish, which was perhaps how Gordon
regarded himself.

I tracked down a dozen of his titles and saw another dimension
they all shared. Although Gordon sold his work as nonfiction, his
writing style resembled melodrama more than journalism. He liked
breathless moments, sudden revelations, and surging emotions—
which was all right, except that when he presented facts, they didn't
inspire trust. Nevertheless, the style seemed to fit Charleston. The
city had papered over its bloody history of slavery with a batch of
Southern legends in which damsels and heroes courted and cavorted.
In this climate, the author's truthfulness didn't matter too much.
People preferred the art of the lie and the lullaby.

Gordon's books also seemed out of touch. The same year he was
sketching the life of "the girl who sculpted Lincoln," 1963, James
Baldwin, on the more timely side of the balance sheet, published a
rattling race manifesto, *The Fire Next Time*. And the year Gordon
wrote *Lady Bird and Her Daughters*, a long chat about Lady Bird
Johnson, the wife of President Lyndon Johnson, Norman Mailer
published a sharp dispatch from the movement against the war in
Vietnam, *The Armies of the Night*.

NUMBER 56 SOCIETY STREET, which Gordon christened the Dr.
Joseph Johnson House, after its first occupant, is a majestic example of
the Charleston single house, with two long porches on its west face.
(After an illogical Italian impulse, the porches were *piazzas* in local jar-

gon, although there was no Mediterranean influence to speak of.) At the time I visited, the present homeowner, Francis X. McCann, a crisp lawyer and family man, had lived in the house ten years and liked the idea that the memory of Gordon and Dawn gave his place extra sizzle. A partner in a small Charleston law firm, with dark hair and a direct smile, McCann cut a respectable figure in society.

On my visit McCann pointed out significant details of Gordon and Dawn's residence. "This is Gordon as a young man," said the lawyer, standing with a painting that showed a boyish, clean-cut face on a green background. Gordon had commissioned the portrait when he was visiting England from New York; it had later surfaced in a Charleston antiques shop, where another Dawn admirer had picked it up, returning it to the house as a gift.

More art from Gordon's tenure survived on an exterior wall, where a carved stone relief the size of a breadbox had been imbedded in the plaster. This, said McCann, was the Whitney family coat of arms: a knight's head with an inscription in Latin, which Gordon had installed and to which he'd added his own and Isabel Whitney's initials.

Even the events of Dawn's life lingered, in the way buildings are remembered for famous happenings. Standing in the carriage house, the homeowner said, "Here's the place where Dawn said John-Paul Simmons proposed to her, after he bought all the flowers at the market and laid them at her feet."

The most conspicuous mementos of Dawn were in the garden. With his large retinue of animals, Gordon had buried many pets; and each time one died, he ordered a granite marker ("Alfred the Turtle, d. 1959"), resulting in a small forest of tombstones in one of the old flower beds. And they weren't small footstones either: each looked the size of an unfolded newspaper.

Gordon had restored his house before moving in, and then he'd opened it to paying guests. For many years, during the spring tourist season crowds walked through the downstairs rooms to ogle the writer's antiques and marvel at the grandeur in which the proprietor lived. Ticket sales were brisk, and one year Gordon decided he would buy the building across the street, a Greek Revival box with big columns, to further showcase his art and furniture. Although the deal went through, Gordon never got around to renovating the second building, but he later sold it for a smart profit.

McCann arrived in his living room, a stately parlor with tall ceilings and a Federal period mantelpiece. A postcard in Dawn's papers, which she'd sent to friends after her sex reassignment, had shown her in the adjacent dining room, outfitted in a frilly Victorian dress, seated in a straight-backed chair, and smiling.

"The wedding took place in the living room, as the pictures show," Francis McCann said. And it was true the room looked different if one knew its secrets.

WHEN GORDON MOVED IN, Ansonborough—a neighborhood just a few blocks square and full of old mansions, corner stores, and little outbuildings—was majority black, not unusual for the city. (Later it turned entirely white, also not unusual.)

In the early 1960s, the white population of Ansonborough had included a small queer elite of decorators, florists, and restaurateurs. Blue-collar gay men, from hair stylists to clothing-store clerks, lived elsewhere in town, and the two classes tended not to mix.

To those who remembered it, Charleston's "gay aristocracy" was characterized by social conformity and discretion, and formed something of a golden closet. The custom, going back perhaps to the Civil War, was that gay sons were expected to move away from the area because the exposure of their sex habits would embarrass their family. If they stayed, they had to be perfectly discreet—and some of the most discreet men had lived in Ansonborough.

Despite the opening of gay life after the 1960s, deeper shelves of the closet had survived, especially if one came from a prominent family, in which the expectation of heirs weighed heavily. A curious society had arisen in Charleston among which it was not rare for a man

to be married, and gay, with children. (Similar arrangements flourished in other sexually choked societies, and they may even have been
modeled on customs in England, the venerated mother country; but
the statistical average in Charleston must have been triple or quadru-
ple that of most places.) In a television interview, Dawn Simmons
described the pattern this way:

> So many of the men in Charleston, especially the mar-
> ried men, walk two roads. They marry a rich society ma-
> tron that might not be very good looking, and try to find
> somebody on the side. When I [as Gordon Hall] showed
> no particular interest in the feminine sex, there were
> those who decided I must be a homosexual. I would be
> invited to a dinner party as a very eligible bachelor, and
> be brought home by the hostess' husband. He would
> suddenly produce a bottle of liquor out of his pocket—
> and I don't drink—and I would practically have to fight
> for my honor on the doorstep.

The rules of same-sex love in Charleston seemed looser for
women. Frequently, two women set up house in a "Boston marriage,"
keeping the public face of spinsterhood on what was actually a form
of matrimony. Such charades didn't upset the heterosexual order very
much; in fact, sympathy for women who never married allowed many
to regard lesbian couples as rather quaint.

GAY NECROPOLIS

It was a cool afternoon, a few miles from the heart of Charleston, and
Ted Phillips, who'd taken me to Dawn's funeral, was pointing out a
back route to his favorite place, Magnolia Cemetery.

"Today I want to show you a nice little nest of lesbians, the
founders of Ashley Hall," he said, referring to a local girls' school.

Ted was a premium resource for Charleston lore. He'd taken me on walks in the cemetery before, but this time I'd asked for a tour with a theme.

Ted Phillips was wearing a gray sweater and a blue button-down shirt, a tan tweed jacket, and a gray wool hat with a narrow brim. The hat and jacket, plus his slouch, made him look like a disheveled Sherlock Holmes. The role fit, to an extent, because Ted was a former public defender and thus something of an expert in theft and drug crime. ("I'm a recovering lawyer," he said.) Since quitting the courts, however, Ted had also become something of a necrologist.

For several years, Ted had researched Charleston's graveyards. It might have been a dreary hobby except that Ted liked the kind of revelations that aired the unseemly truth about the departed. As a result, he'd compiled a host of rumors about the respectable residents of Charleston, a virtual encyclopedia of scandal, which he carried around in his head.

The drive to Magnolia Cemetery took a few minutes, and as we passed a tough neighborhood, Ted pointed and said, "One day I was on one of those streets over there, going to see a client in my role as public defender, and somebody came at me with a gun." His upcountry accent got deeper. "I recognized the guy because I'd previously gotten him off of some drug charge. He was just holding up the first white person he saw, who happened to be me. When he realized who I was, he said, 'Oh, Mr. Phillips, I'm *soooo sorry*. I didn't know it was you!' So I told him, 'Andrew, this isn't going to do much for your parole!' But I gave him some money, anyway, because I didn't want him to feel too bad."

Ted was still musing about the good old days in the public defender's office when we arrived at the gates of Magnolia. Stepping out of the car, he lit a Marlboro and surveyed his domain. "Magnolia Cemetery. Laid out a century and a half ago on this old plantation."

We were standing within sight of the Cooper River. Sweeping his arm across a field of tombstones, Ted went on, "This part was supposed to be wild, so that when you came in you were immediately in the presence of nature. The whole idea of death-in-nature was one of the big draws of the rural cemetery movement, in the nineteenth century. But during the Civil War, Yankee troops set up camp here before they took Charleston. It was wintertime, and cold, so the Yankees cut down a lot of trees, and it was no longer wild when they left."

What remained were sensual, spare wetlands, with young oaks and magnolia trees, a meandering creek through the middle, and wooden footbridges crisscrossing the stream. There were abundant flocks of birds, an occasional alligator peeking from the water, and, after thousands of funerals, granite and marble stones rolling to the horizon.

"Unfortunately, part of Magnolia sits on filled-in marsh," said Ted, blowing smoke in the wind. "No one thought about the consequences of having a cemetery with a high water table. Even today, they have to put a pump in the grave if it's been raining. They pump out the water until the hearse can be seen coming through the gate; then they hide the machine. When they lower the coffin in, sometimes you can hear *slosh, slosh, slosh*—like burial at sea." Ted made a paddling motion, like a swimming duck.

Thanks to this amiable storyteller, a growing number of the dead were being disabused of the notion that their careful choice of a gravesite had provided them with permanent, dignified rest.

When Gordon Hall bought 56 Society Street, he'd found himself among the gay men of Ansonborough at a time when gay life in the South was kept well under cover.

"Ned Jennings," Ted said, stopping at a simple granite stone with a death date of 1929. "A very strange artist who did really wild, almost constructivist paintings, and who lived and painted in Charleston after World War I. Jennings got gassed preparing to go to that war, down in Mexico or something, and he was horribly disfigured, whether by the mustard gas or from something else. And so he would make really bizarre masks, and would come to parties in a mask, where he would entertain his hosts with wild dances."

Inspector's hat cocked, Ted scratched his cheek and bit his lip.

"He was gay, and he was a suicide, at age thirty-one. Shot himself or hung himself, I can't remember—a kind of a lost hope and great promise of the Charleston art world." Ted shook his head at the wasted talent.

In the old days, a handful of young men in every generation would inexplicably commit suicide. Their sense of confinement was such that some men would choose death rather than marry and live double lives.

Pointing at a tombstone with a well-known family name, Ted said, "I remember Willie, the gravedigger, when he dug this one. Willie said, 'That lady's grave, the dirt cut so easy!' "

Walking between the stones, Ted's expression changed—a smile here, a wince there—as he read the familiar inscriptions. "Okay, here's Catherine Drayton Mayrant Simmons, the novelist, who died 1969," he said, flinching. "She had a deputy sheriff she was in love with, and when her parents ran him off, she never recovered."

Waving his hand in a circle, Ted raised his voice and said, "Over here, one of my favorites is that one, a woman who was one of the great Baha'i disciples, Henrietta Imogene Martin."

We walked over to a three-by-six-foot stone tablet with a curious circular emblem on it, like a radiant sun, plus a chiseled number 9.

"Henrietta Martin was a wealthy woman from San Francisco who was converted to the Baha'i faith in Phoebe Appleton Hearst's drawing room—Phoebe being William Randolph Hearst's mother, and a person who had every swami and guru of her day to tea. At the end of her life, Henrietta was still evangelizing. She suffered a heart attack while visiting Charleston, preached from her bed for six months, and then she died."

Ted didn't just visit a graveyard; he riffed on it like a jazz musician. It was a strange power, to be able to talk about the dead in sound bites. When Ted did it, the storytelling felt communal. "These are my friends," he said, sweeping his arm like radar. "Oh yeah, my buddies. And I'm getting more and more friends as the years pass."

A few yards from the Baha'i preacher stood a plain granite marker of unmemorable design. "Helen Gardner McCormack, the art historian, who died in Charleston in 1974, age seventy-one," said Ted. "She was head of the Gibbes Art Gallery for years and years, and she was beloved around town. Never heard anybody say the first bad thing about her. But for our purposes, she was a lesbian. She was the second big lover of the other museum director, Laura Bragg, who was running the Gibbes's rival, the Charleston Museum. Apparently there are love letters and everything else."

There was a crunch of leaves underfoot, a half-mile of terrain had been covered, and Ted was still going. He passed a large stone with the single name "Finger" chiseled on it. "Ah, Dr. Finger," he said. "The gynecologist. I swear."

A gaggle of geese squawked in a nearby stream, and Ted stopped at another stone, took a deep breath, looked concerned.

"Dawn was a sexual mystery, right? Well, here's John Ragsdale—she was the big decorator in Charleston for a long time. She was very tall, and she had a deep voice, and her name was John. People are cruel in Charleston about giving their children an ancestor's last name. So when she called her clients, she said"—his voice dropped an octave—" 'This is John Ragsdale,' and you had to be careful about how you answered, 'sir' or 'ma'am.' "

We came to a narrow, six-foot obelisk that stood straight up, a decidedly erect monument amid many smaller stones. Chiseled on the thing was the epithet "Our King." Ted said, "This man was gay. And maybe he had the biggest one in the neighborhood."

A bit further stood a gravestone inscribed "Lover of Mankind." Ted smiled and said, "Or a substantial portion thereof."

There seemed to be many gay occupants of Magnolia. Although I wasn't sure Gordon had known them during their lifetimes, it's likely he'd been aware of at least some.

"Okay," Ted said, "here's Isabel Heyward, who had a kind of poetry salon in the 1920s. Her bookish group helped to feed the literary scene. She was rumored to be gay. Unfortunately, her girlfriend left her for another woman, and she committed suicide. Took her a while, however. She kept leaving the gas on by mistake, until finally it worked."

We arrived at a peaceful spot, shaded under long branches, where the graves of several women were clustered together.

"This is the nest of lesbians I promised, the women of Ashley Hall," said Ted, lighting another smoke.

The girls' school called Ashley Hall had been set up in 1909, and these were women associated with its creation. "Here's the founder, Mary Gardner McBee, and also Ursula Paret, and then Edna Marie Baker." The last woman's stone read, "violinist and librarian, forty-seven years service."

If they hadn't disclosed it themselves, I wondered, what would lead one to believe these women were lesbians?

"I was just told that by somebody in the past, who had been taught by them," Ted said.

I was surprised that Ted Phillips, the former public defender, relied on hearsay. But on the streets of sexual history, word of mouth was the only lamplight.

Ted adjusted his hat and pointed at a stone with a birth date, but no death date. The monument looked strange, being the sign of a cautious citizen preparing for the end. Ted said, "That woman's forgotten, but not gone."

A flock of birds fluttered nearby and settled on the handrail of a long wooden bridge over the creek. They were sleek and white, with big yellow beaks, and they perched by the hundreds, side-by-side, fluffing and preening, each standing on a single long leg.

"Ibises!" Ted said, and what he said was credible.

JOHN ZEIGLER SAT DOWN on the yellow sofa with the green leaf pattern. The bemused and elegant ninety-year-old was talking about gay life in Charleston during the 1960s.

"I have never 'come out' to this day—and I never discussed it with anybody. But my partner Edwin and I had friends all over town, and nobody would think of inviting one of us without the other." The gravelly voice was soothing. But I noticed for the first time that Zeigler spoke slightly from the right side of his mouth, which made his delivery seem eccentric.

He was describing another aspect of the Southern style, the don't-ask rule, in which gay life was tolerated insofar as it could be overlooked. Zeigler disputed that a social cage had once imprisoned homosexuals in the South. In fact, he thought Charleston in former days was actually an easy place to live, and he had a clever story to prove it.

One night, he said, Zeigler and his friend Edwin went to a party given by some gay friends, where the hired bartender was "a particular older black man." A few days later there came another cocktail party, this one mostly straight, in one of the city's downtown mansions. The same waiter worked the bar, and when it was time to go, Zeigler and Edwin offered him a lift.

"This was sometime in the 1960s," Zeigler remembered. "The bartender was probably seventy or so, and he recognized us from the gay party. In the car, he said something like, 'Mr. John, Charleston ain't nothing like what it used to be. It used to be you could just sleep with *anybody*. But that ain't true nowadays.' " Zeigler smiled lightly. To him, the story meant Charleston back then was sexually wide open, like a Confederate Sodom.

Zeigler's jowls and his avuncular smile gave the impression of a bard sifting his tales. Remembering Gordon, he looked down for a moment and then leveled his eyes. Gordon had come to Charleston and had soon started displaying flagrant behavior, Zeigler said.

"It was a pattern of Gordon's life that he was a masochist—absolutely. You see, in the early years, Gordon was very well known for picking up many, many people. That was his life at night, almost."

I knew Zeigler's ill opinion of Gordon had resurfaced. Nevertheless, I asked, "What kind of people did he pick up?"

"Anybody who would perform anal sex on him. He found men walking around the streets, a lot of them on Meeting Street, in the area in front of Citadel Square Baptist Church. That was the cruising zone. It was the place where sailors would wait for the bus late at night, on the way home to the Navy Yard. He found many young men there."

If Gordon had cruised for sex, as Zeigler said he had, did that mean he *wasn't* intersexual? Or did it merely mean he was looking for love? Either way, Gordon's claim to sexual purity was now badly in doubt.

"We had a very nice black boy who worked for us, named Andrew, a senior from the high school, who did the bicycle deliveries in the afternoon, and some work on Saturdays. Gordon took a fancy to him, and lured him away from his job with us at the Book Basement, and he went over and started working for Gordon."

I made a mental note of this mysterious reference; but Zeigler still hadn't said anything about Gordon's physical identity.

I asked what he thought of Gordon's supposed intersexual nature.

Zeigler laughed. "He was promiscuous, but he was always implying he never had sex until he married. So there's an unrecognized contradiction." The elderly gentleman paused and looked at a fingernail. "I don't know what among the things he said was true and what was not. When he married, he said, his vagina was too small to accommodate his friend."

Dawn, tactfully, would have called Zeigler "one of the doubters." He disbelieved she'd been born with ambiguous genitalia and had been surgically moved over into the distaff. The retired bookseller cleared his throat and offered another story.

"Did Gordon mention in his papers a proctologist?"

Zeigler gave the doctor's name, and I'll call him Dr. Benson.

"Benson used to come in our bookstore, and I think he said something to me about Gordon being a patient. At any rate, two friends of mine were invited to the Bensons' for dinner, and after they ate, Benson wanted to show them photographs. What he showed them was various photographs of the anuses of people, his patients. He didn't tell them who the anuses belonged to, but my friends thought it was a very strange way to be entertained after dinner. Well, I have a feeling Gordon was in one of the pictures."

Whether Zeigler was accusing this Dr. Benson of unethical conduct, or whether he was just looking for a reaction, I wasn't sure. Either way, even in Charleston, this sort of dinner-party game would have raised eyebrows. I didn't know what it said about Gordon's sexuality, and Zeigler, with an enigmatic smile, left the riddle undeciphered.

When Dawn married John-Paul Simmons, Zeigler and his partner Edwin Peacock weren't invited to the wedding. "He had bought a lot of books from us at the bookstore, and owed us a lot of money. It could be he felt somewhat guilty about that," Zeigler guessed. I had a feeling they would have liked to go, because in Zeigler's mind the wedding was an event superior in impact to Gordon's sex reassignment, which had taken place the year before.

"I think people in Charleston could take a sex operation more easily than they could take a marriage to a black man, which was more forbidden, in a way," said Zeigler. "Remember, we still have all these Confederate people all over the place. I don't think the sex switch bothered people nearly as much as it did that Gordon married John-Paul."

This opinion seemed strange. Undoubtedly, to hook up with "a Negro" was for generations the worst thing a white woman could do in the South. But Charleston had little experience with sex reassignment and plenty with miscegenation. One would think a gender switch broke the stronger taboo.

Was John-Paul Simmons gay? "I don't think so," said Zeigler. "I think he was a big old roughneck who was perfectly willing to be seduced, and perhaps Gordon made the change of sex because he, John-Paul, didn't want to be seen as being a homosexual. I'm just speculating, but to me it would make perfect sense that this big butch guy wanted to be seen with a wife."

An interesting theory: Dawn was once a gay man who'd undertaken a sex change to please his boyfriend. But the idea rested on an unlikely assumption: Gordon had been struck by a desire for John-Paul so strong that he'd been willing to become a guinea pig for what was still a relatively new medical practice.

The world Zeigler described didn't seem like one controlled by better instincts. In fact, his speculations made the people he talked about, and their desires, their behavior and justification for it—all of this—resemble a tissue of lies.

Zeigler began to wind down. He was catching a plane to London to visit friends, and needed to prepare. The trip to Europe was one he still made frequently, in defiance of his age.

"I think Dawn or Gordon stayed with John-Paul because he just had a sexual obsession with him," said Zeigler. "If Gordon could have just avoided the operation, and gotten rid of John-Paul, he could have kept writing, and things would have turned out better for everyone."

The elderly bookseller had struck his only note of regret, and he stepped toward the stairs. A few minutes later, I'd left; and a week afterward, there was a note in the mail. Zeigler said he knew a certain man who had also known Gordon Hall. That person still lived in Charleston, and he wouldn't mind talking. He'd had a special relationship with Gordon, Zeigler remembered, and he might be able to say something about the rich dandy who once lived at number 56 Society Street.

Chapter 10

REASSIGNMENT

Sometime in 1966, Gordon Hall acquired a young male Chihuahua, who joined two pedigreed sisters of his kind, Annabel-Eliza and Nelly, bringing to three the number of the breed in the house. The new dog was given the name Richard-Rufus. He'd been rescued from an abusive owner and was convalescing in the mansion when the phone rang with a call from the White House.

The press secretary for the family of Lyndon Johnson had been deflecting Gordon's interview requests, until now. It seemed the Macrae Smith Publishing Company, in Philadelphia, had a deal with Gordon for a book about Lady Bird Johnson, wife of the president. And although the writer had produced much of the manuscript, a small hitch remained: he'd never actually met his subject.

"One afternoon at four o'clock a telephone call came through to the Dr. Joseph Johnson House, requesting my presence at the White House next morning," Dawn remembered. "I was forced to answer: 'I'm afraid that's not possible. I cannot leave Richard-Rufus, my Chihuahua.'"

One assumes the media deputy put down the phone in disbelief. However, she soon called back to say that whereas the First Lady had only the following morning available, and whereas Mrs. Johnson requested that a book about her include at least one meeting with its author, Gordon should bring the dog.

"So Richard-Rufus flew to the White House like a story-book dog, and barked at the President and First Lady," Dawn said. The hour-long meeting evidently being adequate research, *Lady Bird and Her Daughters* came out the following year.

THE DISTAFF

In a radio interview recorded in the late 1980s, Dawn's voice sounded scratchy and old. It was as though she'd rehearsed her story too many times, and in a distracted way she again recalled events of twenty-odd years before.

"The breasts grew, and caused a burning sensation," she said. "And one day I scared the housekeeper, who came in to find me in a pool of blood." Gordon had supposedly had one of his spontaneous menstruations. Recovering from the emergency, he reached a turning point. "I realized it was necessary to see a doctor right away."

Gordon went to a woman friend, Dr. Duncan Pringle (so Dawn said), and the crisis grew into an ordeal. "Even if you have always known that you were really a woman, it still needs some courage to visit even a friendly doctor and announce: 'I think I'm going through some sort of change.' " Judging the situation beyond her powers, Dr. Pringle suggested that Gordon see a Charleston gynecologist, H. Oliver Williamson.

"Dr. Williamson told me that I was a transsexual. I can honestly say that I had never heard the word. Of course, I had heard of sex changes. The Christine Jorgensen story was universal."

Like most of America, Dawn knew about Christine Jorgensen, "the convertible blonde," who'd gone to Denmark for surgery and returned to New York a celebrity in 1953. And it may have refreshed her memory that Jorgensen had just published an autobiography and was once again in headlines.

But Dawn made peculiar use of the word *transsexual*. She didn't mean "a person in transit between the sexes, who might opt for genital surgery." Instead, Gordon saw himself in the throes of an *involuntary change of sex.*

"Even in our English village some years before, a young woman had undergone certain physical changes and become a man," Dawn said. "There was also the rather weird story of a great-aunt who, lying in her coffin, grew a moustache."

Dawn's version of her transformation, which she repeated in articles and interviews, didn't change much over the years. This implied that there was a grain of truth in it, but what about the details? Several people in Charleston remembered Doctors Pringle and Williamson; but both had since died, and only Dawn's testimony remained. She quoted Oliver Williamson as telling her, or Gordon, "Although I was not normal, neither was I a homosexual." It was sometime in 1967.

The law of storytelling requires the narrator to maintain the suspension of disbelief. In nonfiction, if the reader doubts even for a moment that the events being described actually took place—or at least could have taken place—the writer has lost the game. Dawn flirted with disbelief quite a bit, almost all the time. The rumblings in the breasts, the faithful retainer who discovers her mistress in a pool of blood: she gave people plenty of ways to call her a fake.

Yet the individual parts made sense. Dr. Williamson, she said, was a friend of Dr. Howard W. Jones, a gynecologist at Johns Hopkins Hospital, in Baltimore. The hospital had established a new treatment center, the Gender Identity Clinic. Williamson wrote Jones about Gordon. He then told Gordon he was a lucky man, because until Johns Hopkins, patients like him had to go to Scandinavia, even Morocco.

Gordon went home and waited. "I didn't hear for weeks, during which time the breasts continued to grow."

On October 3, 1967, Gordon went to Baltimore for his first examination, believing this was the end of his journey. However, the appointment turned out to be a handshake meeting with physicians, who scheduled Gordon for a weeklong assessment in two months, when complete tests would determine whether treatment would go forward. "I felt a little like a prisoner being called for trial," Dawn said. The next round amounted to an audition, which, if he passed, would admit Gordon to a tiny elite. He would be the only sex-reassignment patient on the Charleston peninsula.

Most people did not regard genital modification as belonging to the Southern way of life. So what, if not necessity, moved Gordon to take the leap? Someone who'd been close to him in those days might be able to say, but by the time I had started looking for people a lot of his friends had died. The person who knew the most was John-Paul Simmons. I had to find him. If, through the haze of antipsychotic drugs, he could remember his partner's change from man to woman, I might have the right testimony. His daughter thought John-Paul was in Albany, New York. When the time came, I'd have to go there.

THE FIRST FACILITY of its kind in America, the Gender Identity Clinic had opened in 1966. Driven by the ambition of a few doctors and fueled by sexual liberation in the culture, the clinic would try to do what Magnus Hirschfeld had done in Berlin nearly fifty years earlier.

In the 1960s, the Victorian glacier of sexual restraint was rapidly melting, and in the ensuing flood tens of millions discovered new sex lives. Sexual minorities, from transvestites to lesbians, stepped into the full sun, blinking from decades in hiding. Despite the loosening of the libido, however, the actual sex organs had remained off-limits. The Christine Jorgensen episode had been followed not by the acceptance of transsexual surgery, but by a decade of backlash. Only a few Americans had managed to get operations, usually in Casablanca or Copenhagen. Sex reassignment remained a dangerous business for doctors, who remembered when prosecutors had stood guard over the penises of men.

For some years Johns Hopkins Hospital, the formidable teaching and research center in Baltimore, had attracted doctors keen to experiment who knew that new therapies could position them for medical fame. By the mid-1960s, this drive had reached the culture of sex. The introduction of the birth control pill (1964) was followed by the publication of the first study of its kind in English, *The Transsexual Phenomenon* (1966), by one Harry Benjamin. A German-born physician practicing in New York City, Benjamin had known some of the sex-change pioneers in Berlin. In America, he'd seen dozens of transgender patients, whom he treated with empathy, although not with surgery.

At Johns Hopkins, when three young doctors came together to create the nation's first transsexual clinic, one can only guess at the reaction in the hospital's executive offices. But no cease and desist order came down, and the men went ahead. Their names were Milton T. Edgerton, a plastic surgeon; the gynecologist Howard W. Jones; and John Money, a psychologist from New Zealand who'd written a dissertation on hermaphroditism. All had used hormone therapy, and people seeking reassignment had previously approached each of them; but so far, none had recommended surgery.

In 1965, the as-yet-unnamed team had decided to carry out its first complete genital transformation on a young man named Avon Williams, an African American who'd been referred by Harry Benjamin. Money for the procedure had come from a wealthy female-to-male transsexual named Reed Erickson, who wanted to promote the cause. When Avon Williams came out of recovery and seemed to be getting along, Reed Erickson agreed to subsidize the whole program. A Texas-born heir to a lead-smelting fortune who'd transitioned from female to male in 1965, at age forty-eight, Erickson offered a monthly stipend, freeing the hospital from having to add a line item in the budget for the weird new specialty. By the end of 1966, the clinic could report that it had operated on five female-to-male and five male-to-female patients.

Physicians at Hopkins preferred the term sex reassignment to sex change or sex modification. Reassignment conveys a basic idea of transsexual medicine, that one's anatomical sex does not form the foundation of the self, even though most people experience it that way. Instead, anatomical sex is like a label imposed on a deeper nature, which flourishes in the mind (and perhaps also in the adrenals, and the chromosomes): one's gender identity, which may be incompatible with the exterior sign. If one's gendered self falls out of sync with one's sexual signage (the meaning of the term *gender dysphoria*), the superficial genitalia can be replaced, and one's sex reassigned.

The main worry of the hospital was bad press. Johns Hopkins faced the accusation that it was providing elective surgery, allowing patients to choose their sex like shoes. Things were complicated because gender identity disorder had not yet appeared as an illness in the *Diagnostic and Statistical Manual of Mental Disorders*. Without a diagnosis, apparently nothing was being treated, and one was in the realm of frivolous surgery, not much different from an eyelift—bad for institutional prestige.

Doctors at the Gender Identity Clinic wanted an observable pathology that would help them justify surgery. Thus, they set up the interview process, a weeklong workup intended to weed out dilettantes (part-time trannies) as well as the truly tormented (schizophrenics with gender delusions). It was at such an audition that Gordon Hall was called to perform.

The story of the clinic proved irresistible to news editors, and in October 1966 the New York *Daily News* ran an item on Avon Williams. When the clinic's switchboard was flooded with calls, the gender doctors, seeing that press was inevitable, offered an exclusive to the *New York Times*. The result was a respectful front-page story that stifled the media's tendency to make nervous jokes and helped reframe the public view of transsexuals. At a news conference after the *Times* story, the clinic doctors faced two hundred journalists in an auditorium; and the writers' bulletins, which were mostly factual and accepting, went out in turn. Whereas transsexual medicine had previously been seen as perverse, it was now being depicted as another miracle of science, akin to organ transplants.

Gordon Hall probably saw one of the friendly stories. In any case, he contacted Hopkins a few months after the *Times* piece. He wasn't alone: the clinic had planned for only two surgeries a month, but hundreds of would-be patients now got in touch. Doctors Edgerton and Money clamped down, intensifying the screening and making it into a kind of college admissions process. Applicants waited nervously at home for word of their acceptance in the freshman class.

ON DECEMBER 11, 1967, Gordon Hall checked into the Sheraton Hotel near Johns Hopkins, accompanied by his twin Chihuahuas, Annabel-Eliza and Nelly. (Richard-Rufus stayed home.) He met seven doctors in the next five days. He was given blood tests, to measure his hormone levels; and he received an electroencephalogram, followed with chromosome tests. Psychiatrists interviewed him in several rotations. Each doctor questioned his desire for surgery. By this time, the clinic was holding weekly meetings, sifting applications and weighing each candidate to determine who should receive the prized patient slots.

Dawn Simmons said the tests weren't particularly hard, with one exception. "The question of my sex life was frequently raised in the interviews. I had not experienced sexual intercourse, and no amount of tests could make me change a story that was true."

At the end of the week, the gender team met and voted Gordon in. "I was placed on female hormone tablets," Dawn said, "and told to dress as a woman immediately."

The names of Dawn's doctors (six of them) appeared on a list of appointments she'd saved. They'd been young men at the time, mavericks making a mark in their field. Could any of them still be found? If so, would they talk?

There were two main questions I wanted to ask Gordon's doctors: Was he an intersexual in transition? Or was he a gay man looking to be a pioneer transsexual? The answers might lie with a retired surgeon, who I hoped would have a good memory.

Had Gordon been a transvestite? I doubted it. There was no evidence in Dawn's papers, or in interviews with people who knew him, or even in rumors, that he'd gone in drag before going to Baltimore. To the contrary, several clues showed that Gordon had approached women's wear like a novice.

He'd written to his mother in England to tell her about his acceptance at the clinic, and she'd written back, dumbfounded. "I cannot believe it now, keep thinking it cannot be true," Marjorie said. But his mom got over her surprise, and in a few weeks, at Gordon's request, Marjorie started sending beauty advice.

"Seven and eight is the popular size in England for women's shoes, so your feet are all right," she wrote. Later, "Another thing—I would like to see you in slim dresses, not full ones."

Because Gordon, as a woman, would presumably spend time in the kitchen, his mother promised cooking notes: "I will let you have the recipe for parsley balls when I write it out. Have not made any for years." But she drew the line at what she saw as Gordon's chief asset: "Don't let the doctors touch your nose, the best one in the family, small and delicate."

Returning home to Charleston, Gordon told a small number of friends about the upcoming operation, but none of them were impressed. (Joe Trott: "What are you trying to prove?" Another friend, sarcastically: "Charleston's such a big city, and nobody talks.")

Gordon was afraid to shop for women's clothes because someone might see him, so he asked one women's store to send things to his house. But the experiment failed. "Boxes of undergarments big enough for a very large lady arrived, with dresses that would have ideally suited mothers-to-be expecting twins," Dawn said. "None of the shoes fit, while to walk even with the smallest of high heels was murder."

An unexpectedly easy part was telling the staff at 56 Society. Gordon employed a butler named Alexander, a cook called Irene, and a housekeeper, Viola. When he brought them together to announce his plan to cross over, I imagine there were murmurs and downcast eyes. However, the only account of the servants' feelings was a remark of Viola's that Dawn recorded. The housekeeper was a minister's widow, and Dawn remembered, "When I showed her my breasts, Viola said, 'I have seen a miracle.' "

A friend from out of town came to the rescue on the clothing front. Richia Barloga, a feisty housewife from Louisiana, had arrived in Charleston for an extended stay. Gordon told her what was happening, and Barloga put herself at Gordon's service, "taking over the organization of the dress problem." It helped that the friend was Gordon's size and could therefore try on clothes for him when the two hit the stores, allowing him to see the likely results. "I looked best in bright colors, reds, orange, and my favorite yellow," Dawn said.

When Barloga gave Gordon some of her nightgowns, he was touched. "They were the gayest and frilliest things," Dawn wrote, adding one of them was edged with six inches of antique lace. Gordon's friend outlined his feet with chalk on paper, and took the stencil to shoe stores, returning with "the highest heels," on which he could practice teetering. Then there were the wigs. After some experimentation, Gordon settled on a dark-haired, shoulder-length look, with a flip at the ends.

But problems surfaced. Throughout the feminine trial run, Gordon found it hard to remember to sit with his legs together. Also, "brassieres seemed to cut into me like knives, though with nature's relentless development in that area, I had to progress to two larger sizes in a remarkably short time."

Within a few months, Dawn said, Gordon had put away his pants and made the switch to dresses and skirts. However, he had yet to go public.

Barloga seized on the idea that the two of them should eat in a drive-in restaurant, where waitresses came to the driver's window and customers ate in the car. That way, Gordon would be in public, but could still remain invisible in the passenger seat.

The experiment worked, and the patient grew more courageous. He walked out alone to the Piggly Wiggly, Charleston's most conspicuous supermarket, on Broad Street in the historic district. He made daily excursions for errands—a framing store here, a bag of potpourri there. Richia Barloga, having done good service, moved back to Louisiana and out of her friend's life.

Salacious talk swept through town. I spoke to one man who remembered the day he saw Gordon at the post office. Gordon was still in men's clothes, but the counter clerks were laughing as he was leaving the building. A postal worker, catching his breath, explained that Gordon had bought some stamps, and then he'd mentioned aloud that his body was changing. He'd asked the clerks if they wanted to see what he was talking about, and then he'd opened his shirt and showed off his breasts.

JOHN-PAUL

There was a photograph of them together, both smiling, each with an arm around the other's shoulders. Gordon Hall, wearing an oxford shirt and short hair, looked boyish and bookish, like an aging graduate student; John-Paul Simmons was a skinny, happy black guy who looked like he'd stumbled into a good time.

Dawn gave a romantic account of the night Gordon met John-Paul, in the late spring of 1967. John-Paul had a date with one of Gordon's young black cooks, she said. He was late, and by the time he arrived, knocking at the kitchen door according to segregation custom, the woman was gone and Gordon answered instead.

"He was a little, smiling man," Dawn wrote, "his cap pulled carelessly over part of his forehead. He never once asked for the cook."

Dawn quoted John-Paul as saying, sometime later, "She was the whitest and most sickly-looking woman I ever did see. Yet I knew from that minute that she was mine. No man was going to lay his hands on her but me."

Joe Trott had said that John-Paul surfaced in Gordon's life as a gardener at 56 Society. Dawn claimed he was a mechanic at Simmons Motors. Whatever he was, the two talked at the kitchen door, according to Dawn, and she asked the man in. The next day, John-Paul allegedly came back with an armful of flowers, and the couple's secret affair began.

In various interviews, Dawn implied she was already living as a woman when she met her future husband, but this wasn't at all certain. First, there was the picture, which showed Gordon and John-Paul entwined. Also, I'd found a telling letter from Gordon's mother, dated October 10, 1967, in which Marjorie had written, "I was very pleased with the photos of John-Paul. He looks very smart." The letter had been sent two months before the screening interviews at Johns Hopkins, when doctors told Gordon to start wearing skirts. So it seemed he was still in men's clothes when they first hooked up.

John Zeigler thought John-Paul was the trigger for the sex surgery, and chronologically this made sense. The affair with John-Paul preceded Gordon's contact with Hopkins by only a few months.

"He was very fair," Dawn remembered of her boyfriend. "He said, 'I've played the field. But you have never had anybody else, because you haven't had the chance. Don't you think you should meet somebody else? Is this going to last?' Well, there wasn't anybody else, and never would be."

Dawn claimed the two didn't have sex, or vaginal intercourse, until they married, a year and a half later. This would have been impossible, she implied, because a membrane hid her vagina.

"At that time, married or unmarried," Dawn wrote, "we could not have had sexual intercourse, for the vaginal passage had not been opened. That such an opening was becoming increasingly necessary was evidenced by the numbing pains I experience whenever John-Paul was tender and close to me."

John-Paul gave Gordon the name Dawn at the start of the affair, the writer remembered, symbolizing the rebirth of his identity. Gordon added a middle name, Pepita, after the Spanish grandmother of his idol, Vita Sackville-West. And in a few weeks, Gordon was calling himself Dawn Pepita Langley Hall.

Was Dawn simply seeking an exhibitionistic thrill? She'd acquired a desire to live theatrically in her youth and had already remade herself several times—from working-class kid, to New York sophisticate, to erstwhile Southern gentleman. But the new persona, woman and interracial lover, far outdid the others in look-at-me-ness.

Or (another Freudian motive), was she setting up a machine for self-punishment? Her life choices looked like a cumbersome masochistic device. This interpretation took support from her notes, in reverse. Dawn insisted, "It will all work out," and she had a self-deceiving faith in happy endings when it came to imagining the future.

Of course, there was still the unlikely possibility that she was who she said she was. If so, all this behavior made a kind of sense and I was looking in vain for the psychological truth. If, as she claimed, she was experiencing spontaneous sexual transition, then she met the criteria for gender dysphoria, and the Hopkins treatment was called for. Concerning the marriage, if one has already made the radical personal choice of sex reassignment, what reason would there be to respect remaining taboos? To a trans-person, the prohibition against interracial sex would appear artificial and trivial—which is, in fact, how it eventually came to be seen after the civil rights movement. In which case Dawn was an intersexual ahead of her time.

Before reassignment, the Hopkins doctors required patients to live for a year in their gender of conviction. They also wanted patients to find a partner, but Dawn Pepita complained her doctors were unhappy about her choice of John-Paul. Dr. Milton Edgerton, the surgeon, had been raised in Georgia. He had a feeling that Charleston's Southern traditions, which included slavery and sexism, might not adapt well to an interracial transgender romance. Dawn quoted Edgerton as saying, "We think you are a fine couple. We're only afraid you will both be assassinated."

*   *   *

NATASHA SIMMONS SAT at her dining-room table, under the brass chandelier, while her young daughter watched television in the next room. The house with its drawn curtains and dim lights smelled of Natasha's cigarettes.

"At this point, I have no idea where my father is," she said. "He, with his sickness, is hard to deal with. He's like another child."

John-Paul Simmons had been missing from his family since before Dawn's funeral, in 2000, and his daughter was worried she'd never find him. "You have to constantly tell my dad what to do and when to do it—and sometimes *how* to do it," she said, shaking her head. Natasha thought he was in Albany. "He goes to the hospital there to get his meds, and his therapy sessions."

In the mid-1970s, Dawn, John-Paul, and Natasha, who was then a little girl, had moved out of the South and to upper New York State. John-Paul soon had a breakdown of some kind and became a patient at the state psychiatric hospital, known as the Central District Psychiatric Center. He rotated in and out of treatment for years, usually on medication.

Natasha seemed weary when talking about her father, as though keeping up their relationship was work. She described his tantrums, and his drinking, and said he had used drugs, "badly for a while." His residence had shifted between Dawn's house, a group home for mental patients, and the psychiatric hospital. "But he has plenty of sense!" Natasha said, lighting a cigarette. "It's when he wants to act like he doesn't have sense that you see his difficult side."

Unexpectedly, Natasha broke into one of her beautiful smiles. "My mom used to call him 'truffle hound.' No matter where she tried to hide money in the house, my dad would find it."

In her midtwenties, Natasha had decided to leave New York and move back to Charleston. Dawn had followed her daughter back to the South; John-Paul stayed in New York. It was at that point he let go of his family.

"Mommy was living with my dad at the time, about 1996, and my dad refused to come back to Charleston," Natasha said. "He didn't want *her* to come back either. When Mommy moved down South, after me, my dad said that he didn't want any of his information released to us by his doctors. So now I have no clue where he is, or what condition he's in."

By "information," she meant her father's whereabouts, and even his state of mind, facts guarded by his psychiatric caregivers.

Natasha looked discouraged. When I asked whether she would allow me to look for her father, she looked down at the table.

"Sure." She put out her cigarette. "It'll be a hunting expedition," she said.

ANESTHETIZED

Marjorie Copper was mystified. Gordon had written her about the surgery plan, but his mother didn't understand it. Writing from Sissinghurst Castle, Marjorie wondered, "No Johns Hopkins wrote to me. Is he a specialist?"

In addition to taking estrogen, Dawn underwent electrolysis to do away with body hair. The treatments removed the beard, and probably more, though no record survived that detailed the pattern. It wasn't unusual for women with congenital adrenal hyperplasia to have some facial hair, but letters Marjorie wrote her son implied there'd been a lot of it.

"My dear Dinky, I do wish you were not having those needles on your face," she said in a note. "It upsets me. Your face is quite nice."

The surgery would be extensive. Dawn's descriptions of what she was experiencing were vague; she also thought it was proper that a lady withhold physical details. Dawn had, or she believed she had—or she stated she had—a uterus (that menstruated once in a while). She said she had ovaries and a vagina (which was supposedly covered by a layer of skin). She also claimed to have a large clitoris. As to testicles and scrotum, she never mentioned them.

The surgery (she said) was to cut the supposed membrane, expose the vagina, and create labia. Something, it's not clear what, was supposed to kick-start menstruation. Her clitoris was also to be cut down. (She rarely talked about sexual pleasure: nowhere did Dawn mention the loss of sensation that would have ensued from her alleged clitorectomy.)

A woman in Charleston said, "I remember he was on TV when he left, getting on the plane—and on TV again when she came home, when she got off the plane, as Dawn."

Dawn Pepita Langley Hall awoke from anesthesia on September 23, 1968, in room B-403 of Johns Hopkins Hospital. In a manuscript, she described taking off the bandages:

> The doctors had removed the dead useless flesh which by a stretch of the imagination might have been termed a penis, and opened up a vaginal tract, which, if successful, could adequately fulfill the woman's physical function in marriage. My vaginal lips were Dr. Milton Edgerton's creation. He had included 'a crease here . . . a crinkle there.' Slowly I let my hands touch lightly the genital areas . . . then I pulled down the bedclothes. Nobody would ever be able to tell the difference. I knew I was like all other women. Not a blemish, not a scar; the vaginal lips perfection.

About her menstrual cycle, Dawn said, "The other bodily function recommenced and continued with clock-like regularity."

Two days after the surgery, Dawn's psychiatrist, Dr. Norman Knorr, wrote a "To Whom It May Concern" letter to help the patient with future paperwork:

> Gordon Langley Hall has been evaluated by the Gender Identity Committee of the Johns Hopkins Hospital. As a result of the evaluation, sexual reassignment was recommended to the patient.
>
> The patient has received surgery to carry out the physical conversion of sex from male to female.

We would appreciate consideration of the patient's request for legal change of birth certificate so that it may be consistent with his correct physical status.

Although Dawn would admit to sex reassignment, it's not likely she would have owned up to physical conversion. Nevertheless, she saved the announcement and used it to revise her vital records.

To judge from her letters, Marjorie Copper found the strength to accept that her son had now become her daughter.

"The discomfort must have been awful," Marjorie wrote, "but thank goodness the op was successful. Many wouldn't have the courage to face it all. Time will help you to forget what you have been through. It must have been so lonely."

Something more could be made of Marjorie's equanimity. If she'd known her son was intersexual (and it's hard to imagine she wouldn't have), then the reassignment wouldn't have seemed strange. In fact, she appeared to have been surprised but not alarmed.

Dawn's mother had given away her son at birth. With the letters, which picked up to a stream around the time of the sex surgery, Dawn must have relished Marjorie's new love, even if it had been purchased at high cost, for both of them. "I still cannot realize this has happened," Marjorie wrote.

Mother and daughter both knew the next stage of Dawn's journey would probably involve the media. "Watch those newspapers. They do write such a lot that's not true sometimes," said Marjorie.

Despite her acceptance, Marjorie occasionally sounded as though she might crack under the strain caused by news of her child's life. When Dawn announced she planned to marry John-Paul, Marjorie sent a rattled stream-of-consciousness reply:

Now you say you want to be married in England. I do think you should get strong again before you think of marriage. Don't think I am against John-Paul. I am not. But at least for three months you should wait before you marry. After all the ops you want rest. Don't upset your-self about John-Paul's race. I never think about it. He's the same as us. What difference does color make? Your hair must look nice. Glad it's wavy. You had lovely hair when a baby. I will write to John-Paul's parents next week. I'm sure everything will be all right for both of you. All my love, Margie.

Joe Trott was sitting at his kitchen table, looking to be in his eighties for the first time since I'd known him. The string tie didn't make him appear more youthful, and he seemed forlorn. After decades, his friend's sex surgery still upset him.

"He had hormone treatments here, the first step," said Joe, wav-ing a hand dismissively. "I don't know if he developed breasts. Gor-don said so, but I never saw him disrobe. I wasn't interested. I think there was all sorts of things that had to go on until he had the final uterus, or whatever you call it, put in, or the dick cut off."

Joe was rambling, and I had a feeling his unawareness of the facts of transsexual surgery was an act. But Gordon had gone to Baltimore at a time when few people had even heard of sex reassignment. Joe picked up a picture of Dawn that showed her standing in her garden on Society Street, wearing a lacy white dress.

He shook his head and said, "Gordon was dressing as a woman at home before he went off to get the operation. Then it finally got to the point where you'd see him walking up Society Street with a dress on. He wore very feminine, matronly, and conservative dresses. They were typical Charleston women's dresses, for ladies—with little white lace collars, in very good taste. And every time he went out in the summer, he wore white gloves; and in the winter, black gloves. He always wore a hat, because of the heat in the summer, and the cold in the winter."

He looked chagrined at the memory. From Joe's perspective, Gordon's surgery marked the start of his decline.

"Everything went along all right, until John-Paul went through the money like Sherman went through Georgia," he said. The army of General William T. Sherman, the Union soldier most hated by Charleston whites, had in 1864–65 burned its way from Georgia into South Carolina and brought the state to its knees.

"John-Paul spent money, and went through that income—millions of dollars! He wanted to go into the fishing business, so Gordon bought him two boats. He wrecks both boats—a total loss, no insurance. Then he wanted a Ford Thunderbird, so he bought him that, and he wrecked that immediately, drunk as a coot. Going down the highway and ran into a tree."

Suddenly Joe stood up. "It's hot in here." He walked out the door and into his garden, behind the house.

It was a familiar Charleston garden, with three walls lined by flowering bushes, and the creeping, fragrant vine known as confederate jasmine. Hibiscus, camellias, and little statuary lined the paths. The garden showed signs of having once been cared for, but recently let go, and Joe frowned at the weeds. "This place has gone down," he said, as though it belonged to someone else.

Joe believed John-Paul had been a gardener. "When Gordon brought Paul out of the yard and into the house, that place declined," said Joe, "until it got to the point that the house was torn up by the animals—excrement on the carpet and everything."

He was getting uncharacteristically worked up, and his voice raised slightly.

"Gordon was not an unattractive man," he said. "Why would he have to go and desecrate himself like he did? John-Paul was ugly as sin. He didn't have enough intelligence to get out of a shower of horse manure."

Joe stopped walking, looked at an overgrown flower bed, and said, as though to himself, "Now, can you imagine a white person in their right mind doing something like this!? They just didn't do that in the South!"

He seemed resigned and sad; suddenly he straightened up, and there came an outburst louder than anything previous. "I told Gordon, 'Nobody in Charleston's interested in that kind of shit!' And he told me, 'But I love the man!' I said, 'That's fine, but don't throw it in everybody else's face! Everybody else doesn't love your man!' "

In Charleston, Joe's ponytail was a sign of an offbeat person, someone who tolerated things. Yet Gordon had mystified his friend by going far across the line.

"A lot of people thought Gordon was a masochist, who liked to be beat on," Joe continued. "He called me on several occasions to come up to the hospital and help him, because John-Paul had beaten him, or thrown him down the stairs. This was after Gordon had started living as a woman. He said, 'Can you help me?' I said, 'I don't know what I can do for you but get you a lawyer.' And I wish I had."

Back in the house, Joe started to lock up so we could leave. In a front hall he stopped beside a picture. The framed piece of old parchment paper, a legal document with a red wax seal, had been signed by his famous ancestor, Nicholas Trott, the jurist, and dated 1703. The artifact gave Joe a leg up in Charleston, a town in which many people bragged about their ancestors but few had the paperwork to back up their talk, and some just lied.

"I think Dawn was trying to do anything to attract attention, but he went at it the wrong way," said Joe. "He had the choice of two doors to Charleston, and he took the wrong door. If he had picked up with a white boy and done this thing, nobody would have paid a bit of attention. But it was the way it was done, and all this hoopla and all. It just put a bad taste in people's mouths. You don't throw your dirty laundry in somebody's face and expect them to come out and say, 'Ooh, that smells so good.' "

Outside and down the street, a horse-drawn carriage rattled past.

GORDON'S MEDICAL DOSSIER, compiled when he entered treatment, supposedly included chromosome analyses and anatomical photographs. I contacted the Alan Mason Chesney Archives of Johns Hopkins Medical Institutions, the repository of case files, to ask the procedure to obtain patient records. On the phone, a discreet and businesslike archivist, Nancy McCall, said records from the Gender Identity Clinic were "especially constrained." Even with permission from the patient's family, their release would have to be vetted by a review committee, which included hospital lawyers.

I asked Natasha Simmons, and she provided the letter of consent, which I forwarded to the hospital. Three months later, I spoke to the archivist a second time.

Choosing her words, Nancy McCall said she'd received Natasha's letter, but now a lawyer on the privacy committee was concerned that John-Paul Simmons would also have to be consulted, as surviving spouse, and his consent also obtained. When I mentioned that John-Paul was missing, the archivist presented another reason why the library might not share its records.

"In any case," she said, "we're trying to find the files from that time, when record keeping at the Gender Identity Clinic wasn't what it should have been. It was an interdisciplinary, interdepartmental clinic, and sometimes the physicians actually kept the records."

In other words, the files had vanished. This supported what the intersex activist Cheryl Chase had said: physicians with sex identity patients sometimes held on to files that might make good material for medical journals. If the paper records were gone, the spoken testimony of Gordon's doctors would become increasingly important.

WHEN GORDON BECAME DAWN, five years after arriving in Charleston, the memory of his initial welcome embarrassed people at the city's finest tables. Old ladies who'd given dinners for the young author now walked with chins in the air, wondering at their judgment. Jokes went around, and the disbelief of Charleston's tastemakers rapidly turned to fear that there was a menacing creature in their midst.

A friend of mine, Tom Tisdale, had observed this development. I'd known Tom for several years and, coincidentally, his father and mine had also been friends decades earlier. One afternoon, I dropped in on Tom at his law office on Broad Street, the spine of Charleston's old quarter, and we walked to lunch.

Tom said, "I never met Dawn Simmons. I think I met Gordon Hall, back in the old days." He was churning his memories.

Tom Tisdale was trim and walked with an officer's carriage. He'd grown up in a town in upstate South Carolina but had gotten a law degree and escaped to Charleston, the city that radiates light into the general dimness of the state. He'd been a judge in the 1960s, confidant of the mayor in the 1970s, and for most of the time a partner in an old-line law firm, Young, Clement, Rivers and Tisdale, which made him a good bit of money. He lived in an eighteenth-century house, had been married more than once, and had children in their thirties. At sixty-three, Tom was considering retirement, and he no longer had to be careful with his words.

We arrived at a posh seafood place, the hostess eased us into a booth, and Tom's tortoiseshell glasses came off for the meal.

"The last time I remember seeing Dawn," Tom said, "she was pushing a baby stroller up Meeting Street, rolling along in front of the Mills House Hotel. It was obvious who she was to anybody who knew anything about the story."

There were two reliable pleasures in Tom's company: what he wore, and how he spoke. He had a rakish style, and on this occasion wore a crisp white shirt, a red-and-black bow tie, and an ironed seersucker jacket, with a folded hanky in the pocket. His perfectly combed silver hair fell onto his forehead in strands, and he kept his square, handsome, smooth countenance locked in a poker face.

Tom didn't really talk so much as he performed his speech. He had a highly controlled, precise diction, slowed by his thick Carolina accent. He was one of the rare Southerners who understood that his accent could sometimes impede communication, especially with people from north of the Mason-Dixon line; therefore, he sometimes repeated certain words, which gave his talk unexpected stops and starts.

"The first knowledge I had about the whole situation of Gordon

Hall was through a man named Bo Morrison, whose father was mayor of Charleston about fifty years ago," he said. "Bo Morrison came up to me in the early 1960s and said a new gentleman had arrived in town, a polished Engleshman." Tom paused and corrected himself, "*Englishman.* This person was being feted at all the great houses downtown, according to Bo, where he was an honored guest. Bo had been to some of these dinners. But there was one problem, and that was that Mr. Hall insisted on calling him, that is, Bo Morrison, 'Beauregard'—as in P. T. Beauregard, the defender of Charleston during the Civil War."

Tom laughed, and then as quickly as it had appeared, his smile fled and the poker face returned.

P. T. Beauregard was a Confederate hero to white Charleston people, including some in Gordon's new circle. But apparently Gordon didn't know that to drop Beauregard's name was too much, something like joining the longshoreman's union and then calling a co-worker *comrade.*

Jazz played from hidden speakers, and an obsequious waitstaff circled the tables like bumblebees. The waitress delivered food and left to alight at another table.

Tom remembered his first real brush with Gordon. "There was an incident, when I was a municipal judge, in the late 1960s. At one point, I received a call from a lawyer called Brantly Seymour, who phoned me in my capacity as a judge," Tom said. "And Brantly Seymour said he represented a gentleman, Gordon Hall, and that his client was having a sex-change operation." Realizing he'd slurred a consonant, Tom repeated, "A *sex-change operation.* Seymour said there were some statutes and ordinances in the city of Charleston that prohibited one sex going out in public dressed as the other, and he was afraid that an incident would occur, by which an arrest would be made of his client. Mr. Hall—or Ms. Hall, however one viewed it at that point—would be arrested for dressing as a woman. And Seymour wanted me to know this in advance, so that I could deal with it in my capacity as a judge."

Tom's eyes were bright beneath his impassive face, a sign he found this memory amusing.

"So I told him, of course in a proper way, that I could not give any advisory opinions, but that I appreciated the reconnaissance! And that if anything came up about it, I would certainly be able to understand the circumstances a lot more easily." Tom broke a smile, which he immediately suppressed.

"To your knowledge, no one arrested Gordon Hall?" I asked.

"I don't think so."

Dawn's recollection of this period was somewhat different, and more to her melodramatic taste. Back in Charleston from Johns Hopkins, she wrote, "I contacted a respected lawyer, Brantly Seymour, who met with the City Fathers. They were sympathetic to my position, and the city police were informed of the unusual situation."

Tom cleared his throat and sat back. Before he became a judge, he'd been in private practice, where he encountered my subject in court.

"Then there was an occasion when I had a matter in litigation on behalf of a veterinarian, in which I sued Gordon Hall," Tom said. "The issue was payment of a bill."

"Gordon Hall was an animal lover, with a lot of pets," I said.

"Everyone said there were a lot of animals around there," Tom answered. "Anyway, Gordon Hall's lawyer was a straight-laced, old-school native of Sumter, South Carolina—and he was quite embarrassed by the situation he found himself in, because by that time Gordon had lost much of his glow around town." Tom repeated, *"His glow around town.* Gordon Hall himself was not there, and I walked into this courtroom, representing this veterinarian, and it was as if a rattlesnake had come into the room."

Gordon no longer attracted friendly newspaper stories; in fact, rumor had it the publisher of the Charleston *News and Courier* had banned reporters from writing any more stories about him. Few people who regarded themselves as respectable wanted to continue being associated with Gordon.

"This other lawyer settled very quickly, so he could get out of there, and out of sight," Tom said.

Why had Gordon failed to pay his pets' medical bills? Was his fortune disappearing? Or did he have less money than he'd said? It seemed Gordon's love for theater extended to his financial life. You couldn't trust what he'd said about his fortune any more than you could believe his claims about the year of his birth.

I asked, "Did Gordon Hall pass from being a colorful figure to something else?"

Tom stopped to choose his words. "I think what happened was so bizarre, relative to the straight line of the community, that it was off the radar screen, almost," he said. "It was so crazy that people said, 'This is really not happening.' It was like another reality, and in another galaxy, that all this was going on."

The crisp lawyer pulled his ear, sipped his iced tea, and folded his arms on the tablecloth.

I asked about Dawn's marriage, and Tom brought up a new name. "Bernard Fielding is the one you have to talk to," he said. "A black lawyer in town, semiretired. He represented Gordon when he needed a marriage license. The probate judge wouldn't give him one to marry John-Paul Simmons. Bernard can tell you about how he solved that problem, I mean, from a purely legal perspective."

Tom gave a smile, which he then managed to erase.

Part 4

QUEEN OF SOCIETY STREET

Chapter 11

BATTLE HYMN OF THE REPUBLIC

In South Carolina, the marriage of a black man and a white woman was technically a crime. The state constitution prohibited "marriage of a white person with a Negro or mulatto or a person who shall have one-eighth or more of Negro blood." In 1967, however, the U.S. Supreme Court had ruled a similar provision in Virginia unconstitutional. Which meant that in January 1969 the path looked clear for Dawn's matrimony.

Another raft of rumors floated through town, from Gordon's old cocktail-party circuit to a hundred church coffee hours; from the trustee meetings of teetotaling black Baptists to the dining rooms of bourbon-happy Episcopalians. Newsmagazines ran stories, and the engagement made Dawn no friends—not that she had many left.

An attorney named Bernard Fielding had eyewitness knowledge of the events. When Dawn had weighed her prospects for getting a marriage license, she'd realized that public disbelief at her behavior vied with private loathing for her. She'd looked for a lawyer to help her marry, and the job had fallen to Bernard Fielding.

About the attorney, Tom Tisdale had said, "Bernard Fielding has two problems in life. First, he has to convince people he's poor, which he's not. Second, he has to convince them he's black, which he's not. Aside from that, his life's not so bad."

Bernard Fielding was a retired lawyer and member of the family that owned the Fielding Home for Funerals, one of several African American funeral parlors in town. He'd been born in 1932, raised in Charleston, and gone to Hampton Institute, the historically black college in Virginia. After two years in the army, he'd attended Boston University School of Law, returning to his hometown in the late 1950s to open a two-lawyer firm. Forty-five years later, Fielding had closed his practice. He was spending his twilight years helping in the family business, which was burying people.

The Fielding family had been well off for generations. Black people with the oldest money in Charleston were funeral directors, since burying Negroes was the first lucrative trade whites had surrendered to black control, in the 1800s.

A two-story Victorian house contained the funeral home, where we were to meet. In a former bedroom upstairs, a long Formica conference table that reached almost the length of the room disturbed the comforting atmosphere created by an old fireplace.

Bernard Fielding, tall and talkative, entered and sat in a red swivel chair. He said he was seventy-one, but he looked in corpulent health, with pronounced jowls, a robust head, and a paunch. His hairline had receded, and his part-gray hair was cut right next to the scalp. Fielding wore a green corduroy jacket, light brown shirt, and striped tie, and his skin was a light tan.

The attorney said he'd met Dawn in 1969, shortly before the wedding.

"One day, my secretary came in my office," Fielding remembered, "and told me, 'There's a Miss Hall to see you.' I immediately noticed there was something strange about this lady, because the stockings didn't quite fit on the legs properly."

Fielding's eyebrows jumped, and other mannerisms implied he was uncomfortable talking about Dawn.

"In other words, she didn't look feminine enough," he went on. "The best I can recall is that the primary thrust for her visit was that Judge Gus Pearlman would not give her a marriage license."

Pearlman, the probate judge responsible for licensing, was a well-liked, gentlemanly lawyer. Dawn had chosen Fielding because he'd done estate work and thus knew Judge Pearlman from appearances in his court. "I became the intermediary, in other words," he said.

The lawyer's discomfort grew, and he began to swivel in his red chair, winding the seat all the way left, and then back again, 180 degrees to the right.

Fielding smiled and shook his head. "I can recall having some conversations with Judge Pearlman in his office, and we joked about how doctors create a vagina, in other words," said Fielding, putting his finger on his temple. "As best I can recall, she explained to me how she had gone up north and had this sex operation, and I think she did verify through some documentation that the operation had been performed, that the operation was successful, and that she was as much a woman as could be created!"

In the 1960s, it would have been unprecedented for a white woman to hire a black attorney—but by this time, Dawn had done enough in her life that minor marvels passed unremarked.

"For the marriage license, they ask certain basic questions," Fielding said, and then he laughed, letting off tension. "The best I can recall, they ask your sex, and your prior marriages, et cetera."

Judge Pearlman apparently worried that if he gave Dawn and John-Paul Simmons a license, he might become the subject of gossip himself.

"The judge was reluctant," said Fielding, "because he'd had bad experiences. He told me that sometime in the past, two females had come in, in other words, one dressed in masculine fashion, and one dressed as a woman. I think he said something to them, to the effect"—Fielding sat up to imitate the judge—" 'Madame, if you drop your pants, and show me that you're a man, I'll give you a marriage license!' " He slumped back down. "That's how he got rid of them!"

Fielding laughed, swiveled in his chair, and pulled the lapels of his jacket.

"Judge Pearlman told me that when he first came here—that is, when Mrs. Simmons came here, when she was Gordon Hall—he had

all this alleged aristocracy, and he became very well accepted downtown. And my wife was an employee of the U.S. Customs Service in
the 1960s, and she also knew him as a *him*, because he did some
import business through the U.S. Customs, before *he* became a *she*,
in other words."

The swivel stopped, and Fielding shook his head. He opened his
mouth to speak and blinked slowly, but no words came. It was all too
unnerving.

In one of her manuscripts, Dawn Simmons had remembered the
same events:

> Dressed in my new fur coat, a white fur hat and the most
> conservative dress I could find, I walked to the county
> courthouse on Cumberland Street. I had my change of
> sex paper with me. Bernard Fielding, the attorney, met
> me, and left me in an anteroom while he went and spoke
> with the judge. Because this was such a controversial
> marriage, on account of my change of sex, and the fact
> that I was marrying a black man, everything had to be
> right. While I waited, I noticed the steel file cabinets
> separately marked *Negro* and *White*.

I asked whether Fielding remembered two sets of records in
Judge Pearlman's office, and he frowned. "The lady had a knack for
exaggerating! She was a good name-dropper, too," he said. "And one
time she even claimed to have a baby! This was something I read in
the paper, in other words."

Judge Pearlman, Dawn said, discarded his reservations because he
identified with her. "Probate Judge Gus H. Pearlman was Jewish,"
Dawn wrote. "After he completed the license, he told me, 'I have
always been in the minority. Now, welcome to the minority.' "

A copy of the marriage certificate, license number 69-151 in the
registry of Charleston County, turned up in Dawn's papers. It
recorded the couple's ages as twenty-one (John-Paul) and thirty-one

In a memoir, Gordon Hall said that in 1967 he had episodes of genital bleeding, and his body began to undergo feminization. Gordon adopted the name Dawn Pepita Langley Hall—*Pepita being the name of the grandmother of Gordon's idol, Vita Sackville-West—and started appearing in public dressed as a woman.*

In September 1968, Dawn Hall flew to Baltimore for an operation at Johns Hopkins Hospital that she said would correct her longtime sexual ambiguity. Dawn later wrote that her doctors had "removed the dead useless flesh which by a stretch of the imagination might have been termed a penis." She posed at the airport after returning to Charleston.

Dawn Hall advertised her altered sexual state with picture postcards sent to friends, including one in which she presided like a lady in her dining room.

In the late 1960s, Charleston teenager John-Paul Simmons was a deliveryman for a drugstore who rode around town on a bicycle carrying packages of aspirin and toothpaste. But in a chance encounter, John-Paul was to meet Gordon-Dawn, an event that would change his life.

Gordon during the transition to Dawn, *with his new friend, John-Paul Simmons, 1967. Dawn would later write that "John-Paul and I could not have sex because the vaginal passage had not been opened."*

Dawn Langley Hall and John-Paul Simmons.

John-Paul with Dawn, his fiancée, in downtown Charleston in 1969; it took special effort to obtain a marriage license.

The wedding of Dawn Hall and John-Paul Simmons took place in the drawing room of 56 Society Street in January 1969, with bridesmaids in blue and the bride wearing a ten-foot train.

A newspaper reporter estimated the kiss lasted thirty-seven seconds.

Ten months after their Charleston wedding, the couple flew to England to reenact their vows in an old church. Afterward, British actress Margaret Rutherford (seated), faithful in her friendship with the former Gordon Hall, hosted a party.

The transgender, interracial couple became frequent guests on television and radio. For a 1970 taping in Toronto, Canadian talk-show host Pierre Berton decorated his studio in the formal style of a Charleston house, hired an actress to play a Southern debutante (seated, left), and invited John-Paul and Dawn to "tea."

A year after the wedding, the money Dawn had inherited from Isabel Whitney a decade earlier was running out.

Dawn began to show signs of pregnancy, and in October 1971, she announced she'd given birth to a girl, Natasha. The mother insisted the baby was her biological child and living proof of her true femininity.

H105.105 Rev. 1/72
(Fee for this certificate, $2.00)

WARNING: It is illegal to duplicate this copy by photostat or photograph.

№ 394482

1. PLACE OF BIRTH

   PHILADELPHIA

   County _____

   Township _____

   Borough _____

   City   **PHILADELPHIA**

COMMONWEALTH OF PENNSYLVANIA
DEPARTMENT OF HEALTH
VITAL STATISTICS

CERTIFICATION OF BIRTH

File No. ____ **150542-71**

Date Filed ____ **11-4** 19 **71**

2. Date of **10-17** 19 **71**
   Birth
   (Month, day, year)

3. Name of Child ____ **NATASHA MARGIENELL MANIGAULT PAUL SIMMONS** 4. Sex **FEMALE**

5. Name of Father ____ **JOHN PAUL SIMMONS**

6. Maiden Name of Mother ____ **DAWN PEPITA HALL**

This is to certify, that this is a correct copy of a birth
certificate as filed in the Vital Statistics office, Pennsylvania
Department of Health, Harrisburg.

J. Dunlap Heller, M.D.
Secretary of Health

JUL 1 2 1972
Date Issued

Dawn made copies of Natasha's birth certificate and sent them to family and friends as evidence of her mother-hood. As a schoolgirl, Natasha carried a dog-eared copy of the birth certificate to show skeptical children.

In 1974, John-Paul, Dawn, and toddler Natasha Simmons left Charleston for the North, moving into a crumbling house in the town of Catskill, New York, three hours north of Manhattan. (Dawn's favorite statue, Saint Teresa of Avila, occupied pride of place on the mantelpiece.) Poor and jobless, except for occasional magazine writing by Dawn, the couple tried to put down new roots and raise their daughter.

38

In 1985, Dawn returned briefly to Charleston for the filming of North and South, a TV miniseries about the Civil War, in which she appeared as an extra in the role of a Southern lady.

39

In the late 1980s, Dawn and John-Paul became grandparents when their daughter Natasha had her first child, Damian (in the arms of his grandfather, John-Paul). By this time, John-Paul rarely lived with Dawn; more often he stayed in or near the state mental hospital in Albany, New York, where he received treatment for schizophrenia. Dawn Simmons died in September 2000 in Charleston, her adopted hometown.

John-Paul Simmons, 2003.

Natasha Simmons.

(Dawn). In the column for "race," there were these words: "Negro & white."

According to Bernard Fielding, Dawn was alone throughout the process, and John-Paul appeared only when it came time to sign his name.

"I had very little to do with the husband," Fielding went on. "He impressed me as being some fellow she met somewhere, who perhaps had an ordinary laborer's job. And I'm sure he didn't know exactly what he was getting involved in. She probably led him to believe she had all this money. After all, she had that big house down there, a good-looking Charleston house, other than the fact she had all these dogs runnin' around." He smiled at the memory of the infamous dogs.

I asked whether Dawn told Fielding that she was a woman by birth, or that she wanted children. The lawyer pursed his lips, and his chin fell to his chest.

"I have no recollection of those things. She mentioned Johns Hopkins Hospital, and I remember seeing some documents of verification from the hospital that she was a woman." Fielding took a breath and raised his voice. "But for those of us who knew what had happened—a sex change and all of that—she doesn't have any female organs! Ain't no way she's gonna have any baby!"

Dawn had claimed that hers was the first interracial marriage in South Carolina, and when Fielding was reminded of this, his manner changed. He was suddenly no longer nervous, and he took on a serious air.

Speaking slowly, he said, "As the secretary of the NAACP so vividly put it, there may not have been integration in the living room in America, but there's been a hell of a lot of integration in the bedroom in America! Her marriage may have been the first legal one, but there was a lot of relationships ahead of it—they just may not have been identified!"

Bernard Fielding, a light-skinned African American, had had family experience with interracial sexual partnerships—and for that matter, so had millions of families in the South, despite laws against interracial sex in every state.

"Twenty miles from here is the town of Lincolnville, which is the oldest black municipality in South Carolina," Fielding went on. He seemed a different person, arguing a case. "It was founded by interracial children. Used to have three schools in that area—one for whites, one for blacks, and the third for mixed-race children."

For the first time in an hour, Fielding had taken command of Dawn, instead of the other way around. He folded his arms on the table and shook his head. "Mrs. Simmons was a publicity hound, in other words," he said. He lowered his chin to his chest and exhaled, a little weary, because even former clients could be demanding.

ONE DAY, I was walking to an appointment at a school in Charleston, and as I crossed the campus, a man trotted up beside me, clutching a manila envelope. He was about fifty, of medium height, and balding, and he seemed agitated. The man said he'd become aware I was investigating Dawn Simmons, and he wanted to do what he could to help. Thrusting the envelope into my hand, he said, "This is about her wedding," and then he hurried off. I'd never seen him before, and I haven't seen him since.

The incident had the feeling of a cold-war rendezvous, complete with the handoff of secrets. In the envelope was a note and a faint photocopy of a ten-page typed text. The note explained that the pages were an eyewitness account of Dawn's wedding, written by a reporter named Jack Leland for the Charleston *News and Courier*, but never published.

The man with the envelope said in a handwritten note that he was a high school Spanish teacher, but that in his youth, he'd worked as an intern for the newspaper. The unpublished Dawn story had bounced around the newsroom for years, acquiring a cult status, and he happened to have a copy. It was a minute-by-minute account of the most talked-about wedding in Charleston. The paper had killed the piece, preferring to run a paragraph about the marriage, as Ted Phillips had told me, on the obituary page.

The news account began with the claim that Dawn's nuptials had been "Charleston's first inter-racial marriage of record." This seemed all right on the face of it, but the reporter had added a weird note in the margin: "This is actually 3rd interracial marriage license issued here; others were Filipino and white, however." In the late 1960s, among educated whites in the South, Filipinos were apparently thought to be a racial group.

Dawn's wedding took place January 22, 1969, late on a Wednesday afternoon when the weather was freezing. According to the reporter, a crowd had gathered in front of 56 Society Street, and many were yelling and cheering, or trying to get a look inside, where the ceremony had been scheduled to get under way.

In Dawn's living room, which was jammed, television cameras and reporters with pads and pencils were posted on the north wall. The service began when someone put on a record of the "Battle Hymn of the Republic." The song was a Civil War anthem sung by Union troops as they marched through the South; by playing it, Dawn was showing her contempt for Charleston's ancient white order. The "Battle Hymn," in the reporter's words, was "the song so roundly detested by Confederate veterans and still an anathema to die-hard southerners."

As the scratchy record was spinning, Dawn and three bridesmaids descended the staircase into the living room.

> *Mine eyes have seen the glory*
> *Of the coming of the Lord;*
> *He is trampling out the vintage*
> *Where the grapes of wrath are stored;*
> *He hath loosed the fateful lightning*
> *Of His terrible swift sword;*
> *His truth is marching on.*

Glory! Glory! Hallelujah!
Glory! Glory! Hallelujah!
Glory! Glory! Hallelujah!
His truth is marching on.

The bride wore a floor-length dress with appliquéd lace flowers, and two five-year-old boys carried her ten-foot train, the account said. At the bottom of the stairs, Dawn met John-Paul, dressed in a tuxedo. When Dawn saw the cameras, she had a word with the minister, who then moved to the opposite side of the room so that the bride could face the television lights.

During the repositioning, the boys with the train ran to get into place, nearly pulling a shoulder-length wig off of Dawn's head. The crisis caused the three bridesmaids to fuss with Dawn's hair until all was back in place, and the ceremony continued.

The room was jammed, the reporter said. "Other than the bride and about ten cameramen and reporters, the entire affair was Negro."

When the minister, an assistant pastor at Shiloh African Methodist Episcopal Church, turned to the bride, he addressed her as "Mrs. Hall." At this, Dawn leaned forward and said, "It's Miss Hall, please."

Wedding rings were passed between the bride and groom, and the television cameras crossed the room for a close-up. Pushing their way between the minister and the bride, the cameramen briefly interrupted the vows.

According to the reporter, at the end of the ceremony, the pastor put his hands on the kneeling couple and said, "I now declare that you is both man and wife." After this, Dawn and John-Paul kissed for thirty-seven seconds.

Pictures were taken, the wedding cake cut, and champagne distributed in tall glasses decorated with tiny flowers. Before leaving for a wedding supper at the Brooks Motel, a local inn with a black clientele, the newlyweds appeared outside Dawn's house and waved to the cheering crowd in the street. But the bride didn't throw her wedding bouquet, saying she wanted to place it instead on the grave of the late Senator Robert F. Kennedy at Arlington National Cemetery. (The late President John F. Kennedy's younger brother had been assassinated the previous summer while himself campaigning for president.)

Afterward, Dawn spoke to the press and let it be known she hoped to be a mother. "I'd like to have three, and the doctors say there's a 50-50 chance that I can have children," she was quoted as saying. If this didn't occur, Dawn added, she and her husband intended to adopt a mixed-race orphan.

I noticed one thing about the wedding story—it included plenty of hearsay, perhaps the reason it was killed. For example:

> When Gordon Langley Hall arrived in Charleston in 1962, he was lionized by the literary and arty segments of the population, and was a guest in the homes of a number of the city's social arbiters. One socially prominent young couple made him the godfather of their child. When Hall's apparent taste for living with young Negro males became known, this prompted a neighbor of the couple to remark, "Well, every boy needs a fairy godfather."

The reporter found Dawn's fertility troublesome, and dismissed it with more hearsay:

> Mrs. Simmons's talk of having children is not new. In June of 1968, in Schindler's Antique Store on King Street, she told Mrs. Singer (Schindler's sister) that a recent fall down the stairs had injured her—and "I'm sure it has caused me to lose my baby." Mrs. Singer took strong exception to the hypothesis at that time. The incident is revelatory in that it happened four months before the sex-change operation was completed.

Dawn had hired Joe Trott to decorate her house with flowers, and Joe had spent hours on the wedding corsages and boutonnieres. On one of our lunches out, he sat across the table and recalled the job.

"The wedding was highly publicized, and everybody from God knows what newspaper was there, doing a story about 'the man who became a woman,' and all that sort of shit," Joe said in his scatological style. "That morning I was at the house making preparations with the flowers. Her bridal bouquet was orchids, and the animals all had different corsages! Some of the smaller animals had things like feathered carnations. The damn guinea pig couldn't carry a full corsage. Damn orchid was the size of a pocketbook, and the guinea pig was the size of your hand."

Joe adjusted his ponytail and rattled the ice in his glass of tea. He set his strong jaw and dug in his memory.

"The dress was very expensive, and she'd gotten it in New York. She'd hired music, too—they had a harp, and they had a viola, and a violin, and I think a flute." As he named each instrument, Joe mimed the movements of the musician playing it.

"People were hanging out of windows across the street, and cameras were rolling, and all this. The police department was there, the fire department. The streets were packed with people waving placards." More miming, this time of protesters with signs.

"I was so scared I would get shot!" Joe stopped and looked wide-eyed.

I thought this was a joke, but it wasn't.

"I was trying to get on a solid wall in case anybody was a sniper from one of the rooms across the street!"

Charleston was not a city where whites voluntarily spent time with blacks, and those who did were shunned. In Joe's view, the shunning of Dawn might have been accompanied by gunfire, an extreme form of ostracism.

Joe twisted his brow, showing some of the anxiety he'd felt decades before. "I was terrified by what these white people might do. There were no white people in the wedding, other than Gordon and me. I could hardly wait for the damned thing to be over with, so I could go home. I was trying to stay away from the windows, because I thought somebody would get killed!"

The anxiety suddenly lifted from Joe's face, and he smiled. "We had trouble before the service with the pets. You see, all of the pets had to have corsages, Gordon told me. Now, his main dog was a German police dog, a very ferocious creature named Jackie, after Mrs. Kennedy. Gordon called me upstairs, and he was very upset. 'We can't get the corsage on Jackie! She's under the four-poster and we can't get the corsage on the dog!' " Joe imitated a nasal cockney accent. "I said, 'Gordon, no way in the name of God am I crawling underneath that bed and putting a corsage on a police dog. If the dog don't ever get a corsage, I don't give a shit!'

"So here comes Gordon with full veil and gown, and everything, and he and I kneel down, and he goes up under the bed, and I'm next to him." At this point Joe bent down under the restaurant table, reenacting. "He takes the corsage and tacks it on the collar of the dog. And I said, 'Come on, Gordon, you're going to be late for your own wedding!' "

Joe got up from under the table and sat down. "Well, the service went on forever, with all the marching down, the bridesmaids, and the animals. Some people carried animals, rabbits and little dogs, little Chihuahuas."

I knew that Gordon had beautiful Chihuahuas, and in one photograph I'd seen them wearing white dresses. They looked very good.

TOM TISDALE, the lawyer, said he knew a man who'd been to the wedding.

"He's named Maurice Krawcheck," Tom said, sitting in the fancy seafood place where we were having lunch. "He's a haberdasher on King Street. Not long after Dawn Simmons died, I was in Maurice's store, buying a jacket or something." Tom paused and repeated a phrase in which he'd lost a consonant. *"A jacket or something.* I had assumed all these years, wrongly, as it turned out, that John-Paul Simmons had perhaps been a tailor for Maurice, because I couldn't figure out any other reason why Maurice would have this relationship with him, and go to the wedding."

It was a puzzle Tom was determined to solve, so he said he went to the men's clothing store and asked the owner whether John-Paul had worked for him.

"And Maurice said, 'Heavens no! Heavens no!' But he was extremely reluctant to talk about it. I said, 'Maurice, didn't you attend the wedding between Dawn Langley Hall and John-Paul Simmons?' And he was very reticent. He said, 'I just sold Mr. Simmons some clothes.' "

There was more to the story coming, and now Tom drifted to the gist, which had to do with the way the wedding party had been dressed.

"Apparently the groom had gone to Maurice's store and bought a bunch of clothes before the wedding," said Tom, "and they had come back several times to get them altered. But it was a horrible job, because it was obvious the clothes had been worn for about three weeks running, without ever having been changed. Therefore, Maurice said he went to the wedding to see the result of his work."

Tom nodded, as though he empathized with his friend's curiosity.

OTHER REPORTERS HAD COVERED THE WEDDING, including one man who worked for a newspaper called the *State*, in nearby Columbia, South Carolina. Bill Starr was a sixty-something journalist with a beautiful baritone voice, a rich laugh, and alert eyes. He'd written thousands of pieces in his long newspaper career, and he said his account of Dawn's wedding was one short item of three or four he'd written during the same week. In 1969, Starr was working for United Press International, the wire service, which sent him to the wedding on assignment. Starr's recall of the day was sketchy, but he did have two clear memories, which he shared over a drink in a cafeteria.

In his low, melodic voice, Starr said that he'd been in the crowded living room that afternoon, and during an hour-long wait for things to begin, he plainly saw that Dawn looked exhausted. (In fact, pictures from the service did show her face looking drawn.) The other memory was more sensual. Starr recalled that when the wedding music finally started (the "Battle Hymn"), he'd moved across the living room to the staircase, the better to watch the bridal party descend. Edging around the minister and Dawn's antique furniture, he arrived at the stairs, and then felt something underfoot. Starr said he looked down and noticed that he'd stepped in fresh dog shit.

"JOHN-PAUL ARRIVED ten minutes before the ceremony," Dawn wrote later. "He was wearing the latest tuxedo and a blue formal turtleneck shirt. I was so grateful to God for answering my prayers, so grateful for being a woman, so grateful to my John-Paul."

Dawn said it was a "wretched insinuation" that she and John-Paul had slept together before their marriage, and she felt she had to rebut the rumors in print. She described her deflowering in a piece she wrote about her wedding night: "All my life I had been a sexless vegetable. Now I had to give myself physically to John-Paul. No woman could ever have been treated with more reverence than I was on my wedding night. Those large, work-roughened hands were soft and gentle. The doctors made me whole—but my husband made me a woman."

Dawn had signed a five-thousand-dollar publishing contract with Doubleday & Company to write a memoir, and had been able to get the advance before the wedding, the better to deflect creditors. She called the book *The Ballad of Dawn and John-Paul*, but the publisher later renamed it *Man Into Woman*, a titled she disliked.

With her marriage, Dawn placed herself further off the keel of Charleston life, if that was possible. She was already the city's resident alien; nevertheless, she'd held on to her sense of humor through the showers of gossip. In fact, she didn't mind spreading rumors about herself if others failed to do so. On the subject of her wedding, she'd even set up the best joke around.

Dawn told people that a dignified aunt of hers back in Sussex had heard about her scandalous marriage, and had been upset. "I am delighted that you have become a woman," the aunt had said, "and I am delighted that you are marrying a man of another race. But I understand that husband you've chosen is a Baptist!"

John-Paul and Dawn had spent their wedding night at home. The morning after, the couple linked arms, went out from the house, and made their way along Society Street. "To walk down the street as a married woman was the crowning moment of my life," Dawn later wrote. They passed the mansions with their crumbling cornices and endured the stares of afternoon peepers. They waved to the cars that honked as they drove by. Turning the corner, Dawn strolled out of white society and into the arms of black.

Chapter 12

ECLIPSE

On January 23, 1969, the *New York Times* reported:

> British-born Dawn Pepita Langley Hall, who was writer
> Gordon Langley Hall before a sex change operation, was
> married tonight to John-Paul Simmons, her Negro
> steward. The bride, an adopted daughter of Dame Mar-
> garet Rutherford, the actress, has given her age as 31.
> The groom is 22.

Dawn normally liked publicity, but this item upset her, with its
reference to her "Negro steward." Pricked that the paper said she'd
married her servant, Dawn told a lawyer to look into a lawsuit; but in
letters to his client, the lawyer talked her down from her fulminations.

The story cascaded, with and without the "steward" part. *Newsweek*
had already run a page-long feature on "the anguished transsexual" and
her marriage to "a Negro garage mechanic." The black weekly *Jet*
magazine ran a sympathetic story about Dawn's affection for her
African American spouse. An American tabloid called the *National
Insider* did a story, as did the Japanese scandal sheet *Shukan Shincho*,
which ran a five-page spread, with photographs.

In England, the London *Daily Telegraph* did a story in its Sunday magazine, and the *Daily Express* ran a piece in competition. After the sex reassignment, Dawn had become a regular topic in the *Sussex Express*, the weekly that people read where she'd grown up, which meant that her family read about her with a mixture of fascination and shame.

But the biggest coverage came in the British tabloid *The People*, which paid a large sum for a serial on Dawn's life. The first installment earned her £3,750, and the editors introduced the series with these words:

> A remarkable FACT has now been established. At *The People*'s instigation Mrs. Simmons was examined by one of Britain's most eminent gynecologists at his Harley Street surgery. He stated: "Mrs. Dawn Simmons was probably wrongly sexed at birth. She has the genital organs of a woman capable of normal sexual intercourse, and she is capable of having a baby." On the evidence of the report of the gynecologist, it is not impossible that she could become pregnant.

The paper withheld the name of the "eminent gynecologist," but Dawn later said he was one Dr. Elliot Phillip. Although I tried, I couldn't find him; and decades after the events, I assumed he was dead. What would his explanation have been of Dawn's fertility?

For a year or two, the tabloid press loved Dawn Simmons. The newlyweds also popped up on radio and television. *The Pierre Berton Show*, on Canadian TV, flew them to Toronto to tape two talk segments; in England, there were television appearances and a BBC radio interview.

After one show, a friend wrote Dawn to say she'd seen the performance. "Mamma and me watched you, and I want to tell you how good you were, and looked," the letter said. "I remember when you came out, looking great, and placed your purse beside the chair where you sat. So very ladylike."

The interviews followed a pattern. John-Paul would shake hands with the reporter, say a few words, and then sit next to his wife and remain silent while she laid out their story.

However well she played elsewhere, Dawn was too hot for broadcast in America. It would be years before cable launched the U.S. market for tabloid television, and the networks steered clear of her, apparently bewildered by her overloaded tale.

The coverage created a halo of infamy around Dawn and led to letters from strangers, who offered support or asked for advice. A desperate woman wrote to say she'd had a hysterectomy and later had gotten engaged. Her fiancé wanted children, but if he found out about her surgery, he'd call off the wedding. The woman begged Dawn to refer her to a clinic where she could "have a transplant of some kind."

Dawn loved her taste of fame, but in Charleston she'd become a pariah. With the exception of a tiny loyal group, white people shunned her. Dawn complained about being hounded on the street, and it's indeed likely that kids yelled from passing cars. But much of the taunting took the gentler form of a social freeze. A note from one Charleston lady, a former head of the Preservation Society, and thus a purveyor of class status, summed up the aversion.

"I received your letter," the woman wrote on social stationery, "but I did not answer it because your life has become too complicated for me. Your style of life is beyond my capacity to cope with, socially or otherwise. I trust you're happy, though I would not think Charleston a happy place for mixed marriages."

And so the newlyweds withdrew into their mansion.

SHE'D GONE FROM MAN TO WOMAN, but when she "married black," Dawn crossed another threshold. Leaving her white life behind, she found moorings in black society.

An African American weekly in Charleston, the *Chronicle*, had run stories about Dawn, and it was the laconic editor of that paper, Jim

French, who shed light on this next part of Dawn's journey by introducing me to another of her small coterie.

Maranda Holmes was a retired city worker who lived in a two-story wooden house near the Citadel, the military college in Charleston. The neighborhood was unusual in the city because it was integrated, a black block here, a white one there. Her house was narrow in the front and long in depth, painted mottled pink, with white doors. Two porches, upper and lower, looked out over a tiny front yard that had been wrapped in a chain-link fence.

She was petite but solid, and to receive a guest Maranda Holmes wore a brown tweed suit with a gold butterfly brooch. She had a combed wig, strong jowls, and narrow rectangular glasses. The pink of her house was echoed in her pink lipstick and pink powdered face.

I put her age at somewhere in her eighties, but Mrs. Holmes had the energy of a bird. She was widowed (her husband, James Holmes, had been a seafood cook in restaurants) and had four grown children ("My youngest is fifty, a professor at Shaw College").

We sat at her dining table, and Mrs. Holmes said, "I been here in this house sixty-two years. See, I graduated from Burke School, right over there." She pointed toward an all-black high school a few blocks away. "After that, I went over to the cigar factory—American Tobacco Company—and stayed there sixteen years. Then, I got married and started having children. Became a seamstress, working in different stores. The children got up in size, and I could leave them alone. So I went to the city working for the playgrounds, spent twenty-five years as a supervisor at the parks department. My working life was forty-nine and a half years! Now I work in the community, as a volunteer. Just finished five thousand hours at the Veterans Hospital, helping the patients. And I been here in this house the whole time, start to finish."

Mrs. Holmes put her elbows on the table and one finger on a temple to prop her head. On one side of the dining room stood a china cabinet full of glasses, teapots, and plates. The walls were lined with trophies and plaques from church organizations, city agencies, and Mrs. Holmes's sorority, the Order of the Eastern Star. Some awards

stood for volunteer work ("Franklin C. Fetter Family Health Center—In Recognition of Outstanding Service as a Board Member,
1979-80"); others were job related ("Department of Leisure Services—1980 Meritorious Service Award"). On one wall she'd hung a
framed poster of the city of Jerusalem, because Mrs. Holmes was a
church lady.

"I can visualize Dawn Simmons right now. She was tall and well
dressed," Mrs. Holmes said. "She used to have her house open to
people who paid. And Society Street was crowded with all these
white folks going in to see the place. Sometimes you could hardly
walk in the street for all the people visiting. So I was aware of who
she was before we met."

Mrs. Holmes said, "Let me get a pen." When she sat down again,
she had a pencil and an envelope, and she wrote down names and
dates as she talked: "Society Street," "1969." She said, "It helps me
remember," and put down the pencil.

"I met her in the late 1960s," said Mrs. Holmes. "When I saw her,
it was on the news, on television. She was at her home on Society
Street, and they had her wedding. I was sitting in my den, and looked
at the TV, and saw my assistant pastor, Reverend William Singleton.
I said, 'Oh, what is Reverend Singleton doing in there with the white
girl?' "

She imitated herself watching television, craning her neck to see
it, making a shrill, surprised voice. "The folks was all over the street
at the wedding! Some was going in all through the windows! Some
looking in, and some were climbing in the house!

"Later that night, I called Reverend Singleton. Dawn must be she
knew he was a minister, because he lived around the corner from her.
So she had asked him to perform the ceremony. He said he didn't
know how it got out, because it was supposed to be private! Reverend
Singleton told me, 'That lady asked me to marry her, and how all
those folks knew that, I don't know!' "

Mrs. Holmes laughed, half at the poor minister, half at her feisty
friend Dawn. She wrote down "Singleton."

"Dawn started to come to church, and she joined our church after the wedding," said Mrs. Holmes.

The Reverend William Singleton was assistant pastor at Shiloh African Methodist Episcopal Church. Shiloh AME stands on two-block-long Smith Street in the heart of the dwindling black section of Charleston. It has a small congregation of two or three hundred, part of the city's largest black denomination. The AME movement was strongest in the Deep South, but it had actually gotten started in Philadelphia, in 1787, when black Methodists, tired of condescension from whites, split off to form their own church.

Mrs. Holmes wrote, "Shiloh."

"She came to a service, and when they called for joining, Dawn just got up and joined," said Mrs. Holmes. "I got to know her because I was the secretary of the church, and all."

Dawn told church leaders she wanted to be an usher, Mrs. Holmes remembered, but the pastor asked her to be a trustee. "You see, at that time, she had still been rich."

Mrs. Holmes cradled her face in her right palm. "She was a good member, came to church all the time. She used to do her tithes, and she took communion." Members of Shiloh each belonged to a study group, and Dawn was required to enroll. "They placed her in class number three, under the direction of a leader, name of Charlie something."

In notes for a memoir, Dawn had remembered things much the same, with some added romantic dressing. "At Shiloh, it took only one service for me to be endearingly called 'their church sister,'" Dawn wrote. "It was a mantle I was proud to wear. I found the services beautiful and satisfying, as the Sunday services had been so long ago in our village church in England. I became the only white member of the congregation."

Maranda Holmes's strong voice started to rise on the strange tide of emotion these events brought with them. At church, Dawn ceased to be an outcast and found Christian acceptance of her nature, perhaps for the first time. Or at least, this is how Mrs. Holmes remembered it.

"She integrated our church! The congregation was glad to have her, you see, because we're all *supposed to be one*," Mrs. Holmes said. "We're not supposed be no black and no white. It's just the color of your skin, but we have the same blood. You're born the same way."

The phone rang, and Mrs. Holmes talked rapidly to someone. She got off and returned to the table. "She's like to talk off your head," she said of the caller.

Collecting her thoughts, she went on. "Dawn Simmons was generous," she said. "She bought the candelabras for the church pulpit, beautiful silver ones. Two of them you still see there.

"Then I went over to Dawn's house, and it was beautiful. Antique furnitures! I never seen furnitures like that! Had all of these settees and buffets—oooh, it was beautiful! And I like coffee, and she used to buy the best coffee for me, because she was a sweet lady. I used to visit her many times at her house, and we sat, and she fixed coffee for me, and I stayed there a good while. But I remember she had about forty dogs, great big old dogs! And they had big names, like president's names."

Charleston in 1969 was actually ripe for an interracial marriage and the integration of a little church. That spring, the city had seen the crest of the civil rights movement, which had been slow in coming to the state. Although "the Movement" had started long before—in 1955, with the Montgomery, Alabama, bus boycott—black protest came to South Carolina only much later, in the late 1960s, which meant that marches coincided with the period when Dawn "became black."

In her tweed suit and among her community laurels, Maranda Holmes didn't look like a frontline demonstrator, but in fact, she'd been a soldier for black liberation. "We wanted to know why, in our school, they had three shifts for black people, and in the white school there was four and five rooms no one was using. We wanted to know why, as taxpayers, if white people come into a store, and we was there first, they served *them*. My husband wanted to know why, at the bus station, you had to stand out behind the station until two minutes before the bus come—and if it rained, you had to stand out in the rain."

Mrs. Holmes wrote "Movement" on her envelope.

The civil rights meetings had taken place at night, and the marches during the day. One night, Dawn came to see Mrs. Holmes. "She said, 'I want to be a part of the Movement.' And we went to the hotel, the Brooks Motel, where we were having meetings, and that's how she joined up."

In early 1969, Charleston's black nurses went on strike for equal treatment and better pay. The strike led to daily marches, which frightened the state's white leaders, who responded with force.

"In the day, we did demonstrations on the street. At night, we used to assemble at a park on Judith Street, and have prayer meetings," Mrs. Holmes said. "Then the police would come and tell the fellows to get up off their knees. But they didn't get up, and they would beat them up and arrest them."

Mrs. Holmes unwrapped a striped peppermint, put it in her mouth, and handed another one across the table. She sucked on it thoughtfully, turning over the good old days in her mind.

"Police would beat up the nurses, didn't care about no women. But we was rough out there. They had a few black police on the force, but the rules were they couldn't arrest no whites, only blacks. Isn't that something?"

The nurses' strike ended when the governor sent in thousands of National Guard troops, leading to street scenes in which soldiers armed with rifles faced down health care workers in white dresses. A curfew was imposed. Charleston filled up with tanks and armored cars, and for a few weeks, the quaint streets looked like the Soviet Union on May Day.

Mrs. Holmes said, "We used to like to see the National Guard with their long rifles, because it meant we got a reaction!"

Martial law proved a difficult sell to tourists, however, and for a time the leisure economy shut down.

Dawn wasn't involved with the marches ("She must have been

afraid she was a target"), but one night she and John-Paul broke the curfew. They were arrested, fingerprinted, and thrown in jail; the next Monday, a judge gave them probation.

Mrs. Holmes mused on her peppermint, her eyes glowing from the memory. "Back in slavery time, when the whites couldn't give the baby the milk, the black momma, or mammy, or what they called her, used to have to nurse the white *and* the black children. And they still treated the blacks like dogs. I think they treated the animals better, in slavery time."

She smiled. "But Dawn was different. The rich people was her enemy. Blacks was her friends."

Mrs. Holmes wrote "Slavery" on her envelope.

DAWN SENT PICTURES of her wedding to England, and her mother, Marjorie, wrote back, "The photo in the white dress is lovely. You favor me, but you are much better looking."

After the wedding, which none of Dawn's English family attended, Marjorie had been hospitalized with pleurisy, and her strength was waning. At sixty-three, she'd worked as a servant most of her life, and for years her marriage had withered. Her husband, Jack Copper, had been having an affair with a woman in Sissinghurst village. Marjorie had confronted him, with the result that he'd beaten her—although not for the first time, according to Dawn. The transformation of Marjorie's firstborn child into a media curiosity and the resulting rude jokes around the village didn't reduce her stress.

Marjorie wrote often, and when a month passed with no news, Dawn worried. During the long season of marches and rallies, no letter came. In August 1969, Dawn's sister Frances sent word that Marjorie had died. It was too late to go to England, she added, because their mother was already in the ground.

Shaken, and bitter at her family for withholding the news, Dawn decided her next drama would have to take place in England. If her family found her embarrassing, she would go home to flaunt. Within weeks she'd arranged a trip, and she was working on publicity that would give it maximum effect. The idea was to have her marriage blessed in a proper English church, with a full court of press to witness. She would make her family come, and she would also take a day to visit her mother's grave.

The actress Margaret Rutherford, whom the bride called her adoptive mother, stepped forward to play host to the pageant. Dawn's relationship with Rutherford spanned fifteen years. It had begun in New York when she was Gordon Hall, and was kept alive by occasional visits Gordon and then Dawn made to Rutherford's home in England. In the Dawn Simmons papers I'd seen letters from the actress, and their tone was always endearing. Now preparing to throw a party for Dawn, and apparently blithe about her own reputation, Rutherford sent out the printed invitation cards Dawn requested and prepared to greet the press.

> Mr. J. Stringer Davis and Dame Margaret Rutherford Davis, O.B.E. request the honor of your presence at the blessing of the marriage of their adoptive daughter, Dawn Pepita Langley Hall to Mr. John-Paul Simmons at two-thirty o'clock Sunday afternoon, November the ninth, St. Clements's Church, Hastings, Sussex, and afterwards at the reception.

The appropriately ancient stone church stood in Hastings, an old fishing village turned tour destination an hour south of Gordon Hall's hometown of Heathfield. At the service, photographers were so plentiful they had to be sent up to the choir loft so that guests could sit in the pews. A handful of Dawn's family showed, but Jack Copper and Frances were not among them.

The ceremony in a Gothic church—replete with organ trills, a second wedding gown (this one yellow), and a cake—was not unlike dozens of Sussex village weddings that Gordon Hall had written about twenty years before, when he was the society reporter for the small-town papers. The service seemed to touch something deep in Dawn that still needed satisfaction, her greeting-card idea of a woman's finest hour. By feeding this craving, the blessing of her marriage by the Church of England gave Dawn at least one day of happiness.

Afterward, Dawn wrote Jack Copper a disappointed note. "My dear Jack—My husband and I came to Sissinghurst to see you and couldn't find you. There was a light. It was raining hard, and dark. Someone lent me a flashlight so what we could find Margie's grave, which we did."

Dawn and John-Paul finished their English trip with a couple of interviews and then returned to their stormy home.

WITH TWO WEDDINGS, European trips, and uncountable luxury treats, Dawn had spent a river of money in twelve months, but she was coming to realize her husband could be even worse with cash than she. "He likes Ford Thunderbirds," she told a friend in a letter, and added that she'd bought him three. When John-Paul said he wanted to fish, she bought him a twenty-seven-foot trawler and two or three other boats (the number varied each time she told somebody new). Dawn claimed she paid to furnish John-Paul's mother's house, and meanwhile she learned that he was giving away money to friends and family.

"A thousand dollars disappeared from a secret drawer in my desk," she wrote. "My old butler kept telling me where the money was going, but love can be blind. Priceless miniatures disappeared from the wall, and other furnishings vanished."

Bernard Fielding, the lawyer who'd gotten the marriage license, remembered a time after the wedding when he started dealing with Dawn's creditors. Swaying in his red swivel chair, looking a little chagrined, Fielding answered a question about whether Dawn had retained him to help her.

"No, she didn't retain me—she *ob-tained* me."

Bernard Fielding folded his arms on the table and laughed. "I may have gotten a token fee, but I know the labor I expended on her behalf was not compensated properly, in other words."

The legal work concerned lawsuits. "When she started to get into financial trouble," Fielding said, "she began referring to me as 'her lawyer.' She had multiple creditors who were bringing suit against her, and I was in the position of trying to fend off temporarily the demands for money. But she wasn't responding or cooperating, wasn't working with me."

Pressure mounted, and Dawn told Fielding about money that was supposedly in train.

"She kept feeding me a line, 'This money's coming from *Englund*, this inheritance from somewhere else.' " On the word *Englund*, Fielding threw his hands forward and laughed. "But these substantial sums never seemed to come forward."

Dawn and Fielding parted company. "My last contact with her was when I fired her as a client," Fielding said.

He gripped the arms of his chair and leaned back with a smile. Despite having lived through the worst possible attorney–client relationship, Fielding seemed to respect Dawn.

"You see, you're dealing with a character actress—or an actor/actress. I think she had that ability to manipulate." His eyebrows went up, and he nodded. "Yeah, she was a performer."

THE SITUATION ON SOCIETY STREET DETERIORATED. A publishing executive named Margaret Stephens, Dawn's editor in the children's division at Rand McNally, wrote to report that she'd received the galleys of a book Dawn was writing; then she added, "The operator at Charleston said your phone had been disconnected."

Housekeeping at the antebellum mansion, never scrupulous, ended altogether when Dawn let her servants go. At the same time, her love for animals grew. In fall 1970, Dawn wrote Jack Copper to tell him about her latest TV appearance—and to talk about the pig she and John-Paul had adopted, and who now lived in an upstairs bedroom.

"Our pig Frances is growing enormous. She is house-trained to paper and she dances, and she bangs the toilet seat when she wants water. She thinks she is a dog. She is a lovely golden color with black spots. We love her so. She is the cleanest animal I ever had."

Life acquired surreal touches, which gradually became the dominant theme. The abrupt changes of the previous eighteen months seemed to have an effect on Dawn's mind, and the line between fantasies and actual events blurred. In a letter she wrote to one family member, the thread of actual events could no longer be disentangled from Dawn's dreams:

> John-Paul is a rough diamond but his heart is in the right place and he is very good to me. In this dreadful deep southern part of America he risked shooting and lynching to marry me. We never know when we go walking if we will be shot in the back; we cannot travel without a gun in the car; and I never go out without the German Shepherd (Alsatian). I've been spat at so many times it is commonplace. But I will never run away and I will never leave him.

She knew she was sinking, yet for her raft Dawn had chosen another dream, the cliché of the long-suffering wife. While her marriage and life unraveled, she made a show of standing firm.

ON A MILD MORNING IN CHARLESTON, when the full sun glowed on the old cornices and facades, I went to see Terry Fox, an acquaintance of Dawn's who remembered the days of her dwindling grandeur.

Terry Fox was a soft-spoken man in black jeans and a black sweater, who lived in an 1840s Italianate house not far from Dawn's old place. He had a full head of auburn hair fading to gray, a young face, and horn-rimmed glasses. We sat in his living room, where the high ceilings and ten-foot pocket doors were offset by contemporary art and modernist furniture, giving the house a lighter feeling than many Charleston homes.

When Fox folded his arms and told his story, I detected a North Carolina accent under the verbs.

"I came to Charleston in the late 1960s, and moved to number 52 Society Street in 1969, two doors from Dawn. I was twenty-three and comparatively naive. Much of what Dawn was about was too peculiar for me."

Fox had a bemused air, which contrasted nicely with the opinion-ated bursts most people offered on Dawn. He lifted his chin in the air and put his left palm up like a cleaver; then he pushed the air from left to right in front of him.

"At the time, part of me thought of Dawn as being a worldly, sophisticated person, who wouldn't have anything to do with me," he said. "And then there was the freak-show part of her, which I wasn't drawn to. But she was always very gracious and friendly when we met on the street."

There was nothing judgmental in Fox's voice, and nothing in awe either. Dawn had appeared in his life and made an impression, which he recounted in his sardonic way.

"After one year of marriage to John-Paul, Dawn decided to give herself a first anniversary party, and she issued a verbal invitation to me on the street to come celebrate her nuptials," he remembered. The party at Dawn's house, which took place in January 1970, turned out to be the signal event that defined Fox's encounter with her.

"I had a friend in the Navy who had a fake fur coat. He was out of town, so I popped on the fur coat, and went over to Dawn's."

Fox remembered that a pretty barren scene had greeted him as he came in through the open front door of 56 Society Street. "I walked in, well after the appointed start time of the party, and nobody was in sight. The place was stenchful, and overrun by dogs. Suddenly Dawn

descended the stairs, dressed in a full length, form-fitting red brocade dress, with long sleeves, wearing some kind of tiara. 'Terry,
Terry, Terry, so good to see you,' she said."

Dawn asked Fox to help her get into her dress, and she turned
around, "as women will always do," while he fastened her. Then
Dawn gestured to the dining-room table.

"She told me, 'We're running so far behind, would you help me set
up the buffet?' And in the dining room were all these beautiful silver
pieces, tarnished to hell, ladened with lunchmeat in plastic packages,
like Oscar Meyer bologna in pull-open packages, Kraft American
cheese, the kind with the slices separated by inserts, and pickle loaf
salami."

As he recounted the setting, Fox never raised his voice, which
remained a monotone. The only sign of his feelings was the slight
look of wonder on his face.

"As the evening played out," he said, "maybe twelve people came.
There were three young gay men. A minister came, John-Paul's
mother came, but John-Paul didn't come for the longest time."

Fox crossed his black-jeaned legs and put his palms out in front of
him, facedown. He was wearing a gold watch on his left wrist and
gold ring on his right hand.

"All at once, the front door of the house burst open, and John-Paul
ran in, almost in tears. I can remember him saying, 'Momma, they stole
my dog! Momma, they stole my dog!' It was an uproar of an entrance.
I don't know whether the dog was actually stolen, or he had lost it."

Fox seemed to see the scene from Dawn's living room in his
mind's eye, and his eyes opened wide. He let his palms drop into his
lap, looked at the coffee table, and allowed a smile.

FURTHER INCIDENTS THREATENED the oasis of marital happiness that
Dawn believed (or at least said) she inhabited. When a crate of furniture arrived from England (whenever Dawn got money, she usually

spent it on antiques), Dawn unpacked it and John-Paul placed the box in the driveway. The hay stuffing was still spilling out of the crate. Later that night, a hissing sound awakened her, and when she and John-Paul looked out, they saw the crate in flames. A fire truck came quickly and doused the flames, but the Thunderbird had been scorched.

"John-Paul discovered the cause of the fire—a homemade fire-bomb made out of a Coca-Cola bottle and tossed by a nameless enemy."

Dawn began to record almost weekly events—a dog poisoned, an attack on the street, theft of art from her house. Some of these things probably occurred, but it was difficult to say how many, or what kernel of event might have taken place beneath her embellishment of it.

"John-Paul was shot at in the street," she wrote in a manuscript. "I was set upon and knocked onto a concrete sidewalk by a white man who had baited me with the words, 'Nigger lover' every time he passed in his car."

Either by theft—or by the need to raise money—the old trove of art and antiques was rapidly diminished.

In Atlanta, I located a woman named Chris Campbell who'd bought things from Dawn during this sell-off phase. I was able to reach her by phone at her house.

"Dawn was selling some pieces from her home on Society Street," Chris Campbell said. "When she needed money, she would call me and offer me something. Which is how I bought an Isabel Whitney painting from her, in oil. And the desk I'm looking at now. It's a French desk with a folding top, superbly beautiful."

Chris Campbell thought highly of Dawn, and her voice betrayed sadness at the memory of her friend's predicament.

"You could tell she'd lived the good life at one time," said the voice on the phone. "She had beautiful manners, but she had made the transition from male to female, and some of the male characteristics had carried over. She had a boyish quality sometimes, more than a woman's. It was hard to get used to at first, but then I did, and I thought she was a lady."

Two years after her marriage, Dawn ran completely out of money. She wrote friends asking for loans, but only a few hundred dollars came back. She asked a publisher in England for four hundred pounds, and the reply came from her editor that he wished he could help—but alas, no. The threat began to loom that she would lose her beloved house.

In JANUARY 1971, Dawn began a diary. At first, she filled it with domestic incidents. "I bought John-Paul some under drawers, size 44. He was quite insulted that I got them so big, but had to admit that they fitted. He weighs 275 pounds. Dreadful and quite unnecessary."

Soon she kept track of the shifting gears of her decline. "The heat went off and I called the heating man, forfeited my last twenty dollars, and the heat went off again five minutes after he left," she wrote.

Dawn knew she might face a day of reckoning with her biggest creditor, First Federal Savings and Loan, which held the mortgage on 56 Society Street, and paranoia entered her mind: "January 24, 1971—They have to have this last pound of flesh and steal this house. May God punish the wicked—those hypocrites."

She wrote that she would prefer to sell the house before facing foreclosure, and she hired a realtor to entice buyers. But the infamy of the owner and the mess of the animals scared shoppers away. (The pig had moved to a proper farm, but a dozen dogs and cats remained, and they used the floor as their toilet.) Thinking the problem would go away, Dawn concentrated on things other than the bank's demands.

"February 14—St. Valentine's Day. My hairstylist set my hair in Grecian style, with curls over the forehead. Now I have to put those wretched curlers in to attain the same curls tomorrow. We then went through my dresses that I'm going to alter to midi lengths. The seamstress is going to put some fur around the bottom, as I hate short dresses. Jacqueline Onassis hasn't got the legs for them, and neither have I."

First Federal gave Dawn a warning, which she didn't take seriously. She seemed to prefer the role of the busy housewife who took time off for a little gossip: "Went to a delightful tea party, the most civilized I have ever attended in this provincial little city, and so much better than those horrible cocktail parties where everybody screams and shouts about their ancestors that nobody outside of Charleston has ever heard of."

The bank announced it would foreclose if she didn't pay off the full loan immediately, and Dawn knew she couldn't raise the money. The house had been her prize, and the sign of her escape from simple roots. Finally, she panicked: "Feb 19—Johnny was very kind to me, otherwise my poor mind would have broken. Those racists think they will win. I do not regret marrying John-Paul. I never saw him as anything other than a *gentleman*."

First Federal foreclosed on 56 Society Street in April 1971 and scheduled the sale of the house. This meant a public auction, which by law would take place on the steps of the courthouse. When the sale ended, a young couple had bought the house for a modest bid, and Dawn and John-Paul faced eviction.

Then came a startling discovery. It happened either the day of the auction or a few days before. Dawn said it was at this point that she realized she was pregnant.

Chapter 13

THE BABY SHOWER

LOVE'S ALCHEMY

To hear her describe it, Dawn's revelation that she'd conceived came like an annunciation:

> I was having coffee in Central Drugs on Meeting Street, where the soda fountain is presided over by Mrs. Madeleine Jenness, when I suddenly became violently sick and slipped off the lunch stool. Mrs. Jenness immediately took charge of the situation, sending the delivery man post haste for John-Paul, who arrived quite breathless a few minutes later.

The sudden appearance of her pregnancy blotted out Dawn's troubles. Despite her fickle partner, and never mind the loss of the house, a baby would be the culmination of her womanhood, which Dawn had cultivated so long and paid so dearly to acquire.

"I have always loved children, for which my animals substituted," she wrote in a moment of self-knowledge.

The eviction took place, landing Dawn and her husband in a faded section of town in a rented house, at 15 Thomas Street. A greatly reduced cache of art and antiques was carried over from Society Street. The new house, a dilapidated wooden box with peeling paint and twenty-seven broken windows, would seem to have been another wound in Dawn's assortment of stigmata. But the expectant mother didn't care too much, because now she had to focus on prenatal changes.

Dawn walked the streets with a growing belly, to the amazement of passersby. Terry Fox, the guest at her anniversary party, remembered seeing her shuffling down the sidewalk in flat shoes, with a swelling in her dress, "the flat shoes being the sensible thing for women in her condition."

No one believed it. Some said Dawn would have a belly one day, a flat stomach the next. "She became a sort of laughing stock," remembered Fox. "People were unkind, said all sorts of cruel things." Another man remembered he saw a blanket under Dawn's dress, "a military surplus thing, and you could clearly see the stenciled words, 'U.S. Navy.'"

As the months passed, Dawn wrote to newspapers and magazines in an effort to interest editors in the event. A letter came back from *Truth* magazine, in Australia. "Thank you for the photographs," said editor Ian Dougall. "Please let me know how your pregnancy is progressing. Also what hospital you're going to, and the date the baby is due."

Defying the doubters, Dawn made preparations to give birth. "The baby was to be born at the University of Pennsylvania Hospital in Philadelphia," she wrote. "I had been warned by two close friends of the danger of publicity had the birth been in Charleston. For privacy I would be registered as Mrs. Marjorie Manigault."

The news of Dawn's baby didn't trigger the gossip frenzy of previous years; the pregnant lady had for some time attracted only derision or pity. Yet her paranoia grew. She thought the white population of Charleston would want to do away with her. Therefore, the hospital had to be out of town.

Of course, another reason to go to Philadelphia, seven hundred miles north of Charleston, might have been to obtain cover for whatever she'd arranged.

*   *   *

MARANDA HOLMES, Dawn's church sister, sat in her dining room, her fingers laced on the table in front of her. Her square face had a slight smile, and her pink blush made her look younger than her eighty-plus years.

"She moved over onto Thomas Street," Mrs. Holmes said, "to a great big house, but it didn't have those nice furnitures in it." Mrs. Holmes wrote down the words "Thomas Street," then looked up. "Whether she sold them to help live, I don't know. I don't know what happened between her move and when she got pregnant."

I asked what Mrs. Holmes knew about Dawn's pregnancy, and she fell silent. She stuck out her jaw, dropped her mouth half open, and lowered her eyelids.

"I don't know anything about that. I've never seen it."

"Some people said she was once male, and became a woman," I said.

"I don't know. I really don't know," said Mrs. Holmes. "They said she had a sex change, but I don't know. I never talked to her about that, and she always looked like a woman to me. She was well dressed, and she wore her hair down, until later on she cut it in a bob."

Mrs. Holmes wanted to stay wide of the subject, and she steered the conversation to safety.

"They used to pay to come to her beautiful home on Society Street. But after she married, there were no tours. So she didn't have no money. Nothing! Because at that time the white folks really hated black people, you know."

She meant the tour groups stopped coming to 56 Society because Dawn had married John-Paul.

According to Mrs. Holmes, when Dawn moved to Thomas Street, she still had pets, but not as many, "because she couldn't afford the dogs no more."

The baby came October 17, 1971.

"I was at the baptism!" said Mrs. Holmes. She scratched her temple. "And as secretary of the church, I took the name down. There were plenty of people from Shiloh, but I can't recall whether Dawn's husband was there, or not. That was the last time I saw Dawn. She was beginning to get poor, and she wasn't coming to the church. Come to think of it, I haven't seen her since she baptized the baby."

Mrs. Holmes pursed her lips and shook her head. She seemed protective of her old friend, like she wanted to shelter something frail.

"IT WAS A LITTLE GIRL," Dawn wrote, "and she had Johnny's bow legs."

The new mother had gone to Philadelphia, and she now had her baby, seven pounds and twenty inches long. She'd named the child (according to the birth certificate) Natasha Margienell Manigault Paul Simmons. Margie was Dawn's mother's nickname; Nell, her grandmother's name; and Manigault, that of a Charleston family Dawn had fantasized about.

Dawn went on, "John-Paul flew into the house and gave one look at the baby and said, 'Whoever saw a blue-eyed nigger?' The blue eyes soon changed to Margie's beautiful hazel eyes."

Natasha's mother sent birth announcements to friends and family, including old Jack Copper, who was alone since his wife's death:

> My dear Jack, she was born with Margie's funny little finger. She has my hair and eyes, same color eyes as Margie, and is dainty like her but she has her father's dimples and good naturedness. It all came right in the end. Incidentally, I have got you a copy of her birth certificate so that you know and can put the ignorant in their place with your usual caustic wit.

Letters of disbelief, and sometimes sympathy, came back to Thomas Street. "The baby. Is it really yours, or did you adopt it?" wrote Anthony Dawson, an English actor the mother knew, who lived in Rome. Helen Mendenhall, a friend Gordon Hall had made in the early 1950s, when he was a writer for the *Nevada Daily Herald*, wrote from Missouri: "I admire your courage in more ways than one. Also, I know Nature sometimes makes mistakes. Did you have a cell chromosome check to see whether male or female cells predominate? Or was it just more of an emotional and mental attitude that made you a woman?"

Natasha became the center of Dawn's world, and the child's beauty pushed the parents' cares to the margin. "Johnny dotes on the baby," the mother wrote a friend. "Her father always calls her 'Red' or 'Emma.' When courting me I was 'Pet'—now it's 'Nigger!' "

When word of the miracle baby drifted out of Charleston and up to New York, the new parents became the subject of jokes on the hit TV show *Laugh-In*, which had forty million viewers. Every week the show's hosts, Dan Rowan and Dick Martin, reviewed headlines in a stand-up routine; one viewer, thinking back decades later, remembered a tart exchange about Dawn. "News flash: Charleston, South Carolina. Noted transsexual Dawn Simmons has just given birth to a daughter," said Dan Rowan. To which Dick Martin responded, "A neighbor was heard to remark, 'We can only hope she grows up to be half the man her mother was.' "

Though Dawn had a new life, money troubles remained, so she struck on the idea of selling a book based on Natasha's appearance. She told an agent in London about a manuscript she wanted to write, called *Letters to Our Daughter*, and alerted people that it was in the works. One friend wrote back, "Your agent should have no trouble in getting you a lot of press here in England, especially if you bring Natasha. There could be television, women's hour, etc."

In other words, Natasha would be good publicity.

VANQUISHED

One night in bed, John-Paul announced to his wife that he was the father of another child. He'd been coming home only about half the time, and now Dawn knew he'd been with Casey, the other woman, and Steven, the child (not their real names). With her husband's confession, Dawn assumed her marriage was broken and that eventually she'd have to become a single mother.

John-Paul wasn't bringing home much money—the big boat had been sold for three hundred dollars, and his wife had made him quit other work—so it fell to Dawn to pay for everything. She'd written a sample chapter of *Letters to Our Daughter*, but no editors who'd seen it took the bait. Most publishers had lost interest in her personal story. Harper & Row had her under contract for a book about Theodosia Burr, a romantic southern figure and the daughter of Aaron Burr, the former vice president who'd killed Alexander Hamilton in a duel. However, the advance was trivial, and only the occasional sale of an antique paid the rent.

Expenses on Thomas Street proved too much, and in 1972 Dawn and Natasha moved (without John-Paul) to a one-bedroom apartment in the shabby Carlton Arms, on run-down Vanderhorst Street. It was still in the historic district, but the building lacked the high ceilings and antebellum style. It also meant shrinking down from ten to three rooms. Baby Natasha seemed to compensate, but the glory was bleeding out of Dawn's life.

She hoped the right publicity would bring in excitement, and much-needed money. "Today I signed a contract with a German magazine," she wrote John-Paul. "This means I will have completed part of the *get-back-on-top plan* and you can have a car or a boat, and me my furniture back."

John-Paul came and went when he felt like it, an arrangement Dawn accepted, though she complained to a TV interviewer that "he was always in someone else's bed." Letters she wrote to friends talked about beatings, which Dawn always blamed on muggers or "racists."

However, reports of the beatings stopped when John-Paul disappeared to his other family.

In summer 1972, an English newspaper flew Dawn to London for a story, and she brought Natasha, using the occasion to arrange a second christening for the girl (after the first one at Shiloh, the black church). Press coverage followed, including an item in the *Daily Telegraph*, and the event took place at the same Sussex church where she and John-Paul had had their English wedding.

After a second visit to the doctor who'd examined her for *The People*, Dawn wrote a relative from her hotel: "Yesterday I saw the same Harley Street specialist, Dr. Phillip. He said everything was normal. He took a pregnancy test. They take saliva from each side of the mouth."

Then she wrote her husband:

My dear Johnny,

I am not upset with you as I know you were not yourself the other night. I have no money left. You know that and you destroyed all of my work when I couldn't give you $30 for your son. I shall never stop you from seeing Natasha as I love you and have always loved you. Nobody would love a man who has tried to kill them several times, gave them 45 stitches in their face, broke their nose, and cheekbone and ruined the eyesight in one eye. But I have never ever shut the door against you and you came back. You were the kindest man I ever knew before that woman ruined you with drink. I am eternally thankful to you for the most beautiful baby in Charleston. You don't have to live with us again Johnny; I don't think you can live with anybody.

Back in Charleston, Dawn told friends she'd been attacked several times on the street, but the incidents seemed to coincide with John-Paul's visits. In December 1973, she said, a masked, white intruder had raped her and broken her arm; yet the only crime she reported that year was a purse snatching, which the Charleston police followed up with polite letters and visits to gather evidence.

Friends out of town told her to leave Charleston. "You really are nuts to just keep on living in that area when all you get is knocked about," wrote Anthony Dawson, the actor in Rome. "I love the antiquities of the South but find the people leave much to be desired," another friend wrote from Maine. Gwen Robyn, in England, summed up the feelings of Dawn's remaining circle when she said, "I am sure you will have a better life in New York. You could get more work from publishers if you are on the spot and do not have John-Paul troubles."

Decades later, Dawn's Charleston friends to whom I talked could remember little about her decline. They hadn't noticed much, probably because she'd been swept off the stage she once commanded. As Dawn struggled, it was her black friends who helped with Natasha, and sometimes with food. She told John-Paul, "You were so happy I would be working again, that I would not be hungry as I have been so often." Neighbors cooked enough to share when the white lady neglected dinner, which happened often.

HEEDING ADVICE, Dawn wrote away for real estate listings, although she was broke. She wanted an old place to start over, and also to be within striking distance of New York City, near her old publishers. A letter came from the National Trust, the preservation foundation, with the names of realtors in upstate New York; a historical society sent fliers on houses.

She told friends she was moving to upper New York State for two reasons. First was escape: she could "hide" in the Catskill Mountains, where her "persecutors" couldn't find her. The more attractive although somewhat random explanation was that she'd opened a copy of *Yankee* magazine and seen an advertisement for the "Uncle Sam house," in the town of Catskill, New York.

Sam Wilson, a nineteenth-century peddler and showman who

passed into folklore as the model for the legendary Uncle Sam, the
U.S. Army huckster ("I WANT YOU FOR U.S. ARMY"), had lived in a
two-story Federal period house that was now derelict and for sale.
Not only did Dawn love old buildings, but to get her hands on this
storied old house would give her a new grip on America.

The deal required only that she put down a two-hundred-dollar
binder. In 1974, Dawn moved with her toddler to Catskill, a tough
town on the Hudson River in Greene County, New York, two hours
north of Manhattan.

Despite their fighting, Dawn's husband had become more
dependent on her, and so before long, John-Paul followed her up the
East Coast, leaving Casey and Steven, his other family, behind. By
this time, John-Paul was showing signs of losing his grip on reality,
but Dawn always took him back.

The *New York Times* chronicled the family's move from Charleston
to Catskill, a historic but beat-up river town, running a friendly article
and homey picture of the odd couple. Natasha, Dawn, and John-Paul
settled in with their scant remaining things, and the Uncle Sam house
continued crumbling around them.

At the prodding of his wife, John-Paul took up sculpture and
began styling himself a folk artist. He made crude busts and figures
from clay dug out of the ground, and in short order, a curator from
the American Museum of Folk Art, in New York, came to see the
results. Dawn was trying to sell a new memoir about her life since
"the change," and Natasha was entering nursery school.

In a red vinyl-covered diary, Dawn kept a record of this short
happy spell, when her family seemed to find peace: "May 7—It
doesn't seem true that we are all together, and we have all been so
happy. Johnny has perfected a glaze for his sculpture and has done
splendid work. I'm so proud of him. He is to have his first one-man
show at the Catskill Library. How thrilled we are! I had my hair
done."

Things were better, a fragrance of normalcy, but money steered
clear of the family. The bigger publishers avoided Dawn after the sex

switch and marriage, and by the early 1970s, she was reduced to dealing with fringe companies—a one-man outfit in New York, a one-woman operation in Pennsylvania. Such companies couldn't give advances, let alone promote her books.

The idyll didn't last, of course, and the first winter in Catskill ended in disaster. Money from her writing failed to materialize, and when a hard freeze came, Dawn couldn't afford heating oil. The pipes burst, and with them, the dream of Dawn's America. The family moved into the Skyline Motel. A dingy place facing a busy bridge, the Skyline would become the scene of Natasha's earliest memories.

Within a few months, Dawn's Johnny fell apart. Dawn told friends her husband was using drugs and acting erratically. She said he would sometimes walk out into the snow at night, barefoot, and end up in jail. "John-Paul has deteriorated badly," she wrote a judge. "There was a time when he was found wandering shoeless in Rockefeller Plaza, New York. Then he turned up in a bus station in New Jersey."

Dawn's husband was delivered to the Capital District Psychiatric Center, the state mental hospital in Albany. The diagnosis was schizophrenia, aggravated by drug use. From his hospital room, he wrote a rare letter home.

FEB 12, 1976

Dawn Dear:

I am not an incompetent (no good) individual.

My "shrink" wrote the above. He made me write it 100 times and hand it in for homework. My whole life is just homework and more homework. If I only had a home to do my homework in, it wouldn't be so bad (I think).

J.

P.S. I love Natasha and you, but I'm incompetent.

I was struck by the letter's tenderness. Until this moment, I'd found no real evidence Dawn and John-Paul had had an emotional bond. Yet here was a profession of love and an acknowledgment their life together had been difficult. Only real couples communicate like this. Perhaps Dawn didn't marry for publicity reasons, but actually for love.

I WENT TO UPPER NEW YORK STATE to get a sense of where Dawn had landed. The town of Catskill stands on a bluff overlooking the Hudson River, and you can see it was once a beautiful port: a smattering of buildings from the early 1800s and blocks of Victorian houses, their bay windows and stained glass announcing early money. But Catskill had fallen, bypassed by change. "This is a welfare county," said a clerk at the courthouse, "and it's not getting better."

The Rip Van Winkle Bridge, a mile-long span across the Hudson, empties into the town, and overlooking its busy off-ramp is a tall, faded sign standing by itself in an empty lot. "Skyline Motel," the sign promises, though the building itself has been bulldozed. Here on the overgrown parking lot, five-year-old Natasha Simmons had once played with her dog, Vita.

On Catskill's main street I passed a half-mile of storefronts, from Chinese take-out joints to little groceries, including one with a misspelled, handwritten sign that said, "We take food stamps and benifit cards."

I'd read in one of Dawn's letters that John-Paul's first stay in the mental hospital lasted several months, after which he came back to his wife and the incidents began anew. When I asked at the office of the town court, the clerk found five or six criminal cases—trespass, burglary, assault—with John-Paul as defendant. The town and the village of Catskill had two jurisdictions, and at the separate village court a different clerk found a second stack of cases similar to the first. In most, if not all of these cases, the charges were ultimately dismissed on grounds of John-Paul's mental instability.

The earliest case against John-Paul, in July 1977, was petit larceny, but the verdict came in as not guilty. Two months later he was arrested for trespassing. Dawn had said her husband had become convinced he owned a certain house, 37 Clarke Street, which belonged to a local dentist, and he'd broken into it. "He moved in and painted pictures of nude people with three eyes all over the walls," Dawn said. He was arrested and spent two weeks in jail; but as soon as he got out he broke in again, and was jailed. Let out after two weeks, he was arrested a third time for breaking into a different house. In a letter, Dawn described the arraignment:

> I think that this evening the judge saw how mad John-Paul is. His was the last case and he came in in handcuffs. Johnny was pleasant to us for a few minutes, as we had some cigarettes for him, and then dismissed us as he had "things on his mind."

The court sent John-Paul back to Albany for psychiatric treatment, but the reprieves were usually temporary.

"I have had quite a time with my husband here," Dawn told a librarian at Duke University. "He was just doing so well with his folk sculpture and then he got into the clutches of another woman. It was the old story of desertion and has ended with frantic calls in the night."

Natasha, smoking a cigarette in her house, remembered what it was like to be a little girl around her erratic father.

"It was big drama," she said. "I was little—five years old, seven, then ten. There was a lot of conflict, and there was this lady who was always around, the woman my dad ran off with that got him strung out on a lot of stuff. My mom said he was never quite right after that."

In Catskill, John-Paul had found a new girlfriend and hardly saw his wife and daughter. "A lot of people were afraid of him," Natasha went on. "My dad's a big guy, and my mom was afraid of him sometimes. He'd do things and not remember doing them. He would hurt her, and anything could set him off."

Natasha looked unhappy thinking about her father's explosiveness. She said she'd feared him when she was a girl, though no longer. "He never did anything to me. He would grab me, and then my mom would always step in and take the brunt of it."

Declared mentally incompetent, John-Paul became eligible for Social Security payments. The monthly checks reduced the outbursts, because he was less dependent on Dawn for money. But the peace came to an end on one bad night. In an article she titled "Madness Haunts Actress's Daughter"—the actress being Margaret Rutherford (who had died in 1972), the daughter being Dawn Simmons—Dawn told the story of her husband's worst collapse:

> On Friday evening, August 22, 1980, the "voices" that for three weeks had been haunting John-Paul Simmons, my black folk-sculptor husband, commanded him to "kill . . . kill . . . ." He took an axe and in a few seconds completely demolished our dining room filled with antique furnishings, slashing valuable Hudson River paintings and tragically for her, our 8-year-old daughter Natasha's prize collection of old cookie jars. Fortunately for us we were eating out or we might well have been killed.

The charge of criminal mischief (destruction of property) led to another psychiatric exam. ("Defendant found to understand charges," said the court papers. "Public defender assigned, but Simmons won't cooperate with any lawyers.") I was unable to learn the final disposition of that case, but in the end it appears Dawn declined to prosecute.

Dawn filed for separation and sole parenting rights. The Petition of Custody stated, "Mr. Simmons is in the Greene County jail for a burglary and an assault on the petitioner and child." It described Dawn as "the natural mother of Natasha Simmons" and John-Paul as "the natural father." Natasha was nine.

"On another day, I was at my typewriter," Dawn remembered, "and he came up from behind and put his hands around my throat. I sat quite still wondering if my end had come. Then his hands slowly traveled to my hair, which he stroked gently. I cried." John-Paul went back to the mental hospital, this time, Dawn said, permanently.

LOOKING FOR RELIEF, and for escape from the Catskill police, who no longer felt love for the Simmons family, Dawn and Natasha moved to the fading town of Hudson, on the opposite bank of the river, five miles upstream. An industrial backwater whose factories had closed, Hudson became a new hiding place, where Dawn found another dilapidated address.

Natasha went to school, Dawn tried to get back to writing, and life settled down. The Charleston lady attended church and found a semblance of ordinary life. But despite good cause, she did not abandon her husband. Mother and daughter visited John-Paul once a month in the D ward of the Capital District Psychiatric Center in Albany, a ninety-minute bus ride. Acting the part of a devoted wife, and also the female masochist, she kept up her marital vows like a stockade.

In Hudson, which had a number of antiques dealers and a sizable gay population, Dawn drew sympathetic curiosity. Attracted by her eccentricity, younger admirers presented themselves as guardians and helpers. People drove her on errands, brought the family food, and enabled Dawn to have friends for the first time in years.

One of several who put themselves at Dawn's disposal was an engaging furniture dealer with the sonorous name of Galen Trembath. Letters I'd found at Duke had led me to him. Hudson had beautiful, if battered, old houses. It also had a decent train link to Manhattan; as a result, antiques dealers fleeing New York City had discovered the town in the 1990s. Galen Trembath had been among the migrants.

We met in a Turkish restaurant in Long Island City, Queens, a section of New York where Trembath had a temporary apartment. He wore a green Barbour jacket against the wet snow, and when we sat down, took it off to show a black corduroy button-down shirt. Trembath said he was sixty, but he looked about forty, with dark hair that showed no sign of being dyed, and tortoiseshell glasses that made him look like a midcareer literature professor. He was thin, had only a few facial lines, and spoke with a refreshing amusement at life.

"Dawn and I would go out for lunch, and conversation wasn't a problem, because she never shut up," Trembath said. "She would talk all through the entrée about her favorite subject, her own life. Then the dessert would come, and you couldn't get a word out of her with a crow bar, because she had a sweet tooth and she was completely focused."

Trembath laced his fingers on the wooden table. An aproned waiter brought grape leaves and hummus, and baglama music played on the speakers. Trembath had an endearing way of talking, with frequent smiles and warm laughs. He was entertained by the world, but not patronizing of it.

"The first time I met Dawn," he said, "I was in a friend's antique shop in Hudson, managing it, and she came in the door. I'd seen photographs of her, and knew her story. But the osteoporosis had definitely set in. She was an ambulatory L, very slight, very small."

Trembath made the shape of an inverted L to suggest Dawn's bent-over posture. Osteoporosis is endemic among older women who've run out of estrogen. I no longer believed Dawn had ever possessed ovaries, but it seemed strange she would have suffered from a classic feminine condition.

"She was very stooped over, very thin, and she had a stick"—he made the motion of using a cane—"with a flash of swooped back hair"—a swirl of the hand to show the coif. "We talked about antiques."

After that first encounter, Trembath became a companion to the much-diminished Mrs. Simmons. She turned out to be so demanding that he enlisted a second person to help. ("A friend and I took her up.")

By this time, Dawn was nearing the end of her journey. To most people, she gave the impression of a person so displaced that she was almost a refugee.

"People took terrible advantage of her," Trembath said. "She had the reputation of being an oddity, and she was very kind, very generous. If she liked you, she would give you whatever rags she had on her back. She gave me wonderful presents, like a dressing table— Georgian, Beau Brummel—a couple of chairs, some daguerreotypes, a wonderful linen tablecloth."

Was her life in Hudson difficult?

"Very. She was impoverished. She lived in unsanitary conditions, which she bore with great aplomb." Trembath pursed his lips to suggest Dawn's endurance. "She was always gracious, always enthroned in some awful chair, and in her lap the cats were all over her." He waved his arms through the air in abundant cats. "She couldn't take them out, so she would spread papers everywhere. And from time to time, we would go over there with garbage bags and pick up the mess."

The town of Hudson, Trembath said, had started off as a whaling port. It was accessible to the ocean via the Hudson River, even though a hundred miles upriver from New York harbor. A few families from Martha's Vineyard and Nantucket had come in the 1790s and in ensuing generations had erected a good stock of architecture. Dawn lived in one of the old houses.

"Wonderful, open, three stories, with woodwork. Dawn's building had been tenementized and was dilapidated," said Trembath. "She was renting three habitable rooms. The bathroom did not work. Kitty litter had been dumped down the toilet."

In Dawn's day, the population of the town was divided between arty furniture dealers (who were white and often gay) and working families (white and black, often poor). Trembath belonged to the first group.

Natasha grew up under Dawn's hand, with occasional visits from John-Paul, who'd been released from the psychiatric hospital into a group home. She attended public schools, except for a brief interval when Dawn sent her to a private academy, which she disliked. Natasha's friends came from black families, Dawn's from the arty white cohort.

John-Paul came and went, using the group home and Dawn's apartment interchangeably, which his wife tolerated. "Dawn had a remarkable gift for self-destruction," said Trembath. "When I met John-Paul, he was always very a mess, mostly inarticulate. There were times he was more lucid than others. When I would bring Dawn food, if her back was turned, he would take the food and eat it."

Trembath had visited Dawn during John-Paul's residence with her, and he described a scene with Gothic overtones: "John-Paul had had many years of madness, and didn't seem capable of prolonged conversation. He would escort her around on the arm, and sit quietly to the side. She would hold court, and she would love to sit in her chair and perform. He would sit nearby, lost in his reveries."

Food came to our table, and the music got louder, now with a zither holding the melody.

"John-Paul's family blamed the madness on Dawn," said Trembath. "From what I heard, the last time he was seen was running around Albany, in a lady's old, worn-out dress." I pictured a man lurching around in one of Dawn's lacy Victorian things.

Trembath pursed his lips and rolled his eyes up.

Dawn's income came mainly from government checks, plus a few stories she sold to British newspapers. She wrote a piece on the boxer Mike Tyson for the Sunday *Telegraph*, in London. Tyson had grown up in Catskill, said Trembath. "And so one of our outings with Dawn was to go to the cemetery to see the grave of the fellow who adopted Tyson, took him off the streets, and showed him boxing." Dawn photographed it.

The friendship with Trembath grew, and he became Dawn's legal caretaker. She insisted that he have power of attorney, and a checking account in her name was opened so he could manage her money. "When her checks arrived, I would take them out and give her the cash," Trembath said. "She would try to keep it from John-Paul, but he would inevitably show up and find it."

There was a period when Dawn would call Trembath every day, he said, and leave long messages on the machine. She talked about what she was doing that day, and her plans for the future. Trembath said he'd kept tapes of the messages, as a kind of memorial.

What did he think about Dawn's claim to femaleness?

"She said she had a hysterical clitoris—that it was enlarged, so that it was mistaken for a penis," Trembath said, repeating Dawn's catechism about her body. "It wasn't something you could ask her, but she volunteered the information."

Dawn became a church lady, active in Christ Church Episcopal, in Hudson; and when Natasha had her first child, Damian, she became a grandmother. Damian was her pride, said Trembath. "He would stay with her, post her letters, run errands for her, and take care of her animals."

As she aged, and the osteoporosis progressed, Dawn's life shrank until it took place largely at her desk. "She made a lot of telephone calls, wrote a lot of letters," said Trembath. (At Duke, I'd seen letters from her friends that began, "Dear Dawn—Thank you for your many letters, and I'm sorry I haven't kept up your pace.") She surrounded herself with newspapers and scissors, and mailed hundreds of clippings to friends.

"She used to sign her letters to me, 'Elizabeth Barrett Browning,' because Dawn was really a nineteenth-century romantic," Trembath remembered. "She loved touting her black marriage, but she was also enamored of the antebellum South, in a romantic way. She always had the stars and bars, the Confederate battle flag, lying over a box in her living room."

The fantasy of the gallant white South touched Dawn, but she also loved to bait the conservative society she'd escaped. One plan from her final years was to write a biography of a black historical figure from Charleston, Denmark Vesey, who'd been the mastermind of an attempted slave revolt.

It occurred to me that in Dawn's mind there wasn't a lot of distance between the Southern belle in a chiffon dress and the leader of a slave uprising: as figures of fantasy, both were appealing. Dawn's most exciting years had been like a dream, and as an older woman, she retreated into her personal fables.

"She was a marvelous embroiderist," Trembath said. "And the older she got, the more the embroidery became the actual fabric." Trembath put his chin on a closed fist.

During her last months in Hudson, before moving back to Charleston, where she would die, Dawn was evicted from her apartment and went to live in a motel. "The Warren Inn," said Trembath, "whose main business was ladies by the hour."

Dawn had heard that John-Paul was in Albany and not in good shape. Natasha, now twenty-five, had already moved to Charleston with her kids. When Dawn followed her daughter, said Trembath, "she bolted for the last time."

On the first move to the South, the rich author Gordon Hall had arrived in a limousine. This time, Dawn took the bus.

WHEN MOTHER AND DAUGHTER LEFT New York for Charleston, John-Paul stayed behind, angry because Dawn's move had deprived him of a home. He gave instructions to his few friends that his life was no one's business, and his family was not to be told his whereabouts.

Dawn had again run from her messy marriage, and she felt guilty. Natasha remembered her saying, "All I worry about is whether he'll be all right." His wife knew John-Paul couldn't make a living and ran good odds of falling apart.

"It got so that whenever I passed a homeless man, I thought it could be my dad," said Natasha.

For the last three years of her life, Dawn didn't know how to reach her husband. When she died, his family couldn't find him to tell him the news.

*   *   *

THE TIME HAD COME to look for John-Paul. Maybe he could say something truthful about Dawn's sex. Or maybe he could answer my questions about Natasha's birth, if he remembered the facts.

By the time I went to look for him, Natasha hadn't spoken with her father in five years. "Are you going to tell him about Mommy?" she said. "That she died?"

Natasha said she thought he was still in Albany. "My dad needs to be close to his meds," she said, "and near someone to watch him." But she added, "I've sent people looking for him, and they found nothing." She didn't know where else to look, and Albany had a population of a hundred thousand.

I was running out of sources, and finding John-Paul felt like a last chance to fill in the blank parts of Dawn's story. Without much more than his name, and with some trepidation, I went to Albany.

Chapter 14

302.85

Reconnaissance

I reached the city at night and drove to the state psychiatric hospital. In the middle of Albany stands the Capital District Psychiatric Center, a two-story 1970s building that weaves like an accordion across a cleared block. It has no feeling of a center, or even of a main entrance. I couldn't be sure along its meandering exterior which door was the fire exit and which the reception.

Privacy for mental patients was tight, and my inquiring calls had yielded little. "We can't say Mr. Simmons is or has ever been a patient" was all that several polite supervisors would give. Natasha had said that in one ten-year stint, her dad had lived in a group home near the hospital. The patients had since dispersed and the house had been sold, but there were others like it somewhere, she'd said, and maybe John-Paul was in one of them.

It was dark and quiet as I walked around the perimeter of the hospital, wondering where to start. A few patients smoked in the night air, lurking on a patio caged with vertical bars. Of course, John-Paul might be one of the incarcerated, especially if he'd crossed with police, by old habit. Across the street a handsome row of houses in the crafts style, circa 1900, faced the copious institutional lawn.

The next morning, I repeated the walkabout and encountered a mailman. He knew the street numbers of two group homes within walking distance. I knocked at the first, a yellow Victorian, and a woman in jeans with brown hair and a friendly manner opened the big oak door.

"Oh, I know J-P!" she said, smiling. "He's a sweetie! He's got his own apartment, on Lancaster Street." She realized she'd broken the privacy rule, and her smile dropped. "I'm not supposed to tell you where he lives."

Behind her, two residents snacked at a big dining room table. I left a note and asked the woman to give it to John-Paul.

Lancaster Street, a mile away, ran through an old neighborhood whose renovated townhouses, some from before the Civil War, wore fancy plaques ("1857, Built by Anthony Madding, blacksmith"). There was ice on the sidewalk, and a gray-haired man emerged from a brownstone to spread sand for traction.

"They gave us two group homes—a double dose, both in these two blocks," he said. He seemed amused that depressed patients on his street might depress property values. "That one, and one there." He pointed out a brick house across the street and a stone building a block farther west.

At the brick, a thin superintendent with short hair said, "John-Paul hasn't lived here in years. But I can't tell you about our clients." She gave me a yellow sticky pad to leave a note. I felt I was closing in on a shadow.

The stone building had a bay window, and a pretty woman with long brown hair appeared at the entrance. When she learned the reason for the visit, her smile turned to a frown and she said, "Thank you," before slamming the door.

One of the women had said that a nonprofit called Rehabilitation Support Services ran housing for patients, "but don't bother going there, because they won't tell you anything." The service agency had a suite on a busy and ragged street within sight of a bar and a check-cashing shop; inside, a staff of ten worked in spartan rooms. A friendly but firm woman repeated the privacy mantra and sent me on my way. I wrote down my address for her, in case someone were to see the nonexistent John-Paul.

*   *   *

BEFORE MOVING BACK TO CHARLESTON, Dawn had published a third memoir, *Dawn: A Charleston Legend*, this time with a South Carolina press, Wyrick & Company. (The first memoirs, *Man Into Woman* and *All For Love*, had come out twenty-five and twenty years before, respectively.) In this installment, the author repeated that she'd been a girl victimized by ignorance, but this time she added a few new "facts." For instance, Dawn claimed she was descended through her mother from an aristocratic line linked to a certain Duke of Medinaceli, from Andalusia, Spain.

When *Dawn: A Charleston Legend* appeared, in 1995, the publishers flew Dawn to South Carolina for book signings and a party at her old house on Society Street. The friendly reception, where a few Charleston liberals treated her well, must have convinced her the situation had sweetened since her escape, and that she was no longer such an outcast.

The feeling grew when Dawn saw the reviews. In contrast to the old tabloid fanfare, the *London Times* ran a gentle piece on the book, as did other tasteful sheets. The most surprising item was the one in the *Spectator*, an English weekly to which Nigel Nicolson, the son of Vita Sackville-West, was a contributor. When we met, Nicolson had mentioned the piece. For years, Dawn had tried to communicate with Nicolson, but he'd avoided the person he called Dinky, who was, after all, the servants' boy at Sissinghurst. Nicolson's review read like an apology for all that. He'd browsed the book, noted that Dawn had only nice things to say about him, and pronounced the former Gordon Hall a worthy eccentric.

Dawn's old trouble spots seemed to be clearing. In the changed climate, she thought she could go home to her adopted town and have some final golden years.

Natasha moved from New York State to Charleston two years before Dawn, and when her mother decided to follow, in 1997, the two got apartments near each other. Dawn's dog, an Akita named

Camilla Parker-Bowles, was sent down from New York to give her comfort. "Mommy wasn't doing too good, and her mobility was going," said Natasha. Dawn was in poor health and had had a couple of falls before she moved. She was somewhere in her seventies.

Back in Charleston, the place most deeply her home, the writer saw old friends, like Joe Trott, and enjoyed the company of her grandchildren; but the hoped-for glory didn't materialize. The aging author lived in federally subsidized housing on the northern reaches of the peninsula, far from sight. Out in the suburbs, where the Charleston landmass widened—it was no longer phallic, but flat and plain—she couldn't find the footing that would restore her legend. Book sales, and therefore income, remained thin. A letter from a publisher reported that Dawn's most recent novel, *She-Crab Soup*, had sold seventeen copies during the year.

She spent her days writing illegible notes to friends (her handwriting had shriveled with Parkinson's) and dictating the occasional business letter. (It was in 1999 that she'd written me about the Ball commode she'd once owned, our toilet in common.) As they had in Hudson, friends looked after her, including a furniture dealer named Florence Haskell, who brought food and sometimes money and who was Dawn's most devoted helper toward the end. And every day Natasha came from around the corner to visit.

"Since I've had children, I realize you can put anything down on paper and have a birth certificate," said Natasha Simmons. She held in hand her own birth record from Pennsylvania. "I've questioned it, but I haven't had the guts to find out."

When Dawn was alive, Natasha had kept things compartmentalized. Mommy had said she was a woman, but common sense made her wonder. Now she'd let herself become curious about the circumstances of her birth.

"When she said her things, she never made me question whether they were true." Natasha leaned forward, imitating herself as a child, asking questions. "'Okay, well, did you have a sex change?' 'No, they just took away the one that didn't need to be there.' 'Then you were sick?' 'Yes.' That made sense."

Dawn tried to keep her age hidden, the better to spread the legend of being a mother. She claimed she'd been born in 1937, which would have made her thirty-four in 1971, the year Natasha was born. But Gordon Hall was actually born in 1922, which made Dawn Simmons a first-time mother at age forty-nine.

I told Natasha, "I can't promise I'm going to find your birth parents."

She answered, "I'm not looking for them. If they exist, I'd like to know. More than thirty years, they haven't come looking for me, so why should I go out of my way?"

Natasha was upset, but trying to bury it. Paradoxically, a search for her parents would mean defying her mother.

With Natasha's permission, and with a release letter she wrote, I contacted the Pennsylvania Division of Vital Records, which handled the state's birth certificates. Then I wrote the Family Division of the Court of Common Pleas, in Philadelphia, which processed adoptions. Both offices could say whether Natasha's birth records were complete or whether there'd been an adoption.

"MOMMY HAD A FALL on a Thursday, and I called and called, but she couldn't get to the phone, because she was lying on the floor, unable to stand up."

Natasha was sitting in her living room, describing the weekend Dawn died. She said she went to her mother's apartment and had to break the window to get in. Dawn was on the floor, conscious but immobile.

People who'd known their relationship said it was one of the gentler points in the picture that Dawn and her daughter had become inseparable. After an emergency room visit, physicians sent mother and daughter home. "Other than her being dehydrated," Natasha said, "they couldn't find anything wrong."

Natasha spoke slowly about what happened next. "That was a hellified weekend. She never built up her strength, and she had trouble swallowing, even soup," Natasha said. "She'd lost twenty pounds in two months, and she was eighty-five pounds."

Dawn stayed with Natasha the whole weekend, her daughter nursing her. On Monday morning, Natasha got her kids off to school and prepared to take Dawn back to a doctor.

"She was in my son's room, in his bed at about eight-thirty or quarter to nine. I was washing her up, getting her ready, and she wet the bed, because she couldn't get up. Then I washed the bed and pulled her to the edge so I could change the sheets. She said, 'Natasha, I feel faint.' No sooner had I pulled her back onto the bed than her eyes rolled back in her head, and her face froze.

"I called 911, and they said I should keep talking to her. She wasn't breathing regularly, she was gasping, and I couldn't get a reaction. Her eyes fogged over—they were the prettiest green—I remember looking at her eyes, and they were almost gray."

Natasha was in a bit of a trance telling this story, as though it had happened to someone else. She lit a cigarette and dragged.

The emergency workers came, and an ambulance took mother and daughter away. But at the hospital Dawn's gurney went through one door, and Natasha, to her alarm, was shown through another. "In a few minutes, the doctor came in and said she was gone, and handed me Mommy's wedding ring." Natasha fingered the ring, on a chain around her neck.

The certificate of death said that Dawn Langley Hall Simmons passed away at 9:16 A.M. on September 18, 2000. It gave her occupation as "novelist." Dawn's friend Florence Haskell made funeral arrangements because, Natasha said, "I didn't know where to start."

The novelist was cremated and her ashes divided. One-third went to New Hampshire, to the friend who made a place in his garden. One-third to Natasha, one-third to England. I'd seen Natasha's container of remains. The New Hampshire man sent a photo of the shrine he'd made, a card table in his yard covered with pictures and mementos.

The English portion was interred on November 25, at All Saints Parish Church, in Old Heathfield, Sussex. Readings at the gravesite included Psalm 23 ("Yea, though I walk through the valley of the shadow of death") and John 14:1–6 ("In my Father's house are many mansions").

THE BUS STATION

John Zeigler, the ninety-year-old bookseller who'd given me his withering opinion of Gordon Hall, had an acquaintance in the Charleston suburbs with different memories. "The person who had a tryst with Dawn has agreed to speak with you," said a piece of e-mail that led me to the man.

I soon found myself a few miles from Charleston in a large garden curtained from its neighbors by trees, with flowers and plantings that looked like a life's work. Julian Hayes came out of the kitchen of his ranch house, a slight man with receded white hair and skin dappled by sun. He stood about five-four, maybe 130 pounds, and wore blue shorts, tennis shoes, and a cowboy shirt with snap buttons and flaps over dual breast pockets. He said his age was eighty-four, but like several men to whom I'd spoken, he looked twenty years younger. Why was this? Why in this story had appearances so often been deceiving? Things had reached a point that it surprised me when a surface sign corresponded to its conventional meaning.

"Two hours of vigorous walking in the morning, then a few hours every day in the garden," Hayes said to explain his youthful looks.

It turned out that Julian Hayes was a specialist in miniature roses, and he led the way down the manicured gravel paths of his flower beds, past rows of rose bushes, each labeled with a little sign ("Elizabeth Taylor," "Minnie Pearl"). After the roses came aisles of gardenias and camellias, banana trees, and bougainvillea. When we finally got to the house, Hayes produced a dish of key limes he'd grown to garnish drinks.

"The gossip when Gordon Hall came to Charleston made him sound like a pompous Englishman," said Hayes, fixing an iced Coke in a glass with rainbow stripes. "I pictured somebody of tall stature, not the small person I later met, accidentally."

Hayes sat down at the kitchen window, which overlooked a piece of the gardens. He had an easy smile and the manner of a Boy Scout, an association reinforced by his shorts. Like John Zeigler, Hayes was widowed: his partner of forty-seven years, Kip, had died in the 1990s.

"I met Gordon about 1963, as I said, by accident."

"Where?"

"At the Greyhound bus station, at a coffee shop there. People went to have coffee, and also for the men's room."

"Men went to cruise," I said.

"It was a very active bathroom in those days, because there weren't gay bars in Charleston," said Hayes. "So often you met people there, nice people. They might become your friends for life."

Hayes and his partner had moved in together in the late 1940s; the encounter with Gordon had come fifteen years later. Hayes said that Kip didn't mind the philandering.

"He would cruise sometimes, and I would cruise sometimes—or, we would do it together." He laced his hands and put his index fingers on his chin, forward body language to punctuate his story.

Although long retired, the vigorous Hayes still had a sexual presence. At one point, he took me to the refrigerator to show off pictures of his current lovers, stuck to the door with magnets. One was a Sri Lankan man in his thirties ("He's in town this week") and another, a black man who looked about forty-five ("A customs inspector in Charleston").

Hayes said he was alone the night he met Gordon. I asked what signals he might have used to advertise himself, and he laughed.

"To somebody who's gay, it's so obvious. A glance will tell you—or, in a place like that, there was a glory hole between the stalls, a big one."

He held his hands in a circle the size of a cantaloupe.

"I mean, a big, much-used glory hole. You would sit down and suddenly there would be someone showing his penis through the hole. I can't remember with Gordon how we communicated, but I didn't want to do it there. I don't know whether we were standing at the urinal, then signaled to one another, 'Okay, let's go,' or something else."

Julian Hayes had been raised in Durham, North Carolina, in the 1930s, and left the South to serve during World War II, which took him to Italy, Luxembourg, Paris, and Berlin. After the fighting he was transferred to New York, where, still in the army, he had a job at the Brooklyn Navy Yard.

"At that time, I had a girlfriend in North Carolina, named Tina. But in New York, I found out I was gay—at age twenty-seven."

This sounded odd, and Hayes shook his head.

"I know. Today you know in high school. I'm sure it was always there. A couple of times during the war, someone knocked me down and dragged me into the bushes, and I loved it. But to be a faggot, you never wanted to be that, and I was always fighting it." A gentle smile with the story.

Tina, the girlfriend, found another soldier to marry. Hayes met his partner Kip in Chicago in 1947, and they landed in Charleston, where Hayes's employer, the American Tobacco Company, had a cigar factory. Hayes worked for decades in office administration.

"After we bought this house, in 1950, people said Kip and I were the first ones to live openly as a gay couple in Charleston," he said.

Hayes's speech was unfailingly cheerful, but to get back to the bus station, I said, "You went to Gordon's house?"

"Yes. I think I'm the only person who will admit that he had sex with Gordon Langley Hall! Everybody thinks he was obnoxious—but at that time, he was not, and he was a nice-looking guy. He was also not Nelly, at all." Hayes was using old code for queeny behavior. "Swishy. He didn't act like a girl. He acted like a young man."

In the early 1960s, in Charleston and throughout the South, there were separate bathrooms for blacks and whites—which meant that black men, cruising, looked for the "colored" sign. Did white men pick up blacks?

"Never, never. I didn't know anyone who did that," Julian Hayes said. However, he added, he'd personally gotten over the taboo after the civil rights movement.

Hayes disagreed with his friend John Zeigler, who thought to be gay had once been easy in the South. It was hard to meet people, Hayes said. There were the fulminations of preachers, and the antisodomy laws meant you could be prosecuted for "the crime against nature."

"They'd use any excuse at all to get you," said Hayes, sipping his Coke. "A little sailor boy I used to know, who was gay—I say little, because the guy wasn't twenty-one—he was cruising one time, and a cop picked him up. Cop was going to take him to jail, so the boy said, 'I'd like to do something for you'—and the policeman, to his surprise, said, 'Okay.' The cop took him out and parked in the woods. The little boy did him in the car, and he didn't have to go to jail! He told me, 'I didn't mind very much, because it was very small.' " Hayes held up his pinky.

In Gordon's day, the bus station stood two blocks from his house at 56 Society. Hayes said that as he and Gordon left the men's room, Gordon led the way home.

"His accent was sort of phony, I thought, and finally I realized who he was. I said, 'Is your name Gordon?' He says, 'Yes.' I said, 'You're famous in Charleston, with your house, and being a writer, and I understand you've made a lot of friends here.' He said, 'No, not enough.' I'd heard Gordon had wanted to get into high society, to go with all the people downtown, but he said he was disappointed."

Julian followed Gordon upstairs to the bedroom.

"I was very much impressed. You see, he was built much bigger than the average man. He had a penis that was enviable."

"He was a slight person," I said.

Hayes answered, "Yeah, I'm small, and I think I'm built pretty heavy, but he was built *much* heavier."

I mentioned Dawn had said she'd been born with ambiguous genitalia. Hayes looked at the floor, and then looked back up.

"There was a penis and an asshole. Those were the two things
that might be useful."

"What was the sex like?"

"I only slept with him once, and we didn't do anything outra-
geous. In fact, I wasn't too turned on by him."

"Was it masochistic?"

"No, it was very mutual."

We talked a bit more about how it was to be queer in Charleston,
how Hayes and his friends played bridge, and what they served at
dinner parties. And before I left, Hayes had remembered another
incident with Gordon.

One night, Hayes and his partner invited Gordon to dinner, along
with some others, including John Zeigler, who came with the novelist Carson McCullers. "Gordon was sitting on the sofa in that living
room, next to Carson," said Hayes, pointing through the door.
"They were talking, and the conversation between the rest of us sort
of dropped, and we were listening to them. I don't know what they
had been talking about, but just then, Carson put her hand on Gordon's leg, patted it, and said, 'You know, you're just a little girl.' "

After an hour, I thanked Julian Hayes, and made my way out,
walking past the Elizabeth Taylor rose, and the beautiful Carmen
Miranda.

I HAD A STACK OF LETTERS and manuscripts from the Dawn Simmons
archive at Duke that I hadn't finished reading. Near the bottom of
the batch was a 150-page novella Gordon Hall had written in 1959
but never published. It was called "The Boy in Washington Square,"
and the story turned out to be an overlooked and obvious clue.

Washington Square, the heart of Greenwich Village, lies two
blocks from the house where Gordon had lived with Isabel Whitney.
The novella opens at night on a street near the square as the protag-

onist, a successful forty-year-old writer named Larry Carson, cruises for men. (Gordon was thirty-seven when he wrote this.) Carson eyes a nineteen-year-old with a suitcase, who looks lost. A few scenes later, the writer is lying awake in bed with him and feeling remorse for what he's done.

Carson hires his conquest as his "secretary," and the book tracks their affair through fairly chaste scenes of 1950s New York gay life, from antiques shops, to cozy cocktail parties, to country houses borrowed for the weekend. The writer becomes obsessed with his boyfriend (who's never named), but the nineteen-year-old eventually leaves Carson in an outbreak of independence. Carson sinks into jealousy and self-loathing, and one night he kills his former lover by strangling him. In a postscript, Carson is sitting on death row for the murder, musing on his confession to a priest. "You have committed a mortal sin," the cleric says—and it's unclear whether he means murder, or sodomy.

I didn't know whether Gordon had tried to publish his melodrama, but after browsing the story I had an idea how much shame he felt.

WHEN SEX-CHANGE SURGERY STOOD at the vanguard of American medicine, in the 1960s, the doctors who performed it were mavericks. Medical rebels are often young, so I guessed that some of Dawn's doctors might still be alive.

I located John Money, a psychiatrist at Johns Hopkins who'd been on the team that had screened Gordon Hall for surgery. He refused to talk, citing privacy. (He seemed to mean his own.)

Then I tried Dr. Milton Edgerton. Dawn had referred to Edgerton, her plastic surgeon, as the "miraculous hands" that had put her sex right. The Gender Identity Clinic had closed in 1979—evidently too risky for the Hopkins executive suite—and Edgerton had moved to the University of Virginia, in Charlottesville, from which, after a long stint, he'd eventually retired. I wrote him a letter and was surprised when the phone rang.

"Dawn Simmons really presented an interesting story," he said in a message.

It was mid-April, and the dogwoods were in bloom on the hills of central Virginia. Handsome houses occupied the ridges, and golf courses had eaten one or two valleys. Milton Edgerton lived on a horse farm where rail fences marked out his paddocks, creating a dark graph pattern over rolling green pasture. Beautiful, muscular horses walked the fences, and tulips were sprouting in the flower beds outside an impeccable ranch-style house.

Milton Edgerton came to the door, and so did a spaniel puppy. He led the way to a big room with a high ceiling and large windows that looked at the pasture; then he sat in a red leather chair and gave me the sofa.

"Transsexualism, even today, is not well understood by most physicians," he started. "When I graduated from Johns Hopkins Medical School in 1944, I'd never heard of it."

Edgerton was trim and fit, a handsome older man with a self-effacing manner. Sitting with his legs crossed, he relaxed and extended his arms, palms up, in a welcoming gesture. He had a square face and strong jaw, a full head of white hair, and pale blue eyes. He said he was eighty, but one could still see the striking young medical pioneer.

He was dressed in khaki pants, a striped polo shirt, and leather sandals. His voice was reedlike, with a faded Georgia accent, and he held his wire-rimmed glasses in his left hand as he talked.

"I was the first resident of plastic surgery at Johns Hopkins, and then became head of the new division of plastic surgery, in 1951," he said, ticking off the timeline. "We were treating all kinds of problems—head and neck cancer, hand surgery, congenital defects—and along the way I became aware of an occasional patient that showed up with gender problems."

Edgerton described the sex-change clinic that had operated in Casablanca in the 1950s, and another in Copenhagen, both run by people he knew.

"I got to know some of these patients because Hopkins was used as a bit of a hospital of last appeal, and we decided to look at the question, should American surgeons be treating them?"

In other words, disappointed sex-change patients returning from abroad had prompted the creation of the Gender Identity Clinic, in 1966.

Edgerton spoke slowly, in paragraphs, but he was modest and allowed himself to be interrupted.

The Gender Identity Clinic had psychiatrists, a urologist, a gynecologist, a clinical psychologist, a geneticist, and Edgerton, the plastic surgeon. Each saw the new patients in a merry-go-round evaluation process, and then all would confer. Initially, the ratio of patients ran about seven male-to-female transsexuals for every one female-to-male.

Gordon Hall came into Milton Edgerton's life in fall 1967, following in the footsteps of the first few cases. "I remember when I first interviewed her, she spent a good deal of time on her upbringing in England," said Edgerton. "Something about the grand dame who had sort of adopted her, an actress." He glanced away and glanced back with the name. "Margaret Rutherford?"

There was little doubt about the diagnosis: Gordon was a transsexual male with gender dysphoria, he said. "She was obviously sensitive and educated, wanted to know a lot about what we had learned, and she was very desirous of having surgery."

Outside the window, the dark horses ran soundlessly along the rail fences, a graceful distraction. Edgerton gestured slightly with his hands, and then laced his fingers in front of him.

"An interesting little surgical tidbit is that Dawn was one of the first two or three patients that we did a new operation on, for building a vagina. In her case we used a flap made of penile skin, which was very elastic and which contained its own blood supply. You actually invert the skin of the shaft of the penis on a blood-vessel-bearing pedical that we leave attached, and place it into the new cavity for the vagina. Penile skin is much better than skin grafting for making a vagina, and the principle of using it is still the dominant technique today." Edgerton added that in earlier surgeries, doctors had used scrotal tissue, but patients had complained about hair in the vagina.

Edgerton had overseen anatomical changes few people had occasion to witness, much less create. Dawn's story had already thrown light on some little-known facts, and now the technique of fabricating genitals took its place in this gallery of obscure knowledge.

When they arrived, the patients at the Gender Identity Clinic, far from being outsiders, received a welcome like friends. "Most of the members of our team felt extreme sympathy for them," said Edgerton. Also, by the time Gordon Hall made his appointments, some procedures had become standard.

"You remove the male testicles," Edgerton said. "You create a surgical channel, which is in the perineal region, posterior to or a little behind the prostate, which is left in place. When you create the vaginal pocket, you have to be very careful not to enter the rectum, the anal canal; if that's done, a fistula into the vagina would occur. Some of the muscles of the perineal have to be repositioned or weakened so there will be room for the vagina."

An entire surgery took two to three hours, including the making of a clitoris. "The clitoris is usually formed from some of the more sensitive tissue of the glans, which is saved along with nerve supply to it," Edgerton went on. "Generally, if the operation has been carried out effectively, the patients not only can have intercourse—we found the majority of them were experiencing orgasm."

"Are you aware that later in life Dawn claimed to have been born a girl, but misidentified as a boy?" I asked.

"That's what all transsexuals tell us," Edgerton said without pause, "that they are girls trapped in a male body. And there's not any ambivalence about it. Somehow their sense of feminine identity is indelible."

What physical exams were performed?

"We did a normal physical workup, but we did not find abnormalities that would be any different from males or females you might examine. In other words, these people were not hermaphroditic, but physically normal males and females."

When Dawn decided she was pregnant, she telephoned her doctor with the news. Remembering the call, Edgerton smiled for the first time. "And I said, 'Dawn, now, don't carry this too far. We'd love for you to be pregnant, but there's nothing we can do at this point to provide fertility.' She said, 'Oh, you don't know how well the operation has worked.' "

His own phone rang, Edgerton answered, and when he sat down again, he gave an interpretation of Dawn's so-called pregnancy.

"Another doctor and I thought she had a condition we call pseudocyesis, which many young women have who desperately want babies," he said. The plain name for the condition is hysterical pregnancy. "The women become convinced they're pregnant, and their abdomens swell. Maybe Dawn had pseudocyesis—either that, or she was just pulling our leg."

Edgerton said he tried to get Dawn to come back to the hospital from Charleston, telling her that hers could be a history-making case. He promised free examinations and treatment, but "Obviously, we couldn't get her to come."

He was smiling a lot now, but they were indulgent smiles, not mocking ones.

"There was another call, and she wanted us to know the baby had arrived!" Edgerton said. "I don't know whether she left town and got this baby somewhere. We could never quite get her to level with us as to where the child came from."

"Dawn did not have a uterus or ovaries?"

"No, there was no suggestion of that," said Edgerton.

"She was not a hermaphrodite."

"Not a hermaphrodite in any sense. Her anatomy was perfectly normal male."

"She claimed to have been born with an enlarged clitoris and a hidden vagina."

"We saw no evidence of that," Edgerton added, shaking his head. "We heard stories like that from a number of the patients, who wanted to convince themselves that everything was just as it should be."

Milton Edgerton folded his arms, a little tired of this line of questioning.

"I think Dawn knew we weren't fooled," he finished.

The surgeon said Dawn was a transsexual, which was not proof that Gordon was a gay man.

"True homosexuals never want surgery, never want anything done to their genitalia. They are a totally different category."

He also said that he'd stored the files of numerous patients, and Dawn's might be among them. But later, after making a search, Edgerton said her records hadn't surfaced.

A glass coffee table stood between us, and on it were various books, along with a black sculpture of a cougar. I looked at the red leather chair in which Dawn's surgeon sat. At the ends of the armrests were carved wooden figures that appeared to be the heads of dogs.

Her doctor had exposed Dawn Simmons, the intersexual mom, as a faker. Or more gently, maybe he'd implied that she was a patient with delusions. Either way, I felt disappointed: I'd wanted Dawn to be the person she'd said she was. Gradually, however, the disillusionment faded and a beam of amazement grew in its place until it canceled the other emotion.

The scale of Dawn's desire seemed astonishing. She'd insisted on her story for so long, to so many people, and at such cost! Her appetite must have been immeasurably vast to put herself through such a gauntlet. I had to feel a tinge of awe.

CHERYL CHASE, THE INTERSEX ACTIVIST NEAR SAN FRANCISCO, had also had experience with transsexuals who invented false anatomical states. One of Chase's stories, which had passed over my head when she first told it, now came back to mind.

She was sitting in her backyard in northern California, a few yards from her chickens, when she remembered the case of Agnes.

"Robert Stoller, a psychiatrist, was at the University of California in the 1950s," Cheryl Chase said, "where he saw a patient named Agnes, who had a man's body." Chase's somewhat masculine features seemed to echo the straight way she told a story. "Agnes told Stoller she was intersex, and that she had started to feminize."

Stoller the psychiatrist interviewed Agnes and examined her body. Therapy sessions continued, and meanwhile, Agnes grew breasts and wide hips. Stoller, flabbergasted, concluded that Agnes had a heretofore-unknown intersex condition that caused her to transition to a feminine identity in midlife, and he published articles asserting the amazing facts.

Cheryl Chase smiled. "Well, Agnes came back several years later and said, 'Nah, nah! I fooled you! I was taking hormones!' Stoller had been strung along, completely taken in, because he wanted to believe her."

Agnes, like Dawn, was an intersex imposter.

I tracked down the Agnes case in an academic journal, and the facts were as Chase remembered. In 1958, the young patient had come to Dr. Robert Stoller in Los Angeles, alleging a sexual abnormality. Agnes had a penis and scrotum, but was growing breasts and hips, and his skin was softening. He wanted surgery to remove his male genitalia and remedy nature's "mistake."

It turned out that Agnes was a genetically normal nineteen-year-old man who'd been raised as a boy, but who had been living as a woman since age seventeen.

Eight years later, Agnes told Stoller that he'd lied, that the feminization of his body was not due to "testicular feminization syndrome." He'd been taking estrogen, stealing hormones that had been prescribed for his mother. Robert Stoller was embarrassed yet also amazed that Agnes could have pulled off the act.

Cheryl Chase said that Agnes's performance wasn't unique. "Some people write me and say they're intersex, and then they tell us a story that doesn't make any biological sense at all," she said.

Chase was talking about mail that came to her foundation, the Intersex Society of North America. She said such people thought their transsexualism would be less trouble if they had a "real" biological excuse.

Intersex fakers, Chase added, don't want to hear medical information. "They want confirmation for their transgender feelings. When this happens, we refer them to a transsexual support group." Chase clarified, "But they say, 'No, those are perverts, and I'm just intersexed.'"

The reason for the deception, she speculated, was stigma. Whereas intersex people were innocently born, transsexualism appeared as a disorder in the *Diagnostic and Statistical Manual*, the mental illness encyclopedia.

Dawn had lied. (She'd asserted a counterfactual medical history, a therapist might say.) But it appeared she was so carried away by the possibility she might really be female that toward the end—and maybe from the beginning—she truly believed she was female.

Chase said she'd encountered other transsexuals with similar delusions.

"We sometimes hear from people who want us to help them recover memories of their sex reassignment," she said, shaking her head. "These are usually anatomic men who have transgender feelings, and penises that look a lot like other men's penises. They think somebody did something to make them a boy when they were a child, and they tell me, 'I know that I'm intersexed, because there's a line that goes along the bottom of my penis. That's where my parents had my vagina stitched shut.'" She smiled at the quaint interpretation.

Dawn Simmons might have been an intersex pretender, but perhaps she couldn't be faulted for her act. She was trying to live in a world that had no place for her.

The person who paid a price for Dawn's fantasies, the real casualty of her trapeze, was Natasha Simmons. Natasha had been raised on the invented self her mother offered others, and it couldn't have been easy, particularly because Dawn wanted her daughter to accept the story.

IN MY FATHER'S HOUSE

Now that Dawn's identity had cracked, the last and most resistant mystery remained—that of Natasha's actual parents. Stories about her origin had already surfaced. John Zeigler had one hearsay version, strange and plausible.

The retired bookseller in Charleston was sitting on the yellow-and-green couch in the library of his antebellum house when he offered me an account of a child's appearance in his croaking gravelly voice.

"Did you ever know Schindler's Antiques, on King Street?" he said. "A big place run by a dealer named Herman Schindler, who's been dead ten years. Herman told me Gordon had paid five thousand dollars for Natasha. Gordon had gotten some person he knew to find him a mulatta child, just born. And for the money, Gordon got Natasha. Schindler told me that in all truth, and I have every reason to believe it's so."

Zeigler was amused by Dawn, but in a caustic way, and the story of the retailed infant gave him a certain gratification.

"Schindler was not the type that would have lied to me. I'd known him for many years," Zeigler said. "If one of his friends told him he'd been part of this, it would have been true."

I'd heard other accounts of Natasha's birth, but none could be verified. Somebody said she was the daughter of John-Paul Simmons's sister. Somebody else made her the child of a sailor from Puerto Rico. But Zeigler's version was the most detailed.

He said, "People hear all kinds of things, and Schindler wouldn't have regarded this as anything unusual, because there were so many unusual things happening around Dawn."

I wondered how Zeigler's feelings about Gordon had changed over the years. "We always regarded him as a nice young man, who became more and more obsessive, lying about everything," Zeigler said, wrapping his case.

*   *   *

A LETTER CAME BACK from the birth records office in Pennsylvania, addressed to Natasha Simmons.

> In accordance with Section 1.49 of Pennsylvania Code, Title 28, the Division of Vital Records can only release information from the original Certificate of Live Birth if both biological parents have filed with our office a Biological Parent Registration Identification Form. Upon reviewing our files, we have determined that neither of your parents has filed such forms as of this date.

This meant that Natasha's birth certificate didn't match the earlier "certificate of live birth" on which it was based. Which meant there'd been an adoption. But the paper keepers wouldn't reveal the names of the birth parents without their written consent.

A second letter arrived from the Family Court Division of Philadelphia County. That notice confirmed the first piece of news. The court said it could initiate a search for Natasha's birth parents, but even if they could be found, the decision of whether to give their names would be theirs.

THE DAY THE LETTERS ARRIVED, the wheel of discovery turned again when the phone rang with a call from Albany. The man on the line said he was the housing supervisor of John-Paul Simmons. "J-P can meet you," the voice said. "He doesn't have many responsibilities, and he might like lunch."

After my failed reconnaissance mission to Albany, I thought John-Paul had been lost to fate. But here he was, or at least someone near him. The man added that John-Paul had his own apartment in Albany in a program for outpatients.

As I drove into Albany, I couldn't quite believe he'd surfaced, and told myself that the elusive John-Paul would never show for an appointment. Following instructions, I went to a branch office of

Rehabilitation Support Services, the nonprofit organization that ran housing for psychiatric clients. In the basement of a large 1970s apartment building, four windowless rooms were furnished with folding chairs, filing cabinets, and long tables for desks. The man who'd called was there, a tall, thin social worker named Rich McCarthy who had a quiet manner and graying hair.

"Some background on J-P," he said. "His diagnosis is schizophrenia, and he takes medicine every day. Also, every Wednesday he gets an injection. The shot brings him way down, and he sometimes slurs his speech."

It was a Wednesday, and John-Paul would be coming to lunch from the shot.

"I don't know how much he'll be able to remember," McCarthy warned.

John-Paul Simmons entered the basement, looking shy. He had a halting step, and there was awkwardness in his greeting because he wasn't used to strangers. He was in his midfifties but had been through a lot, and stress showed in deep furrows on his brow and cheeks. Standing about five-seven, he looked to be 180 pounds, much lighter than Natasha guessed. (She remembered when he'd been up to three hundred.)

Natasha had said, "He used to look like a bum," but at our meeting he looked pretty good. He wore khakis, white tennis shoes with Velcro straps, a yellow cotton T-shirt, and a gray windbreaker.

John-Paul had arrived with Becki Ida, his caseworker, a twenty-something white woman with long brown hair that fell in corkscrew curls. Both she and Rich McCarthy spoke to John-Paul as though they'd been around him a lot. Becki Ida said they'd just left the psychiatric hospital, where he'd taken the shot.

The patient looked at me with his chin slightly up and jaw stuck out, gazing down his nose with clear eyes. The gaze seemed harsh, until I realized this was his customary regard. He had a broad, flat nose and ample jaw covered with a salt-and-pepper beard. His hair was short, with specks of gray; his lips were full, and his skin dark brown.

Rich McCarthy said, "J-P, this man wants to talk about your wife and about Charleston. Do you think you can remember things from that long ago?"

"I remember everything," he answered instantly. John-Paul sat down. "Things won't go away."

He looked at McCarthy, along his nose. His speech was slurred, as though from barbiturates.

"Where do you want me to start?" he said, turning to me. He volunteered that the last time he saw Dawn was when she fled New York State for Charleston, leaving him behind.

"It hurt, because we had the nicest house we'd had in a long time," he went on. "I loved that house, on Union Street in Hudson. And I came home one time, and Dawn said, 'Pack your things, because we have to leave.' Then she went to Charleston, and I was hurt and angry." In shock, he'd cut off his wife and daughter, he said.

John-Paul looked me in the eye without blinking, or smiling, or glancing away. His pattern of speech was to talk nonstop, with none of the usual smiles and solicitation of a first meeting. Instead, he said what he felt, as though talking to a therapist. I guessed he'd been in a lot of therapy.

A prominent feature of John-Paul's appearance, missing from old photographs, was his furrowed brow. Years of agitation had left two deep worry lines on his forehead, which made the shape of two *V*s, one on top of the other, their bottom point landing between his eyes.

John-Paul's speech was muddy, and some of what he said was unintelligible. But beneath the psychotropic drugs and machine-gun delivery, I heard the reassuring sound of a South Carolina accent. The lilt in his vowels transported both of us to Charleston.

"Call me J-P," he said. "That's what my mother named me. Dawn called me Johnny."

He hadn't been to Charleston in twelve years. I told him about buildings pulled down and replaced, and we nodded at the names of streets and stores we both knew. This seemed to relax him, because no one in John-Paul's life in Albany could talk about his hometown, which still stood at the center of his disarrayed personality.

There was one tic. Every couple of minutes, John-Paul opened his mouth wide, stuck out his tongue, then pulled it back in. It was a large tongue and yellow on the top. I asked if he smoked, and he said he rolled his own cigarettes, even though his caseworker, Becki, was trying to get him to quit. "The medicine makes my mouth dry," he said. "That's why I put out my tongue."

We went to lunch, along with Becki, at an atmospheric old bar called the Lark Restaurant (sign on the door: "Established 1933"). It was one long, smoky room with a big bar in the front and a dim eating section in the back. A jukebox spun rock-and-roll CDs, and a pool table stood unused in the middle of things, waiting for the night crowd. We sat at a dark oak table that had been wiped clean of beer, or most of it.

Becki Ida turned to J-P. "Help with the menu?"

He said, "Yes." With coaching, he whittled his choice to fried chicken.

Diminished by the injection, J-P had trouble smiling, but the whites of his eyes were clear. He said he'd been born January 11, 1948. "They helped me find I was really born in 1948, not '47, like I thought."

A scratchy voice, fast, and always the slur. "They" meant psychiatric workers.

J-P talked about his childhood. He said he had seven brothers and five sisters. His dad had operated a crane at the Charleston Navy Yard, unloading ships; his mom was a housewife, and the family lived in a modest wooden house on an old street called Montagu. But J-P's father, not long before he'd finished forty years on the job, was arrested for theft of navy property. He got seven years, which he served at a federal prison in Florida.

The schools were segregated, and J-P didn't know many white people. "Went up to eighth grade, then quit," he said, "because that's when Dad started his stuff, started charging us to live in his house, when we were kids."

Before going to prison, his dad ran a strict house and made his teenaged children pay rent. At age fourteen, J-P got a job as a delivery boy at Henry's Cut Rate drugstore.

"Fourteen dollars a week, full-time, and I gave half of it to daddy."

He was a poor black kid in a city with thousands like him, trying to make it before the civil rights movement, which wouldn't have much effect on things in Charleston anyway. What J-P really liked to do was fish. He borrowed boats or just stood at the water's edge to catch mullet, crab, and catfish, which he sold on the street.

It was delivery hour at the Lark Restaurant. A truck driver wheeled big aluminum beer kegs through a side door. Speakers pumped 1980s pop songs into the large room, which was thinly peopled with sandwich eaters.

Jumping to the present, J-P said, "I love my family, but they disowned me."

After his life had spun into madness, he'd lost touch with everyone and hadn't spoken to relatives for years. He said he knew his father was dead. When I told him his mother was alive, he smiled a little.

After the drugstore, J-P's next job was as a waiter at Big John's Tavern, a funky bar in Ansonborough, Dawn's neighborhood; and after that, as a junior mechanic at Simmons Motor Company, an old car dealership. (The owners belonged to a different Simmons family, a white one.)

We'd reach the point in J-P's life when he'd met Dawn, and he suddenly started using a new tone. His drug-impaired tongue seemed to lie down and behave, and he shifted to a monologue that led me into his world.

"Every night I used to get my bicycle and just ride around the peninsula," he said, leveling his gaze. "And one night, I saw on the side a white man, and a colored girl, and another colored boy. I knew the colored girl. She introduced me to Gordon. Then she said, 'Want to go a party on Columbus Street?' I said, 'I have to go home and take a bath.' I started to pull off, and the man said, 'What's your name?' I told him. He said, 'What are you doing?' I said, 'Going to a party.' He said, 'Don't go to the party, just sit here and talk.' So I sat, and we started talking, talking, talking. He said, 'Walk me home,' so I did—got to his front door and said good night. That was Gordon."

As J-P talked (and he must have gone thirty minutes without a break), it was plain that he'd dwelled on this section of his life.

"Two weeks passed. One night, I passed his house, and he was sitting there by hisself. I said, 'Hello, Gordon.' He said, 'Hello, John-Paul.' We sit there and we talk."

J-P pronounced the name *Gar-den*. I'd seen photographs from summer 1967, when these events took place. J-P was skinny, smiling, handsome, and nineteen years old—a good-looking package. Gordon was forty-five, boyish but getting on.

"Then he start—she start getting beside the point."

For the first time, J-P called Gordon both *he* and *she* in the same sentence. "Beside the point" meant that Gordon had come on to him.

"So I told him, 'I don't play that way.' He said, 'Why?' And I said, 'I never had any use to go that way with anyone.' I only had messed with women. I jumped on my bicycle and go on."

J-P had his arms folded on the table, and he nodded lightly at every plot point. His delivery was controlled, but gradually it intensified, with hand gestures pushing the air.

"She had a friend named Gussie, and she made Gussie search the whole of Charleston to find me. Gussie find me, and said, 'You know, that man's in love with you.' I said, 'Gussie, don't mess, don't start! You know I don't play! I'm not going around him.' But next morning, I'm going to work, and she come back like that, Gussie come with him to my work!"

J-P looked sheepish, bowed his head, rubbed his scalp with his palm and smirked.

"I said, 'Gussie why you bringing him in the place where I work? Now he knows, he could be a menace! She said, 'All right,' and they go. The boss said to get to work, so I tried to. Got off that night, a car pulled up. She got out the car, with Gussie driving. 'You like this guy?' said Gussie."

J-P smiled and shook his head, like he thought he was telling a story nobody could trust. He held his hand parallel to the table, then turned it upside down.

"You just can't believe this!" he went on. "I said, 'Gordon, I'm trying to tell you, not trying to be funny, it ain't going to work!' So I pull off, go walking. Next day, another car pulls up, and it's Gussie and Gordon. Man! Finally, I went to a preacher, because this was getting stupid. The preacher said, 'Do what you want to do, not what I want you to do.' I said, 'Charleston is too little to do something like this.' I told my old friend from my street, Rufus, and he said, 'You're going to get into this, and you ain't getting out.' "

I realized that not only did J-P remember things almost photographically, but he'd been obsessed with the past. It was as though he'd composed his life with Dawn into a film and memorized every frame. To tell the story, all he had to do was turn on the projector.

The telling had an inevitable drive, as though he could only push to the end. The caseworker, Becki Ida, looked on as J-P talked, but her eyes were distracted. She didn't follow his convoluted tale, didn't know the people or places. The only thing J-P's caregivers knew was that a long time ago, he'd had some sort of strange marriage.

"So I go to work, at Simmons Motor Works," J-P said, "and got off about four-thirty. I was sitting there in Market Street, and another car pulled up. And he got out the car dressed like a girl!"

J-P paused, looked straight for a moment while this registered, shook his head, and laughed.

"Man! I said, 'What are you doing?!' " J-P shivered and laughed, because he still found this funny. "I knew it was Gordon, you couldn't mistake it. And he said, 'I want to give all this to you, if you will only love me.' I said, 'I can't do it! I can't play this game in this fucking place! People see me with you, they say I must be mad!' "

According to friends, Gordon had shown no sign of being a trannie before he met J-P. Which meant the speculation of John Zeigler, the elderly bookseller, was right: Gordon thought he could please his man with skirts and heels.

"So he's standing at the car, crying, and he got in the car and go." J-P waved his hand to show Gordon riding off. "I'm sitting there, and saying, this is getting absolutely crazy! This man, he insist he's going to do this. What am I going to do?

"I go talk to my momma, and she said, 'Boy, don't get involved with those people, because they're hard.' "

J-P's face fell a bit, and he swallowed. By "those people," his mother meant white people, or maybe gay whites.

"Momma said, 'You can't get loose from them.' So I said, 'All right.' And after that, every time I see him, I walked off."

The food came to the table, and in front of J-P there was now a big pile of chicken. He took a bite and slowed down.

"A few days later, I was sitting in Brooks Restaurant, where some of the high-class colored people go, dressed up, eating chicken. When who walk in that door dressed like a clown? Her!" He reached out with his right hand palm up, and then put his hands together as though to pray. The clown part meant women's clothes.

"I said, 'How you find me?' Everybody in the restaurant turned right around, looking. I dropped my fork, and said, 'Dawn—Gordon. This isn't fair.' I said, 'Come on, let's go.' " He followed Gordon to Society Street, the point of no return.

At the mansion, still in women's clothes, Gordon showed J-P his antiques, and impressed him with his servants.

"I told him, 'You come around like this again, I'll throw a punch. You gotta put man's clothes on,' " J-P said. "So she stopped and went back to a man's clothes."

Gordon and J-P started going out to movies, or on walks. They couldn't go to restaurants, not because they were two men, but because no white kitchen served black people, and J-P was too shy to show up at a black restaurant, where he'd be targeted for gossip.

"She said, 'When are you going to live with me?' And I said, 'When you move away and go up north, because we can't live down here. Somebody will kill me, or kill you.' She said, 'Johnny! Ha-ha! Nobody going to kill us!' "

It sounded strange, but when J-P gave these lines, he used an effeminate voice, like a macho man imitating a fag.

J-P said, "Before that, I didn't know what 'gay' was." More gestures, a finger waving behind his right ear.

Suddenly, I remembered Gordon Hall's 1959 manuscript, *The Boy in Washington Square*, and it seemed uncanny how the novella's forty-year-old protagonist and his nineteen-year-old object of desire fit so cleanly over J-P's story, though the book had been written eight years before these events.

Gordon and J-P were living together off and on. "Next thing, I'm sitting in the house, waiting for him, and he come in the room and said, 'I gonna have an operation.' " Again the swishy voice. J-P dropped his jaw and shook his head in disbelief. "He came in and announced this! I slapped her back, because I didn't want to beat her up. I knew that in Charleston, it's bad enough working a white man. You work a white lady, you're dead. You ain't got a chance."

Weeks passed when Gordon dropped the subject. "I thought it was out, and she forgot about it. But he come in, said, 'I'm going to Hopkins to get a checkup.' She went to Baltimore, called me two weeks later. I went to the airport to pick her up, and she's there dressed to kill—in women's clothes! I looked at her, and I said, 'I'm dead.' "

The story had sped up. Previously, J-P had remembered individual scenes, but now weeks of detail went past with small mention.

When Gordon returned from Hopkins—this had been his second visit, when his doctors told him to live as a woman—he and J-P drove home. They went upstairs. "And she get out of these clothes. There was no operation yet, it was the same as before. I said, 'You ain't changed a bit,' and she said, 'I gotta go back.' I knew something was going to happen."

J-P went with Dawn to Baltimore to see Dr. Edgerton and others at the Gender Identity Clinic. Maybe this way, he could prevent it. At

Johns Hopkins, Edgerton sized up the white, middle-aged Gordon and his black, teenaged friend, and tried to talk the patient out of surgery. J-P remembered Edgerton saying it would be a mistake.

"He said, 'We don't know how long you're planning to live, but it ain't going to be a whole time like a normal person, because you're gonna catch all kinds of pain. You going to be every way but the way you want to be. We don't want to do the operation.' And also he said, 'But if you say so, we'll do it.' "

J-P put on his imitation of effeminate Gordon, and held his hands together in a prayer. "Gordon said, 'I want the operation.' "

Back in Charleston, J-P lost control, he said, because he was scared. "I beat her until she cried, 'Have mercy!' and she ran off. I go all around Charleston looking for her, bring her back home. After that, she didn't want the operation, because I told her not to."

He thought he'd put an end to the sex change. Also, he thought it was time to get out. "I said this was enough for me, so I rented a little house on Johns Island."

Johns Island is rural farmland a half hour from Charleston, with creeks that finger through marshes, and plenty of places to fish. J-P moved there alone, but Dawn found him and coaxed him back. She promised not to have surgery if J-P would live with her and allow her to wear women's clothes.

"I said, 'You ain't going to get the operation?' " J-P went on. "And she said yes, that she'd be staying the same. Then she went right back to Hopkins, and had the operation!" J-P pushed back in his chair, disgusted.

A year had passed from the start of their affair to the surgery. After the sex reassignment, Dawn became an attraction in Charleston, an oddity people went out of their way to see.

One night, J-P and his friend Rufus were sitting in the yard on Society Street, drinking. "There was people crawling over the fence, up on the railing, just to see her! Rufus said, 'John-Paul, go home to your family before you get killed. She's not worth it.' So I left her, after the operation. Next thing, She come around my house, dripping with sweat. She said, 'I want you back.' But I said, 'Till hell freezes over!' "

IT MIGHT HAVE BEEN QUIXOTIC to ask for Dawn's truth from a schizophrenic. Was any of this real, or was it another pail of dreams? J-P's life was wreckage, and for all I knew, he lived half the day in fugues. He received $640 a month in Social Security payments for his mental illness, and he said he took Clozoril, a strong psychoactive compound, every afternoon. (Becki Ida, his caseworker, brought the drug every day and watched as he took it.) The weekly injection of a neuroleptic further sedated J-P to passivity.

But the hallmark of sanity is an ability to narrate a credible story. In this, J-P outclassed his former wife, and for that matter, most others who'd aired their version of Dawn. When he talked, his mind came alive, and his story carried strong emotions—shame, amusement, curiosity—all of which he still felt. I could see him shaking off the sedation, like a man coming out of the waves, trying to breathe, and holding his truths above the water.

One also couldn't overlook the possibility that Dawn Simmons might have aggravated J-P's madness. She seemed to have been delusional, and as she pulled the kid J-P deeper into her life, first her demands, and then her transformation from man to woman, descended on the young man-child.

What might have become of the cute auto mechanic had he not bicycled into the sights of Gordon Hall?

The day after our lunch at the Lark Restaurant, I made a visit to J-P's apartment. When I arrived, he was sitting on the stoop outside the building, watching cars go by.

John-Paul Simmons lived in a three-room apartment in a four-story brick building that was showing its age. Outpatients occupied most of the apartments, several on each floor. "I don't see the other people," J-P said. "Don't go anywhere either. To the grocery, then back home."

The apartment was about four hundred square feet, with a little bedroom, tiny living room, closet-sized kitchen and bath. Second-hand furniture filled the rooms somewhat randomly, and a broken TV tube sat on a table ("I'm trying to fix it"). Dirty dishes sat in the kitchen sink, an unfinished plate of food rested on the bed, and shoes and clothes lay scattered on the floor. There were no books or maga-zines anywhere, except a single Book of Mormon on a table, which I guessed an evangelist had handed to J-P.

When asked, J-P brought out some of his artwork. He could no longer make sculptures—no space or materials—but he could draw, and he put a stack of eleven-by-seventeen-inch drawings on the table. Each consisted solely of a woman's face, an oval for the head, and squiggly additions for hair, ears, mascara. The faces had no back-ground, and the drawings, dozens of them, seemed to be a record of obsession.

J-P sat on a low sofa and told the story of how he and Dawn lost the majestic house on Society Street. Then he said how the baby came.

"After the operation, she talked about it all the time, having a baby," J-P said. "So we move, they kick us out of Society Street. We living there, on Thomas and Warren Streets. I'm out in the living room one day, and I go to the bedroom to find her, but she's gone. I find a little baby on the bed! With the navel string ain't even dry!"

Dawn had gone out and left Natasha, newborn, with a wet umbil-ical cord. Waving his finger back and forth, J-P pushed his head for-ward, stopping in midair for effect.

"She said, 'How do you like it?' I said, 'Where'd you get this from?' She said, 'I had it.' Oh, man!"

He shook his head and rubbed his palm over his hair, coughed.

"I said, 'Dawn, we'll get arrested if you don't do something fast with her.' I took the baby from her, took her home to my parents, and I said, 'Momma, the little girl gonna die, and we're going to go to the electric chair.' "

"Where do you think Natasha came from?" I said.

J-P pushed his chin up and looked along his nose. "She didn't give birth to no baby, because she stole it!"

He made eye contact.

"I had another girlfriend, light skin, like a white girl, but she was black."

John-Paul told me the woman's name, and I'll call her Delores.

"I'd been going with her for eight months—constantly had sex, sex, sex, all the time with this girl. She was about twenty-three. She got pregnant, and she told her daddy who the daddy was." J-P pointed at himself. "Delores's daddy said, 'You already got kids, take it to that white woman.' So that's why Dawn got ahold of her. That was Delores's baby. *Delores is Natasha's mother.*"

In a minute, J-P mentioned Delores's full name, said where she lived, and laid out the rest. As J-P told it, when Delores went into labor, she took herself to Charleston's Roper Hospital, on Calhoun Street, where she registered as "Mrs. Simmons." Within a day or two, Dawn had come to the hospital and taken the baby home.

J-P said he went to Delores later, angry, and asked her, " 'Why you didn't take her and give her to me?' "—meaning give *him* Natasha. " 'How much money did Dawn give you?' Delores said, 'A thousand dollars.' I told her, 'I thought so!' and I walked off."

"You're Natasha's father?" I said.

"I'm her father."

He smiled a sweet smile, nodded, and for the first time since we'd met, the tension went out of his face. He looked proud. "Tell me about Natasha. Is she eating all right?"

Delores's father had made all the arrangements. He knew Dawn wanted a baby, and Delores was light-skinned enough for it to work, so he'd gone to Dawn with an offer.

J-P added, "I don't know how much money he got—but he got something."

"Why did Dawn go to Philadelphia?" I asked.

"To publish a book! She didn't go there to get a baby!"

One of Dawn's publishers, Macrae Smith, was indeed in Philadelphia. But Natasha's birth certificate also came from Pennsylvania.
Why?

J-P looked across the room into the kitchen.

Suddenly it made sense. Dawn needed papers for Natasha, but
securing a new birth certificate in Charleston would have been
impossible. Dawn was notorious, and she would have been recognized and questioned. Also, the mandatory race classification of all
infants in South Carolina would have caused trouble. Where had the
white lady gotten a black baby?

Natasha was born October 17, 1971, but the birth certificate had
been issued November 4. It was an excellent ploy. Dawn had flown to
Pennsylvania to see her publishers, bringing along her infant girl.
She carried the original record of birth, which listed the mother as
"Mrs. John-Paul Simmons," the name Delores had assumed in the
hospital. In Philadelphia, Dawn showed up at the vital records office,
an infant in her arms and papers in hand, with her own married name
on them. She flew home with government-issued proof of her motherhood.

The child was named after a Tolstoy character that Dawn had
admired in *War and Peace*. As for child care, J-P left everything to his
wife.

"She didn't want no help—all she wanted was that baby, who
would call her 'Momma,' " J-P said, stretching out his arm for emphasis. "She wanted to be the first man ever bring a baby up!"

Sitting on his sofa, J-P looked at the wall and shook his head. "I tell
you, if I was a drinking man, they'd have put me in the nuthouse. If I
was messing with dope, I probably would be dead!" he said. He could
hardly believe it himself. "It used to make me so damn confused."

And for the rest of the story, J-P confirmed what I knew. They'd
moved away from Charleston, and things had spun out of control in
Catskill. He was sent to the hospital for long stretches of time. "I
loved it," he said. "Clean bed, all the food I can eat, stayed clean, give
them my clothes, they wash them."

But they were lost years, and he knew it.

Dawn's choreographed life had turned him inside out, and he'd never recovered. "She can be pretty close to a woman," he said. "But I actually stood there and saw this man *change* from a man to a woman. I sit there with both eyes open and saw this!"

His eyes were wide as he said these things, showing old shock.

He asked, "Did you ever talk to her?"

"She wrote me a letter, but I never spoke to her," I told him.

"You're luckier than me."

It was getting to lunchtime, and J-P had to take his medicine for the day, so I made to go. His angry voice stopped for a minute, and he looked wistful.

"Don't get me wrong," J-P said slowly, his feelings pushed to the surface. "I fell in love with her. And I prayed nobody would harm her. She was like a dream."

I thought I saw a change in his eyes, a dimming of his presence in the room, and he retreated into his memory.

NATASHA NEEDED TO KNOW what her dad had said. At her dining-room table, she looked expectant as her three-year-old daughter tramped around. She finally told the little girl to go to the next room, and she closed the door.

I asked whether Natasha had heard the name Delores, and I recited the full name, which J-P had given.

"No, who's that?"

I repeated John-Paul's story, and Natasha's eyes filled with water. But she didn't cry. (I hadn't seen her weep at Dawn's funeral, either.)

"All this time I was thinking—" She broke off but then added, "Mommy must have had her reasons, and I have to respect that."

Natasha said she wasn't eager to find her biological mother, Delores, who seemed to have sold her. But she wanted to talk to her dad. J-P was her real father, and not, as she'd come to think, her adoptive one.

"It'll take me a while to process," said Natasha, nodding. I gave her J-P's whereabouts and phone, and Natasha's little girl came back from the next room.

CHANGELING

Sometimes she referred to Natasha as "my greatest achievement." Indeed, Dawn had turned out to be a performer who lived an elaborate script, and her finest role had been "mother."

The drama had called for frequent changes of character. Role number one: Gordon Kenneth Ticehurst, who would change his name to Gordon Hall, the skinny, rejected boy with a likely future as a servant. Little Gordon had been Dawn's core, which she spent years trying to transcend. Born in rural England four years after Britain had buried seven hundred thousand in World War I, Gordon had grown up in an immobile, hierarchical society in which class was destiny, much depended on conformity and reputation, and deference to one's superiors was demanded at all times. His was a frozen world in which the son of an unmarried shopgirl would suffer whispers and knowing looks, the gossip harvest of his mother's sexual desire.

Barred from upward mobility, Gordon moved laterally into fantasy, which led to role number two: the teenaged performer who entertained the troops. While dancing in the light, this "chorus girl" probably learned the lessons of sex and shame. The two were inseparable if you were queer in a place where everyone knew you and it was still thirty years before Stonewall.

When Gordon fled Britain for Canada and the United States, he learned to edit his life to impress strangers. To new friends he played role number three, the writer who'd grown up at Sissinghurst Castle. (He didn't specify that he'd written about the jams and jellies competition at the county fair, or that his family had done the mistress's laundry.) Gordon carried his writerly pose to New York, where he presented it to Isabel Whitney, the manor-born American. Whitney probably saw through the disguise, but she liked the young man's chatty manner and affectionate nature, and her money gave him the clothes and street address he needed to enlarge his dreams. In 1956, Gordon went home to England to buy Beecholme, the fine house in Heathfield, and by doing so succeeded in modeling his literary self for his childhood friends.

The several pieces came together perfectly in Charleston, which provided Gordon with role number four, the Southern gentleman-author. He lived in a mansion, wrote books, and bossed servants. By this time (he moved to Charleston in 1962, the year he turned forty), Gordon trusted his embellished biography, which in turn made it more believable to others.

America is the land of self-invention, where you are what you do, or what you look like you do, and, if the facade sticks, no one probes deeply into your past. Gordon's manufactured life wouldn't have been possible in England, where he'd have been betrayed by his cockney accent and half-education, and put back in his place. But Charleston didn't know any better, and the early years of his residence there gave Gordon a stage for his script, which is why he loved the place.

"Charleston is a city with Gothic tales, and what they don't know, they make up," Dawn once said in a TV interview.

It might have ended there, in a refrain of dinner parties with black waiters and buying trips for antiques. But Gordon had another character in the wings, one that would undo him; and that was role number five, the sexual libertine. Cruising for boyfriends actually caused him little trouble, however, until it brought him to John-Paul Simmons.

He must have known that the business with John-Paul could sabotage his constructed self. On the one hand, it is possible that self-destruction was what Gordon wanted, because he felt he really didn't deserve what he had. On the other hand, John-Paul proved to be an unlikely boon, because he would provide the two best roles in the repertoire.

Role number six was Orlando. Returning to childhood for his model, the Virginia Woolf character, Gordon was fortunate that sex-change medicine had become available when he had the desire and money to do it. The decision to switch genders must have had many motives behind it—it was what psychoanalysis calls *overdetermined*—but I counted three chief ones. First, it would be an adventure, like teaching the Ojibwa in Canada. Second, Gordon thought it was about time (at age forty-seven) that he assumed a place in the firmament among his idols, like Bette Davis and Margaret Rutherford, and sex reassignment would make him famous. Last (the unconscious attraction), it would punish Gordon for the rest of her life. The part of Orlando, a character that could make Dawn a starlet while inflicting suffering, fit all the requirements.

Her friends had said Dawn was a masochist, but to become a woman wasn't merely to be the victim of bigots and homophobes. It was also to start the journey to role number seven, motherhood. Dawn had a strong and I think genuine maternal drive; yet to most people, a man presenting himself as a woman who wants to bear a child cannot be regarded as he/she regards herself, namely, as a loving human being. Such a person appears diseased. To a psychiatrist, he/she is "302.85," the numerical label in the *Diagnostic and Statistical Manual of Mental Disorders* for a transsexual with gender dysphoria. To Natasha, however, Dawn would be "Mommy."

It cannot be a coincidence that Dawn's father of record, the Sissinghurst chauffeur Jack Copper, had also claimed to have been a parent where (presumably) he wasn't. When Gordon, at age seventeen, had added Copper's name to his own birth record, he'd altered official files. Thirty years later, Dawn reenacted this scene in an American vital records office, offering another false story of conception by making herself the parent of Natasha. The subject of Gordon's paternity, translated by Dawn into maternity, apparently trailed her to the last.

What makes the ego crave punishment? Often the appetite is caught up with the image of the father, and Gordon's fatherlessness had been a source of his earliest anxiety. The most remarkable thing was that she asked her daughter to consent to the fantasy. ("Mommy always said, 'You're not adopted.' ") Had Dawn been a little mad to insist on a lie to her child? Was she cruel to use people, including her husband, John-Paul, in her therapeutic charade?

Dawn's very American act of self-invention failed in this, its last role. At the end, she was still reaching for an audience. It was only a year before she died that Dawn wrote me her letter, the message about the Ball family toilet she'd once owned. By the logic of her world, if I'd been able to locate the antique commode, I'd have become a spectator at her performance. Better, I'd have been a character witness, testifying to her expert impersonations.

IN DAWN'S PAPERS, I'd found a letter from an old friend named Rita Coakley, an actress she'd known in the 1950s. They hadn't seen each other for decades, but the friend said she'd been thinking about the sex change, and she wrote from Canada to resume contact.

"Despite all the things that have happened to you," Coakley said, "the essence of your personality does not seem to have changed. You always had an air of naïve innocence. So please don't change *that.*"

The personality of an actress is often credulous, and Dawn Langley Simmons, the changeling, eventually believed her own inventions. "It'll all work out in the end," she said. Dawn occupies a grander place as an artist who suffered for her parts, larger than if she'd simply been born intersexed. To be a hermaphrodite requires no exertion, but to design the self is a hero's tale.

ACKNOWLEDGMENTS

This book, more than most, is a group portrait. I'm grateful to the people I interviewed and who appear in the story, very few under pseudonyms. Others I talked to that didn't show up in the book also deserve thanks: Murray Barnes, Claire Behr, Ted Ellis, Bill Erwin, Florence Haskell, Peter McGee, Sara Rentschler, Nina Stanton, and Joan Trimbath. A number of people helped with referrals and papers about Dawn Simmons, including Chris Campbell, Tim and Jemma Fairhurst, Jim French, Elaine Janes, Francis X. McCann, Robert Rosen, James T. Sears, James Wilmot, Ken Wissoker, and Connie and Pete Wyrick. Thanks to my effective researcher, William von Reichbauer, for helping to locate people; to the Morris Museum in Augusta, Georgia; and to the staff at the Rare Book, Manuscript, and Special Collections Library of Duke University, in Durham, North Carolina. A special appreciation to Tania Diez as well as Jack Hitt for long-term care of Dawn's story. My agent, Kris Dahl at I.C.M., has been superb as usual. Thank you to Geoff Kloske, my editor at Simon & Schuster, who is wise and had immediate faith in this book. Without the help of Natasha Simmons, the telling of Dawn's life wouldn't have been the same. My wife, Liz, encouraged my interest from the beginning, as did her mother, Katherine, which made the recovery of Dawn's eventful time on earth an easy part of mine.

Picture Credits

Part I gateway photo, page 1 (Gordon Hall in school blazer): private collection; Part II photo, page 51 (Gordon Hall with Ojibwa children): Rare Book, Manuscript, and Special Collections Library, Duke University; Part III photo, page 119 (Dawn Hall poses next to column): private collection; Part IV photo, page 179 (John-Paul Simmons tosses veil): private collection.

Inserts

1: private collection [p-c]; 2: p-c; 3: Rare Book, Manuscript, and Special Collections Library, Duke University [Duke Univ.]; 4: National Trust Photographic Library/Eric Crichton, U.K.; 5: Beinecke Rare Book and Manuscript Library, Yale University; 6: Duke Univ.; 7: p-c; 8: p-c; 9: Isabel Lydia Whitney Papers, Morris Museum of Art, Augusta, Georgia; 10: Duke Univ.; 11: p-c; 12: p-c; 13: Duke Univ.; 14: courtesy of Francis X. McCann; 15: Everson Museum of Art, Syracuse, New York; 16: p-c; 17: William Struhs; 18: courtesy of Francis X. McCann/photo by Jack Alterman; 19: p-c; 20: p-c; 21: Duke Univ.; 22: William Struhs; 23: Associated Press, 1968; 24: p-c; 25: p-c; 26: p-c; 27: Duke Univ.; 28: Duke Univ.; 29: Duke Univ.; 30: courtesy of Francis X. McCann; 31: courtesy of Francis X. McCann; 32: Duke Univ.; 33, Duke Univ.; 34: Duke Univ.; 35: p-c; 36: p-c; 37: Duke Univ.; 38: p-c; 39: Duke Univ.; 40: photo by the author; 41: William Struhs.

About the Author

EDWARD BALL was born in Savannah, Georgia, raised in the South, and graduated from Brown University. His first book, *Slaves in the Family*, won the National Book Award in 1998. He is also the author of *The Sweet Hell Inside*.